YOU TALKIN' TO ME?

YOU TALKIN' TO ME?

The Unruly History of New York English

E. J. White

OXFORD
UNIVERSITY PRESS

OXFORD
UNIVERSITY PRESS

Oxford University Press is a department of the University of Oxford. It furthers
the University's objective of excellence in research, scholarship, and education
by publishing worldwide. Oxford is a registered trade mark of Oxford University
Press in the UK and certain other countries.

Published in the United States of America by Oxford University Press
198 Madison Avenue, New York, NY 10016, United States of America.

© Oxford University Press 2020

Library of Congress Cataloging-in-Publication Data
Names: White, E. J. (Elyse J.), author.
Title: You talkin' to me? : the unruly history of New York English / E. J. White.
Description: New York : Oxford University Press, 2020. |
Series: The dialects of North America | Includes bibliographical references and index.
Identifiers: LCCN 2019039334 (print) | LCCN 2019039335 (ebook) |
ISBN 9780190657215 (hardback) | ISBN 9780190657239 (epub) |
ISBN 9780190657222 (updf)
Subjects: LCSH: English language—Spoken English—New York (State)—
New York. | English language—Dialects—New York (State)—New York. |
English language—New York (State)—New York—Pronunciation. |
English language—New York (State)—New York—Slang. | English language—
Social aspects—New York (State)—New York. | Americanisms—
New York (State)—New York.
Classification: LCC PE3101.N7 W45 2020 (print) | LCC PE3101.N7 (ebook) |
DDC 427/.9747—dc23
LC record available at https://lccn.loc.gov/2019039334
LC ebook record available at https://lccn.loc.gov/2019039335

1 3 5 7 9 8 6 4 2

Printed by LSC Communications, United States of America

How to talk. America: *Meiguo*,
second tone and third.
The beautiful country.

—Adrienne Su
at the Nuyorican Poets Café[1]

CONTENTS

CONTENTS

NOTE ABOUT PHONETIC SYMBOLS

This book sometimes uses International Phonetic Alphabet (IPA) symbols to indicate specific sounds.

For an up-to-date guide to IPA symbols, the reader should consult the website of the International Phonetic Association: https://www.internationalphoneticassociation.org.

To listen to the sounds that IPA symbols represent on an audio player, the reader can access this website belonging to the Department of Linguistics at the University of California, Los Angeles: https://linguistics.ucla.edu/people/keating/IPA/inter_chart_2018/IPA_2018.html.

The symbols that appear most often in this book are:

ə—mid central vowel or schwa: the "uh" sound in "what."

ɑ—open back unrounded vowel: the sound you make when a doctor puts a tongue depressor in your mouth and tells you to say "aah."

æ—near-open front unrounded vowel: the sound you make when someone sneaks up on you.

ɔ—open-mid back rounded vowel: the sound you make when you see a kitten.

e—close-mid front unrounded vowel: the sound The Fonz makes.

ɪ—near-close near-front unrounded vowel: the vowel in "it."

i—close front unrounded vowel: the sound you make when you say the fifth letter of the alphabet.

ʊ—near-close near-back rounded vowel: the sound a ghost makes.

θ—voiceless dental fricative: the sound at the beginning of "thing."

ð—voiced dental fricative: the sound at the beginning of "that."

d—voiced dental/alveolar plosive: the sound at the beginning of "duh."

f—voiceless labiodental fricative: the sound at the beginning of "fuck."

Chapter 1

How to Talk Like a New Yorker

It was in New York that I learned to tell people to fuck off, and I think I'm a better person for it. From what I have seen, New Yorkers are connoisseurs of the word *fuck*. They use it as an obscenity, as an insult, as a qualifier, as a term of respect, as an adverb, as an interjection, as a method of asserting personal space, or simply as punctuation. They create new words based on it: according to data from Twitter, it was New Yorkers who created, or at least helped to popularize, one of 2014's trendiest new words, *fuckboy*.[1] A friend who works with Wall Street bankers told me that they talk about trying to get *fuck you money*, which may be defined loosely as "enough money for a Wall Street banker."[2] Another friend, also a New Yorker, argues that the word's very flexibility in local usage has dulled its capacity to offend: he can't insult people, or even get the attention of people he wants to insult, by shouting *fuck* or calling them *fuckers*. This has forced him to search out alternative forms of provocation. (He's had some success with political language—with success defined as whether someone takes a swing at him.)

I grew up mostly on the West Coast, with my family moving from small coastal town to small coastal town. The first time I ever heard a New York accent in real life, I was eighteen years old, stepping off the plane in Newark Airport on my way to college. I'm ashamed to admit this, but I was astonished: as a woman walked past shouting something in Brooklynese, I suddenly realized that I had not known New York accents were *real*. I had thought they were made up for television. That's how green I was, and if the spread of internet use—in particular, online videos, which allow us to see and hear ordinary strangers living far away—has made such raw ignorance less probable, my simplicity at least gave my iteration of the coming-to-Oz scene, which Dorothies from around the world replay hourly at Newark, JFK, and the Port Authority Bus Terminal, an additional element of magic. At that moment, the world seemed full of possibility. Seek and you will find; knock and the door will be opened to you (although, since the crowds are fearsome, keep to the right as you move through the door and lead with your shoulder).

Learning how to move through a big city has entailed learning new expectations, new fashions, and new forms of courtesy: how to ignore a celebrity; how to walk defensively; how to watch a traffic light for the first sign of change (the red light turns off; by the time, a New York hour later, the green light turns on, you should already be crossing the street); how to know, upon a stranger's unwanted approach, whether to offer help, to look sad and say, "Sorry, sir", or to say, "Fuck off." Because I teach the history of language, I took special interest in exploring the city's linguistic ecosystem: the slang, the place names, the conversational styles, the code-switching strategies in multilingual communities. New York City's eight million inhabitants speak, in aggregate, some 800 languages. The city's most famous local variant of English—what I just referred to as *Brooklynese*—has more vowel sounds than any other language in North America ("variant" is now the preferred term for "dialect"). And, as I knew when I first arrived, that variant has a rich history in film and television. Brooklynese, or New York City English, is the variant of Travis Bickle, Nathan Detroit, Archie Bunker, Detective Bobby Goren (but only when he wants the suspect to think he's an asshole), Vinny Gambini, and Mona Lisa Vito. It is also the variant of the physicist Richard

Feynman; the comedian Rodney Dangerfield; the actors Denzel Washington, Whoopi Goldberg, and Fran Drescher; and many ordinary New Yorkers besides.

This is a book about why New Yorkers talk the way they do, reaching from mundane matters like cursing and low slang to subjects as high as the fine arts, as complex as code switching, and as human as navigating class and social difference through language. The book tells the story of the development of a distinctive speech community in New York City—a history that encompasses social class, immigration, culture, economics, and, of course, real estate. In the process, the book explores both the workings of the English language and the social history of the city. Social creatures that we are, we register social details in every facet of our speech, in ways that we do not always recognize. In the 21st century, as the "urbanization" of the world's population continues apace, we have an ever greater need to understand how language moves and changes in urban spaces.

The book moves from *New York speech* to *New York words* to the *New York state of mind*, with each chapter exploring specific topics, ranging from the music machines of Tin Pan Alley to the sociology of department stores, that incorporate New York's history from the city's colonial settlement through to the 21st century. The book as a whole intertwines a cohesive set of arguments, drawing on a rich linguistic literature, about the English language in New York City: to wit, that metropolitan spaces are important cauldrons of language change; that language transforms in conversation with group identity; that the performance of language reveals important information about how Americans respond to class, race, and identity; and that the language history of New York City is deeply entwined with the language history of the United States as a whole.

Inevitably, the varieties of English in New York City, and the communities of speakers who use them, share features with every speech community and every language. As such, they demonstrate important truths about the rules of syntax, morphology, and phonology that govern all languages. But the variant known as New York City English is unlike the local variants of other world-class cities: in few other places do listeners (both inside and outside the city) respond to its sound with such scorn and ridicule. New Yorkers are very aware of the distance between New York City English and the language of the outside world. New York, as New Yorkers are happy to acknowledge, is the nation's capital of fashion, finance, gossip, and literary life. And yet many New Yorkers, when they go to college, start work on ditching their New York accent.

Take the lawyer Alan Dershowitz, who grew up in Brooklyn and attended Yale Law School in the early 1960s. In a 2013 interview, Dershowitz recalled, "I didn't know I had an accent until I went to Yale Law School. The first day I was called on at Yale Law School, the students laughed hysterically. I didn't know what they were laughing at. I thought *they* all had these funny accents."[3] Like many New Yorkers in this situation, he got with the program and "corrected" his speech. Today, Dershowitz has no audible New York accent except for the vowel [ɔ] in words like "thought."

"My Irish accent was one of the many things I forgot at Oxford," Oscar Wilde once said; he meant by it that one of the purposes of going to Oxford is to lose one's Irish accent.[4] That a New York accent is, as the Irish accent would have seemed in Wilde's Oxford, an embarrassing parochialism to be gotten rid of is a plot point of many films about upwardly mobile New Yorkers: for example, *Working Girl* (1988), in which Melanie Griffith's character, who is trying to rise from secretary to executive, listens to recordings of her boss and carefully imitates her, trying to reshape her chewy New York accent into her boss's Wellesley-brushed Standard American. The perfect film *My Cousin Vinny* (1992) uses the same widespread attitudes regarding the city's accent to the opposite effect: in the early scenes, we're meant not to know whether to take the title character seriously because, although he's been to law school, he still talks like a longshoreman from Red Hook. That the variant of a world capital is so stigmatized is one of the weirdest things about New York City English; but both New Yorkers and outsiders recognize the force of this stigmatization, which has a history that's deeply bound into the history of New York City itself.

This stigma has long penetrated the city's own schools, which have historically placed great emphasis on "correcting" the poor English of local students. The sociolinguist Deborah Tannen, a New York native, cites a letter to Ann Landers from an elementary-school teacher in the city who grumbled about the "speech habits" of her students, writing, "For example, I am now struggling with a student who says, 'Vot's the kvestion?', 'It's vorm ottside'. This boy was born in the U.S. (Brooklyn) and is nine years old. Another boy in the class says he is 'heppy as a boid.'" Landers replied, "With consistent effort, bad speech habits can be unlearned. I hope you will have the patience to work with these students. It's a real challenge."[5] Tannen recalls, for her own part, "Not so long ago one of the requirements for a license to teach in the New York City public schools was passing a speech exam, which entailed proving that one did not speak with the indigenous 'accent.' I myself recall being given a shockingly low midterm grade by a speech teacher in a Manhattan high school who promised that it would not be raised until I stopped 'dentalizing.'"[6]

The stigmatization of the city's local sounds is one reason why the local variants have changed so quickly, and why sounds that once defined, in F. Scott Fitzgerald's phrase, "voices full of money" are now gimmicks belonging to low comic characters. People are often surprised to learn that the Old New York upgliding diphthong in words like *third*—as in the famous phrase *Thoity-Thoid and Thoid*—was once a marker of upper-class speech. But it's true: in the days when Mrs. Astor held balls in her home on Fifth Avenue, the sound identified posh speakers like the "four hundred" she invited. (You can hear

Theodore Roosevelt, who grew up in New York City's upper class, using this marker in old recordings, as when, in a 1912 campaign speech, he spoke of men "whose souls bɔɪnɛd the fire of lofty endɛvɜ.")[7] It is also a reason why, in today's popular culture, heroic characters from New York City rarely have New York accents. Captain America, who grew up in Brooklyn in the 1930s, speaks, both in comics and in the recent Marvel films, without a trace of a New York accent. The same goes for Bruce Wayne, even though Harley Quinn, a comic villain who likewise grew up in the Manhattan-lookalike city of Gotham, speaks with an incredibly chewy New York accent. If these heroes spoke with New York accents, the reasoning seems to go, they would have to become different characters: mouthier, pushier, more aggressive, less polite.

But here's the thing. New Yorkers understand their conversational style to be polite. They take a certain pride in rebuffing adversaries efficiently, but when they're speaking to friends and peers, they use as a gesture of friendship the same conversational techniques that outsiders identify as rude. (When I showed my students a list of complaints that, according to polls, Americans in other states have about New Yorkers, they took the complaints as compliments: "That's right," said one, "We tell it like it is.") A vast sociological literature shows that New Yorkers treat straightforwardness as honesty, argument as engagement, loudness as enthusiasm, and interruption as a sign of listening. The literature also shows this to be a deep cultural tradition that extends across different language communities in the city. In a 2013 documentary film about the New York accent, an interviewer asks a deaf New Yorker whether American Sign Language is, in New York usage, freer with curse words than ASL usage in other regions. The interviewee explains that it is, because New Yorkers are "nice and straightforward":

INTERVIEWER: Here in New York, do they curse more?

INTERVIEWEE: *(speaking American Sign Language)*: Yes. In New York, there's a lot of cursing. *(Grimaces to signify, "Oh yeah, definitely.")* For example, *fuck*; some say *motherfuck*—that's the sign for *motherfuck*—or *motherfucker*. In New York, it's very different from other places, other states. Maybe they don't sign that, I'm not sure what they do. But here it's, you know, cause it's very nice and straightforward, here there's cursing a lot.[8]

WHY ARE NEW YORKERS SO [RUDE] [AGGRESSIVE] [LOUD] ⬎

The bad reputation of New York City speech is long-established and widely held. Polls have shown it to be the second most disliked accent in the country, just behind that of the American South.[9] A 2011 poll that asked Americans to judge whether people with specific accents seemed *nice, honest, intelligent,* and *well-educated* found that 51 percent of respondents judged speakers with New York accents to be "rude," while only 7 percent judged them to be "nice." (Respondents also judged speakers with Southern accents to be nice and uneducated; people with Midwestern accents to be honest, nice, and well-educated; and speakers with British accents to be sophisticated.)[10] According to Tannen, when New Yorkers leave the city for good, they often find it useful to play down their native speaking style, and may even begin to characterize that style as rude and aggressive: "New York Jews who have moved away from New York may be heard to proclaim that they hate New York accents, hate to go back to New York or hate to go home, because 'no one listens to anyone else' or 'it's so loud' or 'people are so rude.'"[11]

Within the city, however, New Yorkers see their speech conventions very differently.[12] Tannen showed how they work in practice by making a formal study of the conversation at a Thanksgiving dinner to which she had been invited. The event brought together three guests from New York City, one from England, and two from California. Following common practice for researchers of conversational style, she recorded the exchange and then translated the recording into a transcript that registered, by means of special annotations, details of expression as fine as stuttering, changes in pitch, and the overlap of multiple speakers talking at once. As the transcript showed, three of the dinner guests used the following stylistic conventions in their conversation:

Topic (a) prefer personal topics, (b) shift topics abruptly, (c) introduce topics without hesitance, (d) persistence (if a new topic is not immediately picked up, reintroduce it, repeatedly if necessary).

Genre (a) tell more stories, (b) tell stories in rounds, (c) internal evaluation . . . is preferred over external (i.e., the point of a story is dramatized rather than lexicalized), (d) preferred point of a story is teller's emotional experience.

Pacing (a) faster rate of speech, (b) inter-turn pauses avoided (silence is evidence of lack of rapport), (c) faster turntaking, (d) cooperative overlap and participatory listenership (i.e., interrupting).

Expressive paralinguistics (a) expressive phonology, (b) pitch and amplitude shifts, (c) marked voice quality, (d) strategic within-turn pauses (i.e., changing pitch, volume, and so forth in ways that outsiders may find dramatic).[13]

Guess which group this was: New Yorkers, or non–New Yorkers?

The answer is New Yorkers, of course; and, as Tannen noted, the differences in conversational style between New Yorkers and non–New Yorkers led to frequent hiccups in the conversation.[14] For example, the New Yorkers took for granted that pauses between conversational turns would be shorter than the others expected: "It happened frequently that while the Californians and the British speaker were waiting for a pause that would signal an open floor, a New Yorker, perceiving that the turn-exchange length of pause had come and gone, began speaking." Because of this, the non–New Yorkers believed they were being interrupted, talked over, ignored.[15]

Moreover, during a given speaker's turn, the New Yorkers would often add side commentary, which linguists call *cooperative overlaps: of course, I hate that, I would have done the same.* "Because the non–New Yorkers did not use overlap in this way, they frequently mistook these 'cooperative overlaps' as attempts to take a turn, that is, to interrupt." Thus more hiccups in the conversation: a non–New Yorker would be holding the floor; a New Yorker would make a comment *sotto voce*; the non–New Yorker would pause, tactfully, to yield the floor; the New Yorker would fail to take the floor; and the non–New Yorker would continue. After the conversation, one Californian commented that he had often struggled to "fit in." Though he had often held the floor, he had proceeded in jerky starts and stops, never feeling, he said, like "part of the flow."[16]

Another cause of disruption was *overlapping questions*: New Yorkers sometimes asked rapid-fire questions while someone was speaking, a practice meant to signal involvement and interest. When a non–New Yorker heard an overlapping question, he would stop and ask for clarification, treating the question like an interruption. When a New Yorker heard such a question, he would finish his thought and then answer without pausing. If the question led away from his conversational direction, he ignored it without expecting to signal offense. Referring respectively to her friends from California and New York, Tannen explained that the dinner guests interpreted these conventions as polite or not in accordance with their cultural expectations: "Indeed, the very aspects of these questions that make them intrusive to David—fast pace, high pitch, and overlapping or latching timing—are precisely the aspects that have the opposite effect with Steve and Peter, for whom they signal casualness, as if to imply, 'Answer if you feel like it, but if you don't feel like answering, then don't bother. My only purpose here is to encourage you to keep talking' ".[17]

Even from a perspective of broad cultural contrasts, we can see that both groups of speakers at the dinner were being polite. One group practiced politeness by signaling interest, while the other group practiced politeness by signaling considerateness, that is, respect for the independence of others. According to the linguist Robin Lakoff, who studies communicative politeness, the style of politeness that belongs to your specific community comes down to the relative weight that your community gives to three conflicting rules: *don't impose* (don't intrude on others); *give options* (respect the independence of others); *be friendly* (embrace others).[18] Tannen recalls the shock she felt when, as a new hire at a California university, she discovered that her manner read entirely differently in her new community: "As a native of Brooklyn, New York, of East European Jewish background, I was experiencing culture shock in northern California. In New York City I had been regarded as so diffident, polite, and indirect that one friend habitually referred to me as a WASP. In California I was surprised and hurt to realize that I was sometimes perceived as aggressive and even rude."[19]

All of this happens on a spectrum, of course. Californians perceive New Yorkers as pushy; Alaskans perceive Californians as pushy; and Europeans perceive Americans in general as pushy. But as we Americans know, we're just being friendly. The writer Bill Bryson, a Midwesterner who lived in Britain for almost two decades, confessed that, even after all that time, he found the British emphasis on *not imposing* as a part of politeness to be discomfiting: "I don't know how you strike up conversations with strangers in Britain. In America, of course, it's easy. You just offer a hand and say, 'My name's Bryson. How much money did you make last year?' and the conversation never looks back from there."[20] As someone who travels to England sometimes for work, I admit to feeling the same discomfort and uncertainty.

As Tannen's use of the term *WASP* suggests, scholars have also attributed aspects of New York conversational style to the conversational styles of specific communities within New York City. Tannen has suggested that we might attribute the speech norms of New Yorkers, in part, to the influence of Eastern European Jews.[21] Another linguist, Deborah Schiffrin, recorded a group of Jewish Americans in Philadelphia in conversation. She argues, based on transcripts similar to the one that Tannen produced, that the speakers often introduced disputes to the conversations—and further, that for the speakers this was simply a conversational correlate of latching and overlapping questions, a way of signaling interest in the proceedings: "One of the first things I noticed about the talk in my corpus [that is, her recording of the conversations] was how frequently the speakers disagreed with each other: Utterances often contradicted, denied, or negatively evaluated each other." Schiffrin argues that this comfort with disputation is a culturally Jewish conversational style, one that enables speakers, without fear of offense, to make disputes of "topics of talk not inherently defined as disputable." Questions that gentile speakers would simply *answer*, she suggests, gave rise here to friendly disputes: "questions about the location of a family doctor, belief in fate, educational background, solutions for personal problems, childhood games, location of friends and family, evaluation of local restaurants, who to invite to a party."[22]

Schiffrin also noted that the speakers in her study used, as further signals of involvement, *contextualization cues*, like higher volume, higher pitch, faster tempo, and "exaggerated intonation," that often signal that a speaker is arguing. As we saw in the case of Tannen's study, this is a feature of New York conversational speech, with its "exaggerated phonological and paralinguistic cues." (Television shows often make this way of speaking a trait of characters who are supposed to be bone-deep New Yorkers, like Fran in *The Nanny* and Janice in *Friends*.) At her Thanksgiving dinner, Tannen says, this way of speaking, which outsiders interpreted as angry, was yet another conversation-stopper: "For example, my question 'What's that?' is loud and high pitched. When any of the New Yorkers uses such features with Chad or David, the result is that they stop talking in surprise, wondering what caused the outburst. When used in talk among the New Yorkers, introduction of exaggerated paralinguistics spurs the others to follow suit, in a mutually escalating way."[23]

Although Schiffrin and Tannen emphasize their role in Jewish culture, we can also find significant overlaps between these features of New York City conversational style—comfort with latching, with simultaneous speech, with personal anecdotes; a conversational style in which speakers feel comfortable when they are disagreeing, in which they can take for granted that such disagreement is sociable, and in which they continually negotiate degrees of seriousness within disagreements—and the conversational styles of other ethnic and cultural communities with substantial populations in New York City. For example, scholars have identified simultaneous talk as a feature of conversational style among many communities that speak Romance languages: Puerto Ricans,[24] Italians,[25] Spanish-speakers in general,[26] and French speakers in general.[27]

The idea that silence between turns is a universal ideal and the opposite is rude or disruptive hindered decades of linguistic research. In 1981, for example, the social theorist Erving Goffman used for his definition of defined "a turn" in conversation "a stretch of talk, by one person, before and after which there is silence on the part of the person."[28] His characterization of silence between turns as a universal norm of conversation was standard for the period in which he was writing. However, in the decades since, research in linguistics has moved decisively away from his approach. Rather, scholars now accept simultaneous talk as, in many cases, a cultural norm that does not disrupt conversation. In different cultures, differing norms govern such tacit rules of conversation as how to take or cede a conversational turn, how to show interest as a listener, what topics are acceptable for small talk, and whether simultaneous talk will disrupt a conversation.[29] In other words, the features themselves aren't rude or polite; it's whether you're part of the community that shares them. If you don't grow up with a given conversational style, these features signal the opposite of communication. If you haven't experienced cooperative overlap, then you think overlap is simply changing the subject. If you haven't experienced cooperative interruption, then you think interruption is a sign of uninterest. Among non–New Yorkers, these features stop the conversation. Among New Yorkers, they keep the conversation flowing.

NEW YORK NICE

If you want to know whether someone is being *New York Nice*, you need to keep your ears pricked for specific markers. Is the speaker animated? Is she asking rapid-fire questions? Is her speech clipped? Is she making small talk in the form of complaining, thus welcoming you into the good fight against the world?[30] If she seems to be disagreeing with you, is she using her tone and manner to frame the argument as friendly and lighthearted? Schiffrin observed that the speakers she studied continually framed their speech in ways that indicated varying levels of seriousness; even at moments of disagreement and competition (friendly disputes are part competition, part dance), the speakers showed cooperation with, and support for, each other. Even at moments when they used what, in a genuine argument, would be considered fighting words, they *glossed* (performed) them as non-serious. For example, one speaker told another, "I hate you," but combined those words with what sociologists call a laughter "flood-out," showing that the words were meant as a joke: "I hate you hhhhhhhhhhhhhhhhhhhh."[31] New Yorkers excel at forms of expression, like shrugging, sighing, and sardonic grimaces, that are, like jokes themselves, displays of good humor and amiability that enable the speakers to reassure each other of their friendship amid ordinary conflict. If you're a New Yorker and your forms of politeness include features that, played straight, might read as forms of hostility, expressive displays of humor and amiability are a good way to demonstrate that you're not being hostile.[32]

In other words, there may be some truth to the old joke that in Los Angeles, people say "Have a nice day" and mean "Fuck off," while in New York, people say "Fuck off" and mean "Have a nice day."

The British philosopher of language Herbert Paul Grice famously proposed that the speakers in a conversation will, if they're working together, adhere to what he called the Cooperative Principle, or a set of tacit rules that allow them to communicate productively: these can be summarized as *be informative, be relevant, be straightforward, be clear,* and *be orderly.*[33] Studies show that speakers in language communities that use simultaneous talk are cooperative in Grice's terms. For example, simultaneous talk usually entails two speakers overlapping, even if many people are part of the conversation, and it usually ends with just one speaker speaking. Speakers who overlap tend to repeat established information while the overlap is happening, which makes their speech more useful overall. (Giving redundant information during an overlap means that if your listener can't hear you clearly, she won't miss anything important.) Speakers who make side comments, either in the form of "backchannel cues" (*I knew he was trouble*) or interpolations (*ay, mm hmm, oy, uh huh, uh oh*), do so with the knowledge that the speaker will not interpret them as interruption. True interruptions, or "terminal overlaps," take place when the following speaker senses that the first speaker is coming to an end. On occasion, a speaker with the floor *may* offer to yield his turn to another speaker who has made a side comment, but when that happens, he does so by indicating, by gesture or question, that he will yield his turn if the next speaker will build on the first speaker's point.[34] In this case, offering and accepting the floor are acts of respect, showing that the speaker and the listener are quick enough on the uptake not to need lengthy, drawn-out explanations. In the 2013 interview, Alan Dershowitz was quick to affirm this point:

DERSHOWITZ: Quick, funny, intense, honest, direct, no B.S.,
   that's the New York accent.
INTERVIEWER: Are there any, uh—
DERSHOWITZ: One more point. Interruption. Interruption.
   That's a very important part of the New York accent. Never
   let a person finish a sentence. You interrupt the second you
   get their point. And the smarter they are, the quicker you are
   to interrupt them, because *you got it.*

THE COLOSSUS OF NEW YORK

Living in a city is an increasingly normal experience for modern humans; scholars estimate that more than half of the world's population lives in cities. As such, the dynamics of cities can help to illuminate our linguistic future. More than this, however, attending to the workings and history of metropolitan language can help us to better understand how to live among, and communicate with, diverse communities of people.

Because this is a book about the speech community of New York City, I want to start with some necessary caveats. To begin with, in a city as large and diverse as New York, the *idiolects* of individual speakers are certain to show great variation. An idiolect is an individual's speech pattern, and it may differ from the norm of the speaker's speech community due to the influence of factors as broad as gender or age and as specific as what clique the speaker belonged to in high school.

The idiolects of New Yorkers show so much variation, in fact, that linguists used to assume that New York City represented a massive case of "free variation," meaning that the city was an anarchic maelstrom rather than a consistent speech community. In the 1960s, the great linguist William Labov conducted a series of studies that showed that New York City is indeed a speech community, that is, a community of speakers who *share linguistic norms*. Different groups of people in the city may have different variants, but they have shared standards (that is, a shared understanding of what should be "correct," even if their own speech is different) and a shared rate of change. Indeed, he showed that the differences of style among different groups in the city—he was looking especially at differences of social class—were "highly systematic." Systematic though their relationships are, the variations in styles and variants of English that the city contains are immensely complex. If you're a New Yorker, your speech in English may differ from the speech of your neighbors in accordance with your age, your social class, your ethnic background, your other language competencies, your place of origin, and even your gender. (For example, men give more force to the pronunciation of plosives (sounds made by opening a barrier like the lips or the tongue to expel air), like /p/ and /b/.[35] They even turn /th/, which women, like speakers of Standard English, pronounce as a fricative (sounds made by forcing air through a constricted barrier like the lips or the tongue), into a "voiceless plosive": *the* becomes a sound that many listeners casually transcribe as "da." Women, in the meanwhile, extend diphthongs, or sequences of two vowels in one syllable, for longer beats than men do; when they pronounce *dog* as a diphthong, you can really hear two vowels in the word.) Your speech may change from context to context and from audience to audience, a common practice that linguists call *code switching*. Your speech may also differ from the speech of your neighbors simply because you come, as I did, from somewhere other than New York City. Indeed, the coexistence of so many kinds of speakers has helped to make the city's variety of English, even at its most structured and formulable, what it is. New York has a different accent from the standard accent of the Northeast for the same reason that Chicago has an accent distinct from the standard accent of the Midwest, that Boston has an accent distinct from the standard accent of the Northeast, and that Los Angeles has an accent distinct from the standard accent of California. City speech is distinctive speech, regionally speaking, because cities are magnets for migrants and immigrants.

The city's immigrant identity is famously symbolized by the Statue of Liberty, which stands in New York Harbor, visible to all ships and to many planes entering the city. The statue's sculptor, Frédéric Auguste Bartholdi, anticipated, correctly, that Americans would interpret the statue not only as a patron of safe harbor, but also as a statement of support for universal rights and the freedom for all peoples. Slavery was unlawful due to the passage of the 13th Amendment just two decades earlier, but many Americans, especially in the South, still resented that change. Indeed, some public opposition to Bartholdi's statue proposal came from the belief that the statue would represent freedom from slavery.[36] It was during conversations with French emigrants in New York that Bartholdi recognized that he would best be able to win approval for the project from American politicians if he pitched the statue as something noncontroversial: a tribute to American independence, given in celebration of the Declaration of Independence's centennial. Once he received approval, he went around publicizing the statue in New York Harbor as "a personification of hospitality to all great ideas and to all sufferings." And he placed under the statue's foot, where most people wouldn't see it, a broken chain. His reason for keeping the chain partly hidden was likely that he understood that Americans would recognize the meaning he invested in the chain in the same way that they recognized the meaning he invested in the statue as a whole: that the chain stood, not only for liberty from tyranny, but also for emancipation.[37]

These layers of meaning are appropriate for the avatar of a city that has often been racialized, in American culture, as itself nonwhite and therefore un-American. Many of the people who appear in this book are people of color, or were considered, in their own time, to be people of color because they were Irish, or Italian, or Jewish.[38] As scholars of American immigration such as Nancy Foner have discussed, living in a city in which the majority of the population belongs to ethnic minority groups has made New Yorkers more comfortable with ethnic diversity and "ethnic succession" (that is, the rise of new ethnic majorities) than inhabitants of many other American cities.[39] This history has sometimes prompted out-of-state politicians to make a red-meat issue of decrying what they called "New York values," which they implicitly contrasted with American values. It has also helped to shape the (often antagonistic) relationship between New York City English and what became known as Standard American English.

Yet despite their different backgrounds, and *because* of their shared experience in the city, New Yorkers share many expectations about speech and communication. And if they come from elsewhere, they will find themselves gradually absorbing those expectations.

There's something ineluctable about becoming part of a speech community; it doesn't happen deliberately, or at least not entirely deliberately. Tannen reports that a participant in one of her studies—a
woman born and raised in Greece who then moved to the United
States—found, as she returned to her former home for holidays over
the years, that the conversational style that Greeks took to be natural was harder and harder for her to understand: "She found herself
wondering, 'What are they getting at?' and 'Where are they getting
THAT from?'"[40] Or again, a change to one part of your accent will
sometimes result in unconscious changes to other parts of your
accent. As I worked on this book, I noticed that a part of my brain
started to "correct" standard pronunciations, when I heard them, to
New York pronunciations: *water* became *wɔdə, strong* became *strɔng,
Long Island* became *lɔŋg island*. I suppose that if I stay here long
enough, eventually I'll be telling people to *fuck ɔff.*

TAWKIN NOO YAWKAH

For the aid of readers, I should open this book with a brief outline
of the outstanding features of New York City English (NYCE), the
term that linguists use for the city's distinctive local variant—and
I will make such an attempt here. But the features that define NYCE
have changed many times through the decades. Moreover, the way
one speaks may change according to social class, social clique, gender, sexuality, ethnicity, the performance of traits such as expertise
or authenticity, dozens of factors that may not stay consistent—as
one person relates to another, as an individual relates to a crowd—
from hour to hour, let alone from year to year. In a city of more than
eight million souls, the chatter that flows from person to person, up
the avenues and down the streets, in and around the department
stores and delis and bodegas, will always be in a state of change,

rebellion, adjustment to new conditions. Some New Yorkers, being many decades older than others, use pronunciations that belong to the historical past rather than the leading crest of linguistic change. Some ethnic variants in New York maintain sounds that other ethnic variants are discarding.[41] The history of language does not move in a straight line, but rather in circling eddies and countercurrents that temporarily stay older forms even as they are borne into the past. This book charts the history of living language that changes as one social class takes up another's pronunciation, or as popular fictions preserve old sounds as city stereotypes, or as speakers otherwise use the past to charge the present with meaning.

Despite historical changes and individual variations, New York City English *is* a distinct and identifiable variant. The outstanding features of NYCE remain the same regardless of where one lives in the city, contrary to popular belief. Many people believe, erroneously, that a connoisseur of local speech can tell by a New Yorker's accent which borough they come from: Brooklyn, the Bronx, Manhattan, Staten Island, or Queens.[42] Linguists have pushed against this myth for decades, without much success in the public sphere.[43] In 2005, William Labov, the dean of New York linguistics, told the *New Yorker* that city-dwellers often asked him to identify their borough, even their block, by their accent, as though he was the fictional Henry Higgins: "People want me to tell them which block. The fact is— but don't write this, because it will enrage people—Brooklynese is exactly the same whether it's spoken in the Bronx, Queens, and Staten Island or in Brooklyn. Or the Lower East Side."[44]

In 2018, two linguists published the results of an experiment in which New Yorkers listened to audio recordings of other New Yorkers and tried to determine which borough the speakers hailed from.[45] The listeners mostly guessed incorrectly; moreover, the listeners who were native New Yorkers had no greater success than the listeners who were not native New Yorkers.[46] One interesting finding was that the listeners were not guessing randomly; rather, listeners seemed to imagine that speakers without New York accents lived in Manhattan and that speakers with New York accents lived in the outer boroughs. A sensible guess, if one associates "proper" (i.e., non–New York) speech with the wealth, privilege, and elite education that pervade Manhattan—but still incorrect.[47]

The three most noticeable features of NYCE, Labov told the *New Yorker* in 2005, are the vowel in *talk*, the vowel in *bad*, and the final sound in *water*. Linguists often call the first feature a "raised BOUGHT vowel": speakers raise the vowel, or move the tongue towards the roof of the mouth, in words like *thought, bought, coffee,* and *talk.*[48] (This feature has inspired innumerable jests about New York "tawk," from the *New Yorker* headline "Tawking the Tawk" to the *New York Times* headline "Unlearning to Tawk like a New Yorker" to the title "Tawkin Irish," for a chapter about the New York Police Department, in Tom Wolfe's 1987 novel *Bonfire of the Vanities.*)[49] The second feature is what linguists call a "split short-a": speakers pronounce the vowel in the words *bad* and *bat* very differently, raising the vowel for *bad* and lowering the vowel (moving the tongue low in the mouth) for *bat.* Which words have raised vowels and which have lowered vowels largely depends on the type of consonant that follows the vowel. Most speakers of NYCE are not aware of their reasons for choosing one vowel sound or another, but they make that choice in a consistent pattern, rendering *bad* as "bi-uhd" and *Harold* as "Hi-uh-rold."[50] The third, and perhaps the most famous, outstanding feature of NYCE is the "variable nonrhotic / r/." In certain circumstances—namely, after a vowel—speakers do not pronounce the sound /r/. Instead, they replace the sound with a schwa (a colorless vowel: the vowel in "uh"), so that *water* becomes "wattah," *four* becomes "foah," and *park* becomes "pahk." The iconic New York–ism *fuhgeddaboutit* ("forget about it") relies on the non-rhotacism of New York speakers.[51]

Careful listeners may identify a range of other features, less famous but still distinctive, that make New Yorkers sound like New Yorkers. One is the use of metathesis (switching the sequence of a pair of sounds) in the word *ask*, which becomes "aks." Another is the use of a glottal stop in place of a medial /t/: instead of pronouncing the /t/ sound in words like *written*, speakers briefly stop the flow of air in the throat, producing a sound that one might transcribe as "wri'en." A third is the use of dental stops (a type of consonant that entails stopping and then releasing air at the teeth) for words like *thirty*, *this*, and *think*, which in Standard American use dental fricatives (a type of consonant that entails releasing a hiss of air at the teeth). Speakers of NYCE may alternatively use a dental affricate, which combines a stop and a fricative; but in any case, as the linguist Michael Newman observes, most outsiders will hear them saying *todee*, *dis*, and *tink*: "Actually, most hearers do not notice any difference between the affricate and fricative, but the stop is quite salient, and thus leads to stereotypes like '*toidy-toid and toid*' and '*dis and dat*' for *this and that*."[52]

When the researchers who tested New Yorkers' ability to hear one's borough of origin had to write for the test a passage that included "as many features of NYCE as possible," this is what they came up with:

> Please call Don. Ask him to carry the things he bought back from the store: half a pound of coffee, six cans of sauce, a scoop of ice cream, five hats, a jumping robot for the kids, and a copy of "Career Source" magazine. He can hang the bags on the door before we go see his boss, arriving at dawn in Korea town. What time is he coming?

This passage, as its creators note, elicits many of the sounds that characterize NYCE: variable nonrhoticity (*before, door, store*), raised

BOUGHT vowels (*boss, coffee, dawn, sauce*), split short-a's (*bags, half, hats, have*), dental stops or affricates in place of certain dental fricatives (*things*). It also includes an abundance of what linguists call "minimal pairs," that is, pairs of words that, in a given variant, are distinguished by just one phoneme, and which thus reveal meaningful phonemes in that variant: *career* and *Korea, coffee* and *copy, Don* and *dawn, half* and *have, sauce* and *source*.[53]

This book includes these sounds and their histories, but it also includes phenomena from a much larger universe of language, such as naming, slang terms, language mixing, the teaching of language, the social stratification that often causes people from different backgrounds to speak differently, and the stigma that often causes speakers of NYCE to feel ashamed of their diction. It includes the cultural meanings that color pronunciations and affect their use: for instance, the reason that men, in general, give more emphatic pronunciation than do women to the dental stops that initiate *thirty, this*, and *think*, is because harder consonants sound "tougher," men often hit their consonants hard in order to sound tough.[54]

To capture these many and varied aspects of New York speech, each chapter in this book focuses on specific institutions and case studies set in New York City. Chapter 2 discusses the relationship between the speech of New York City and the Standard American accent that prevails in films, higher education, and broadcast news—the accent that sounds, to listeners across the country, like English "without an accent." New York City is an anomaly among world-class cities: normally, the variant that a nation takes as its "standard language" comes from its center of finance and culture; but in the United States, the national standard accent comes from (relatively speaking) the provinces: the Midwest and the West. Rarely do speakers from a world-class city respond to their own speech with such suspicion.

Chapters 3, 4, and 5 move from the *way* New Yorkers speak to the *words* they say. Chapter 3 focuses on place names, examining how historical shifts, such as the American Revolution, wrote and rewrote the geographical text of the city. Chapter 4 explores the slang and colloquialisms coined in New York City, with special focus on the language of the city's criminal underworld. American English has absorbed a great deal of slang from the 19th century—a period of explosive growth for America's cities, New York City included. The chapter asks why so much underworld slang—words that were once too rough to say in polite conversation—has been folded into ordinary American English. Chapter 5 provides a lively historical view of the city's music industries, which export the city's idioms to the world.

The last two chapters look at social uses of language and how New Yorkers use speech to both reflect and shape their surroundings. Chapter 6 examines linguistic phenomena that arise where different language communities rub shoulders. When you walk down the street in New York City, the people around you are as likely as not to be speaking languages other than English. Even English speakers are likely to be mixing registers or adjusting their variants to fit the occasion. As a center of immigration, New York City has always been polyglot, but only recently have language mixing and code switching gained wide cultural favor. Chapter 7 examines a single fascinating study of speech behavior and economic class in New York City, which researchers have repeated many times over the decades, and which reveals how changes in our social environment can affect the way we speak.

BODY LANGUAGE

The book that follows is the linguistic path that one newcomer cut through the city. As a Westerner, I can hear some elements of the city's speech that may not catch the notice of the city's speakers.

But as a newcomer, I know as well that I will miss elements of the city's sound. In the year that *Fiddler on the Roof* (1964) debuted on Broadway, a gentile reviewer wrote of one of the musical's songs: "But he does permit himself one small musical daydream ('If I Were a Rich Man') and when Mr. Mostel dreams he dreams in vocalized snuggles, not in words. For every other line of the lyric he simply substitutes gratified gargles and coos until he has arrived, mystically, at a kind of cabalistic coloratura." A Jewish reviewer, writing that same year, correctly identified the musical style in that song as a reference to synagogue cantillation: "When Mr. Mostel sings 'If I Were a Rich Man,' interpolating passages of cantillation in the manner of prayer, his Tevye is both devout and pungently realistic."[55] One listener heard "cooing"; another heard prayer.

The historian Henry Bind generously describes such gaps in interpretation as a result of *double coding,* a term that refers to methods of speech or performance by which members of a group (here, Jewish people) can communicate different messages to in-group and out-group audiences.[56] George W. Bush famously did this when he sprinkled his speeches with words that held special resonance for Evangelicals. As a description of how people sometimes speak, double coding helps to explain how *Fiddler on the Roof* became such a hit with non-Jewish audiences while drawing on the culture of Ukrainian Jewry. But an account of the difference between the reviews that focuses on how people *hear* might say simply that when we listen to others, we often miss meanings that we don't understand. I have no doubt that this book will include examples of this failing.

The odd truth about language in New York City is that most of the speech you encounter there is not heard but overheard. Out on the street, New Yorkers live in collective solitudes: bodies fold inward, shielding against any interloper looking for an excuse to step into someone's personal space. To address a stranger directly is to see a step back and a wary look.[57] This practiced aloofness, which is a matter of personal safety for the members of such a vast and anonymous crowd, has been remarked upon since the earliest years in which New York deserved the designation *city*. Edgar Allan Poe, who lived in New York City during its first period of massive expansion, registered the unease of living amid so many strangers in the short story "The Man of the Crowd" (1840), which describes city life as disturbing precisely because it is anonymous: the narrator claims that wickedness becomes undetectable when it is generalized across a thousand faces.[58] Nathaniel Hawthorne, who lived in Boston during the same years, wrote a story about a man who lives in a city for years one street over from his family, without their ever meeting him or guessing he lives so nearby.[59] Today, some 175 years later and with a population some 25 times greater, we rely more than ever on anonymity to survive. We avoid eye contact, we avoid small talk with strangers, we keep pace with the undifferentiated flow of bodies through the streets.

Still, New Yorkers find ways to communicate with strangers. They hold poetry readings; they mount one-person shows; they publish in tabloids, in literary magazines, in underground zines; they whisper over radio channels late in the evenings; they perform at concert halls, fringe festivals, and hole-in-the-wall pubs. People who can't talk with their neighbors on the subway strive to make those neighbors fall in love with them on the stage. Alone together, New Yorkers reach out to each other by talking . . . and this book will show you how to hear them.

Chapter 2

New York vs. the Rest of America

JACK
The television audience doesn't want your elitist, East Coast, alternative, intellectual, left-wing—

LIZ
Jack, just say Jewish, this is taking forever.

—30 Rock (2009)

That Americans talk the way they do is, from a global perspective, amazing. In most nations, as one observer writes, the variant that speakers treat as the national standard belongs to those nations' capitals of finance and culture: in France, the standard accent, the accent of newscasters on television and radio, comes from Paris; in England, it comes from the "golden triangle" that connects London, Oxford, and Cambridge. According to this pattern, the standard American accent should sound like a New York accent. Or it should sound like a mixture of the New York accent and the Boston accent, since both cities were major economic and population centers in the 19th and early 20th centuries, a time when developments in media and education were exerting standardizing pressures on cultivated American speech. In other words, American newscasters should use nonrhotic, or "r-less," speech, as New Yorkers and Bostonians do. (*Pahk Avenue; I pahked the cah in Hahvid Yahd.*)[1]

But instead, in the United States, the accent of news broadcasting, the accent of prestige education, the accent that's meant to sound like English "without an accent," is the accent of the West and the Midwest. The standard American accent is rhotic; that is, we pronounce the sound /r/ not merely after consonants, but all the time.[2] We use the sound /æ/ in words like *rather* and *grass*, making them sound like *hat*—not like *father*, the historical New York sound. We pronounce words like *hawk* and *dog* with /ɑ/, rather than an "open o" (/ɔ/). And we have no "intrusive /r/," which is to say that we don't insert an "r" sound at the end of r-less words in certain contexts: *the idear of it!*[3]

"It would be strange," writes the language historian Thomas Bonfiglio, "to imagine British emulating the speech of Yorkshire or German emulating the Alpine dialects. Yet, this is basically what happened in the standardization of American English. The pronunciation of the economic and cultural centers of power was not taken as a model. Instead, the pronunciation of a largely rural area, the midwest and west, was preferred."[4] Why?

In this chapter, drawing substantially on Bonfiglio's analysis, I discuss both the place of the New York accent within standard American speech and why standard American speech broke away, unexpectedly, from New York City. In the process, I explore a history in which a nation of immigrants sought to define itself against its capital of immigration.

WHAT MIGHT HAVE BEEN

There was a time when cultivated American speech had a New York sound. If you grew up in New York or New England in (say) the 1940s, you would have learned, either in public school or in a private or finishing school, a cultivated accent that was known as "General

American." Like the New York accent, General American was non-rhotic. To contemporary listeners, it actually sounded rather British, as though the speech of Southern England had been brushed over the top of New York speech. While some people disliked the artificiality of this school-taught accent, they agreed that it was pervasive; as late as 1952, a linguist could take for granted the "'elocutionist fiction' which prescribes for cultivated usage a mixture of eastern New England speech and Southern British English."[5]

In other words, the possibility that New York would set the standard for American speech was still to be found almost into the mid-20th century. Nonrhotic speech dominated stage plays, radio plays, and early sound films. Frances Robinson-Duff, a famous speech coach based in New York City, taught cultivated speech to actors including Katharine Hepburn, Clark Gable, Mary Pickford, and Miriam Hopkins, as well as many patrons outside of show business: in New York "flocked to her amateurs and chorus girls ambitious to become actresses, actresses ambitious to become better actresses, opera singers with acting ambitions, ministers craving the better to exhort their flocks, public speakers, politicians eager to ease their deliveries, even society girls pelvically frail and seeking vigor."[6] For these customers, good speech was aspirational; it sounded like money, like sophistication, like patrician ease, like New York's upper classes.

It's no coincidence that the accents of New York and Boston were, like the speech of Southern England, nonrhotic. Many historians of language argue that the nonrhotic accents of certain parts of the United States—New York City, Boston, the Tidewater South—are linked directly with the rise of nonrhoticity in 18th-century London.[7] Received Pronunciation, the nonrhotic cultivated variant of London, only came into being in the late 1700s. Before then, Londoners were rhotic—which means, for instance, that the standard American accent probably sounds more like the accent of

William Shakespeare than does Received Pronunciation. Nobody's really sure why Londoners switched over from rhoticity to nonrhoticity. To a great extent, the history of spoken language is a history written on water.

As the historian John Hurt Fisher notes, the parts of America that became nonrhotic during the 18th century were anchored in major port cities that had regular contact with London. By the turn of the 19th century, nonrhotic pronunciation was the speech habit of the educated and the upper classes in New York, Boston, Philadelphia, and almost all of New England (with the exception of Connecticut and Vermont), along with every social class in the Tidewater South.[8] The particular form that nonrhoticity took in these cities matched the form of nonrhoticity in London, further supporting the theory that American nonrhoticity was an imitation of London. Speakers did not merely lose the /r/, but rather replaced it with a schwa; they also lengthened the vowel before the schwa.[9] More rural and inland regions in the United States, not connected so readily with London, held on to the older rhotic pronunciation, in what one scholar calls a "linguistic 'lag.'"[10]

Indeed, by this accounting, a number of features that distinguish the speech of the Midwest and Appalachia from the speech of New England and the South—rhoticity, the long [æ] in words such as *grass*, the lack of a difference between the vowels in *dawn* and *Don*—are speech habits preserved from the 17th century, unchanged by commerce with London.[11] Conversely, many features beyond nonrhoticity connect the speech of old port cities with each other and the speech of London. For example, the pronunciation of *bird* as [bɜ˞d], and similar uses of ɜ˞ for /r/, is an old stereotypical feature of New York speech: Woody Allen uses it in movies like *Manhattan* (1979). In 1948, a linguist remarked that the same pronunciation was "an old feature of speech in the southern plantation area, in such communities as Charleston, S.C." In other words, Southern plantation owners used to sound a bit like Woody Allen.[12] Or again, the New York pronunciation of *water* (ˈwɔːtə) uses a London sound in the vowel; New Yorkers pronounce the word more like Australians, who also have an accent derived from Southern England, than they do like Midwesterners.

Or again, New Yorkers, Bostonians, and Southerners are, or were, united in an old pronunciation, Southern English in origin, that outsiders tended to mishear as *erster* (oyster) and *terlet* (toilet). The sound gets a shout-out in the Broadway musical *Newsies*, in an exchange between two of the eponymous newsies:

> RACE: You're famous, and the world is your *erster*!
>
> HENRY: Uh, your what?
>
> RACE: Your erster! Your erster! You know, your fancy clam with the poil inside![13]

One of my colleagues tells me that his Boston mother-in-law used to say something that he would mishear as *terlet*, because she had that peculiar pronunciation of [oy]—a pronunciation that dates to the 18th century, which is why it was found in old coastal cities: Boston, New York, Charleston, Savannah. The actual sound that speakers used was a schwa. Yes, there were people who pronounced *oyster* and *erster* identically, but they were in the minority. Most locals kept the pronunciations distinct, but the sounds were so close and so peculiar that to an outsider they sounded the same.

The classic song "Let's Call the Whole Thing Off," the work of the New York songwriting team George and Ira Gershwin, registers the confusion that the differences between varieties of American speech could cause. In the film *Shall We Dance* (1937), where the song is performed by Fred Astaire and Ginger Rogers, Astaire takes the more British variants of *either* and *tomato* (ˈaɪðə, təˈmɑːtə) and gives

Rogers the less British variants ('iðər, tə'meɪˌtɑː). The divergence shows the lingering effects of London's example on American speech (while incidentally corresponding with the general rule in their films that Astaire uses more "cultivated" speech than Rogers):[14]

> You say either ('iðər) and I say either ('aɪðə),
> You say neither ('niðər) and I say neither ('aɪðə) . . .
> You like potato (pə'teɪːtɑ), and I like potato (pə'tɑːtɑ),
> You like tomato (tə'meɪːtɑ) and I like tomato (tə'mɑːtɑ) . . .

Confusingly, the two switch positions midway through the song, so that Rogers takes the more British variants (posing haughtily and holding her sunglasses like an opera glass) and gives Astaire the less British variants. Well, early sound films aren't famous for their linguistic accuracy. During her time as the more cultivated speaker, incidentally, Rogers lays claim to the port-city pronunciation of *oyster*:

> So if you like oysters
> And I like ersters
> I'll take oysters
> And give up ersters. . . .[15]

NEW YORK DAINTY

The cultivated accent that children learned in schools would have overlaid the native New York accent, already somewhat British in its features, with a layer of further Briticisms. I think we should call this artificial variant "New York Dainty," following a term that the linguist J. K. Chambers borrowed from the dialectologist Rex Wilson. Chambers wrote seminal articles on the cultivated English that Canadians affected over the airwaves, which was an imitation of the speech of Southern England.[16] In the case of Canada, the use of Briticisms related partly to the influence of Loyalists who moved north following the American Revolution, who were eager to avoid excessive Americanisms in their speech. In the Victorian era, as Chambers notes, schoolchildren took "enunciation lessons," which taught them to burnish their speech with British sounds: "*schedule* with SH, *tomato* with AH, *student* with YOO, *whale* with WH . . . and many others." Every city had its own version that the comfortable classes adopted, a similar "veneer of Briticisms" transposed onto the local accent: *Halifax Dainty, Toronto Dainty, Winnipeg Dainty,* and so forth. In 1936, when Canada established a "national radio network . . . announcers adopted these pronunciations as a matter of course." *Britannia rules the (air)waves.*[17]

In New York as in Halifax, on the stage and screen as in the classroom, the dainty was an artificial variant—and thus was subject to tremendous unevenness in performance. Adults and adolescents are just not good at learning new variants and accents.[18] (We don't have dainties anymore, but you can see the same unevenness, with the directions reversed, in the case of British singers who use Americanized accents in their singing in an attempt to get that "rock and roll" sound. In their first studio album, The Beatles used what must have seemed to them like American sounds, for example using a rhotic sound for /r/ in contrast to the nonrhotic variant of their native Liverpool. Even so, according to one study, they only manage to pronounce /r/ where an American would around 47 percent of the time.[19] A few albums later, after their own music had made Brit Pop into a recognizable and even a prestigious category, the Beatles had stopped worrying about sounding American and sang as their nonrhotic selves.)[20] This unevenness is one reason for using the term *dainty* rather than, as some people have called this variant with reference to the stage and screen, *the Mid-Atlantic accent*, which suggests a uniformity that did not exist in practice. Indeed, Katharine Hepburn, who is often presented as the queen of the Mid-Atlantic accent, wasn't using the same accent as most of her costars; she was speaking in what one might call Connecticut Dainty, which differs in marked ways from the New York Dainty that the majority of film actors used.

What were the features of New York Dainty? In 1948, Yakira Frank, later a distinguished linguist, wrote a dissertation that touched on what she described as the "cultivated speech" of New York City.[21] She observed, to begin with, that in words such as *row* and *road*, speakers used the diphthong [əu]—a feature that does not belong to any variety of New York speech, and which Frank suggested was an imitation of British speech.[22]

For the vowel in *bird*, Frank says, the prestige pronunciation is [bɜˑd]—the Woody Allen sound. This sound had only recently entered the curricula of finishing schools; a generation before, the prestige pronunciation had been [bɔɪd].[23] For reasons that will soon become clear, the sound [ɔɪ] fell to the status of a comic stereotype—and worse, a comic *lower-class* stereotype—with incredible speed, so that what was once a prestige marker became, for speakers raised with it, a source of embarrassment. When, in the 1960s, the linguist William Labov conducted an in-depth study of New York speakers, many of his elderly informants used [ɔɪ] for words such as *bird, burn,* and *work*. These speakers were chagrined to be using what was, by then, a stigmatized usage, but they were well past the window for changing their habits of speech. Labov wrote, "One older Italian woman was particularly embarrassed at her own inability to distinguish *earl* and *oil*, which had apparently been a point of ridicule for many years in her own family. She cheered up considerably when she learned that this was once the prestige pronunciation of the highest levels of society."[24]

AN ENGLISHMAN'S WAY OF SPEAKING

The quickest way to show the extent of the connections between American dainties and the speech of Southern England is with a chart (see Table 2.1) comparing the pronunciation of a variety of words in old "stage English," modern London English, and modern Standard American English. I have taken the stage pronunciations from a speech manual published in the 1950s.[25]

	aunt	bar	far	board	careless	hot	flour
American Stage English, 1956							
	aunt [ant]	*bar* [bɑ]	*far* [fa]	*board* [bɔd]	*careless* [kɜəlɪs]	*hot* [hɒt]	*flour* [flauə]
	banana [bənanə]	*berry* [bɛrɪ]	*farm* [fam]	*door* [dɔ]	*forfeit* [fɔfɪt]	*not* [nɒt]	*here* [hɪə]
	dance [dans]	*stir* [stɜ]	*far away* [fɑrəweɪ]	*four* [fɔ]	*palace* [pælɪs]	*what* [wɒt]	*our* [auə]
	example [ɪgzampl]			*more* [mɔ]	*minute* [mɪnɪt]		*require* [rɪˈkwaɪə]
	rather [raðə]				*tourist* [turɪst]		*there* [ðeə]
British English							
	aunt [ɑːnt]	*Bar* [bɑː]	*far* [fɑː]	*board* [bɔːd]	*careless* [keəlɪs]	*hot* [hɒt]	*flour* [flauə]
	banana [bəˈnɑːnə]	*berry* [bɛrɪ]	*farm* [fɑːm]	*door* [dɔː]	*forfeit* [fɔːfɪt]	*not* [nɒt]	*here* [hɪə]
	dance [dɑːns]	*stir* [stɜː]	*far away* [fɑːr əˈweɪ]	*four* [fɔː]	*palace* [pælɪs]	*what* [wɒt]	*require* [rɪˈkwaɪə]
	example [ɪgˈzɑːmpl]			*more* [mɔː]	*minute* [mɪnɪt]		*our* [aʊə]
	rather [rɑːðə]				*tourist* [tʊərɪst]		*there* [ðeə]

Standard American English

aunt [ænt]	bar [bɑr]	far [fɑr]	board [bɔrd]	careless [kɛrləs]	hot [hɑt]	flour [flaʊər]
banana [bəˈnænə]	berry [bɛri]	farm [fɑrm]	door [dɔr]	forfeit [fɔrfɪt]	not [nɑt]	here [hir]
dance [dæns]	stir [stɜr]	far away [fɑr əˈweɪ]	four [fɔr]	palace [pæləs]	what [wʌt]	require [rɪˈkwaɪər]
example [ɪgˈzæmpəl]			more [mɔr]	minute [mɪnət]		our [aʊəe]
rather [ræðər]				tourist [tʊrəst]		there [ðɛr]

American Stage English, 1956

bear [bɛə]	heard [hɜd]	ought [ɔːt]	Wash [wɔʃ]	dew [dju]	city [sɪtˈɪ]	board [bɔd]
fairy [fɛrɪ]	herd [hɜd]	ball [bɔːl]	watch [wɒtʃ]	duke [djuk]	attitude [ætɪtjuːd]	door [dɔ]
hare [hɛə]	whirl [wɜl]	bought [bɔːt]	water [wɔtə]	neutral [njutrəl]	telephone [tɛlɪfoun]	four [fɔ]
	worthy [wɜþ]	daughter [dɔːtə]		new [nju]	getting [gɛtɪŋ]	more [mɔ]
	bird [bɜd]	fall [fɔːl]		tune [tjun]	hotter [hɒtə]	

British English

bear [beə]	bird [bɜːd]	Ball [bɔːl]	Wash [wɒtʃ]	dew [djuː]	city [sɪtˈɪ]	board [bɔd:]
fairy [feəri]	heard [hɜːd]	bought [bɔːt]	watch [wɒtʃ]	duke [djuːk]	attitude [ætɪtjuːd]	door [dɔː]
hare [heə]	herd [hɜːd]	daughter [dɔːtə]	water [wɔːtə]	neutral [njuːtrəl]	telephone [tɛlɪfəʊn]	four [fɔː]
	whirl [wɜːl]	fall [fɔːl]		new [njuː]	getting [gɛtɪŋ]	more [mɔː]
	worthy [wɜːði]	ought [ɔːt]		tune [tjuːn]	hotter [hɒtə]	

Standard American English

bear [bɛr]	bird [bɜrd]	Ball [bɔl]	Wash [waʃ]	dew [du]	city [sɪti]	board [bɔrd]
fairy [fɛri]	heard [hɜrd]	bought [bat]	watch [watʃ]	duke [duk]	attitude [ætə,tud]	door [dɔr]
hare [hɛr]	herd [hɜrd]	daughter [dɔtər]	water [wɔtər]	neutral [nutrəl]	telephone [tɛlə,foun]	four [fɔr]
	whirl [wɜrl]	fall [fɔl]		new [nu]	getting [gɛtɪŋ]	more [mɔr]
	worthy [wɜrði]	ought [ɔt]		tune [tun]	hotter [hɑtər]	

We can take away several points from manuals of this kind. First is the necessity of such manuals in the first place. Because dainties did not exist in the wild, speakers had to learn them through professional coaching: speech manuals, pronunciation dictionaries, elocution teachers, the New York City Board of Education's "Bureau of Speech Improvement." Second is the deliberate brushing of London speech on top of regional variants that had already included some London elements since the 18th century, and the presentation of this further Londonizing as a more correct style. The book just cited, called *The Bases of Speech*, remarks that "the Eastern American dialect," which appears to mean cultivated speech in New York, Boston, and environs, "strongly resembles South-of-England speech."[26] The elocutionist Edith Skinner, whose primers were standard textbooks for stage diction, recommends the imitation of Southern English usage in a range of contexts, including the postvocalic /r/: "The consonant r is pronounced in Spoken English ONLY before a vowel sound." (In fact, she dislikes the sound /r/ so much—it corrupts "the purity of the vowel," she says—that she curtails it more than London's nonrhoticity prescribes, insisting that if /r/ comes "between two vowel sounds," the speaker should arrange matters so that "the consonant r is always spoken with the SECOND vowel sound." Thus one should say *spi-rit*, not *spir-it; me-rry*, not *merr-y; gingerale* or *ginge ale*, not *ginger ale; faraway* or *fa away*, not *far away*.)[27]

Third, the results of these primers were often distractingly uneven. Many speakers failed to apply the rules entirely in step with other speakers, or even with themselves. Consider the case of Fred Astaire and Ginger Rogers, perhaps the most iconic costars in American cinema during the 1930s and 1940s. As a general rule, Astaire uses more "cultivated" pronunciation than Rogers, even when that difference flies in the face of the story's plot. In *Top Hat* (1935), Astaire, who plays an American, has the more English sound of the pair, while Rogers, who plays an Englishwoman, has the more American sound. But they also shift unpredictably into other accents: Rogers tacks from inland American pronunciations (*driver* [draɪvər], *horse* [hɔrs], *course* [kɔrs], *can't* [kænt]) to pronunciations that are English (*can't* [kɑːnt]) and even upper-class English (*back* [bɛk], *hat* [hɛt]).[28]) One student of film variants suggests that Rogers's accent was deliberately kept a notch "lower" than Astaire's as a way of reinforcing their distinctive screen chemistry: "There is linguistic truth to the often quoted saying about Rogers and Astaire attributed to Katharine Hepburn that 'he gives her class, and she gives him sex.' "[29]

Fourth, the elevation of dainties entailed the lowering of regional variants that were not dainties. *The Bases of Speech*, for example, devotes space to the brow-furrowed censure of what the authors call the "urban substandardisms" of New York City. (Notice the use of the word *urban* to refer to white ethnic minorities.) The authors record these features as a way of warning readers not to use them: speakers should "use [ɔɪ], not [ɜɪ] or [ɝ], in words spelled with oi or oy plus consonant": [bɔɪl] for *boil*, instead of [bɜɪl] or [bɝl]. New Yorkers who haven't cleaned up their speech use [t] instead of [θ] ("Toity-Toid and Toid") and [d] instead of [ð] ("dis" instead of "this"). Perhaps most shamefully, they use [ɜɪ] or [ɔɪ] where they should use [ɜ]. An *urban* speaker would pronounce *bird* as [bɜɪd] or [bɔɪd]; but a correct speaker would pronounce it as [bɜd].[30]

These attitudes permeated the city's schools. Since at least the 1920s, teachers in the local public schools trained their students in better speech using "speech improvement texts and brochures" written by elocution teachers of the same kind as those who wrote the primers just mentioned. By 1925, speech was a regular discipline in New York City public schools, where it was often taught under the aegis of English literature with the title "Oral English." "The Board of Examiners scheduled special examinations for speech-improvement teachers in the elementary schools," writes the historian Arthur Bronstein, "where teachers worked under the jurisdiction of a special Bureau of Speech Improvement, with headquarters at the Board." Under the bureau's guidance, teachers worked to free their students from speech habits that, as they were told and told the students in turn, were "careless," "slovenly," and "uncultivated." (When Bronstein was writing in 1962, the city's public schools were still using texts that described the untutored speech of New York City as "careless" and "substandard.")[31]

The city's archives contain copies of course guides and other teaching materials that the Bureau of Speech Improvement distributed in the 1930s to teachers in day and evening elementary schools. (They were *evening* elementary schools because the students apprenticed in vocational trades during the day.) These materials keep in the foreground the fact that most of the reader's students will be immigrants or the children of immigrants. Speech improvement, they seem to imply, will help to tame this foreign and perhaps dangerous population. One booklet from 1933 suggests that teachers should hang posters with slogans that present speech improvement as a patriotic task: "He who would be great must use one language correctly." "Better speech for better Americans." "The keystone of Americanization is the language of our country." "Show your patriotism by improving your speech." "A free country! A powerful language!" "America! Speak English!"[32] Another, from 1931, describes the "characteristic racial errors" that students of various ethnicities are apt to make in their speech, using language that suggests that nonstandard speech derives from flaws of ethnic temperament: "Italians, Spaniards and Cubans have a characteristic languorous drawl. We notice, in their speech, an elision of syllables and consequent slurring, following the custom of the mother tongue."[33] In order to break the students of their bad habits, the teachers are instructed to give them regular drills in pronunciation, as well as in reading aloud and recitation from memory.

These booklets also suggest "speech slogans" to aid students in remembering good pronunciation—for example:

"Hend" for hand should never stand,
"Terl" for toil your speech will spoil.

"Lenth" for length lacks proper strength.

Daisy wore a stylish dress,
But she would say "Yeah" for Yes.

Not "dooty" but duty
Gives added speech beauty.[34]

Nobody tells American children anymore to say *duty* so that it rhymes with *beauty*. To our modern ears, the pronunciation sounds just a little British. But with a dainty, a slight British timbre was the explicit goal; and because the city's speakers were already nonrhotic, New Yorkers, despite their substandardisms, had a shorter distance to go to have voices that sounded like American money.

DECLINE AND FALL OF THE BRITISH KNICKERBOCRACY

How, then, did the prestige pronunciation of the United States move away from New York City? In the 1930s, the outlook for New York English was promising. Broadway actors, trained in dainty for the stage, made nonrhotic syllables part of the new music of the silver screen; Paramount maintained a studio in Astoria, Queens, the better to utilize New York City's acting talent. As an ordinary, if not universal, matter of course, preachers, pundits, and politicians went to school on the same sounds; indeed, Franklin D. Roosevelt, elected to the presidency in 1932, was entirely nonrhotic for twelve years in the nation's highest office without that fact attracting, it would seem, much in the way of contemporary commentary.[35] In those years, too, the nation's cultural and economic strongholds were uncontestably the great port regions of the Northeast (and the South, though that region never regained the power it had before the Civil War).[36]

Thomas Bonfiglio explains the historical factors that drove this change in part by referring to a set of changes that elite colleges like Harvard and Yale were making to their admissions procedures during the same period that New York Dainty began its slow fade as a prestige pronunciation. This comparison may seem odd at first, but it proves to be quite useful. As gateways to prosperity and training fields for the upper class, elite colleges participated in the same world of social distinction and display as finishing schools, aspirational media, and elocution teachers like Frances Robinson-Duff. As such, they can serve as a representative segment of a larger ecosystem. Above all, the issues that pervaded policy discussion among American elites during this period were immigration, ethnicity, and regional demographics.

In 1918, the Association of New England Deans, which included the presidents of Harvard and Yale, gathered to discuss what the association called—not at all ominously—the "Jewish problem."[37] At issue was the future of Jewish students at their schools. Strictly speaking, their problem was not with Jewish students as such, although many of the gathered administrators shared the anti-Semitism that pervaded American society, but rather the effect that Jewish students might have on undergraduate enrollment. At the time, these schools based admissions primarily on indicators of merit like grades and test scores, and a large, growing number of Jewish students were getting through the gate. The president of Harvard, Lawrence Lowell, argued that something had to be done about this—that if too many Jewish students enrolled at a given school, upper-class Protestants would send their sons elsewhere.[38] This was a problem because the primary business of an Ivy League school is the manufacture of alumni, and, to Lowell, the national leaders and alumni donors who would give the school its cachet and cash would necessarily come from the Protestant elite.

For Lowell, Columbia University presented a cautionary illustration of what could happen if a school admitted too many Jewish students. Based as it was in New York City, Columbia had access to a large local Jewish community, as Jerome Karabel writes; especially after 1910, the college enrolled large numbers from this community, more than any other Ivy League school. In response, it seems,

Protestant students went elsewhere; though Columbia was "still attracting 16 percent of the sons of New York's elite between 1900 and 1909, the proportion dropped precipitously the following decade to 6 percent.... In the 1920s, just 4 percent enrolled at Columbia; meanwhile, 84 percent matriculated at the Big Three [Harvard, Yale, and Princeton]."[39]

For writers and politicians who believed that Jews were actively dangerous, New York City itself looked like a cautionary illustration. During the first decade of the 20th century, the rate of immigration to the United States was at a historic peak. Not for the last time, politics and the press abounded with race-based anti-immigrant sentiment—which focused in particular on Jews from Eastern Europe, who were painted as potential terrorists: dangerous socialists who might bring violent ideas into the country and foment an underground army of revolutionaries. In 1913, a trustee of Columbia University wrote, arguing against the school's admission of Jews, "They form the worst type of our emigrants, they supply the leaders to anarchistic, socialistic and other movements of unrest. In the recent election the socialistic vote was confined largely to the East Side and to Brownsville, in Brooklyn, where they live." In 1921, the Senate Committee on Immigration saw testimony that included, an observer reported, "a map of New York City that coded in red neighborhoods with high levels of radical activity [and] revealed that these neighborhoods were 'chiefly inhabited by Russian Jews.'" [40]

As always in these cases, there was a lot going on under the surface of this immigrant discourse: fear of otherness, fear of change, fear of losing the privileges of majority status to a new group of people. In 1911, a congressional commission on immigration published a report that described, in ostensibly scientific terms, "the inferiority of the heavily Catholic and Jewish immigrants of southern and eastern Europe compared to their sturdier, more industrious, and predominantly Protestant 'Teutonic' predecessors from Britain,

Scandinavia, Holland, and Germany." White-nationalist books began to hit the bestseller lists: for example, in 1916, *The Passing of the Great Race*, which argued that the immigrant city of New York was becoming dangerously mongrelized. ("The man of the old stock," it warned, "is literally being driven off the streets of New York City by the swarms of Polish Jews.")[41] In 1920, a similar book, *The Rising Tide of Color against White World-Supremacy*, not only became a national bestseller, but also won praise from Warren G. Harding and Calvin Coolidge.[42] Political action followed: in 1917, Congress passed an act that aimed to reduce immigration from Southern and Eastern Europe while retaining immigration from Northern Europe. In 1921, Congress passed another act that aimed to limit immigration, this time restricting the entry of Jews from Poland and Russia as well as Italians, "who were thought to produce anarchists," in order "to keep political radicals out of the United States."[43]

The solution that elite colleges came up with to the "Jewish problem" created the most recognizable features of modern college admissions. Beginning with Harvard, in 1922, colleges began to ask applicants to fill out forms that included "questions on 'Race and Color,' 'Religious Preference,' 'Maiden name of Mother,' and 'Birthplace of Father.'" They asked for letters of reference from teachers and headmasters to attest to the applicant's "aptitude and character." Was the student an athlete? Was he leadership material? Was he *agreeable*? In short, they found ways of determining elements of an applicant's background that allowed them to enforce de facto ethnic quotas.[44]

But there was a second part to the new procedures that elite schools, the Big Three in particular, implemented in the quest for ethnically agreeable student bodies. They expanded their recruitment zones to include areas beyond the Northeast, where they began to send recruiters and cultivate high-school administrators. "Designed to facilitate the admission of 'a new group of men from the West and

South,' the top one-seventh plan seemed to [critics] a thinly disguised attempt to lower the Jewish proportion of the student body by bringing in boys . . . from regions of the country where there were few Jews." It was a strategy that explicitly used geography as a proxy for race.[45]

NETWORK ENGLISH

Just as elite colleges responded to the "Jewish Problem" by turning their recruitment away from the Northeast, elite institutions in the United States at large shifted their preference for prestige pronunciation toward the "purer" regions of the West and the Midwest, where Protestants of "Nordic" descent were more likely to live. This shift was gradual and disorganized, Bonfiglio says: "It is analogous to the phenomenon of the post-war 'white flight' to the suburbs, which was a process of gradual and incremental gravitation, the ethnocentrism of which can generally be read only on the level of submerged or coded discourse."[46] Yet incremental as this change was, and unaware as many individuals were as to why or how it was happening, the standards for educated speech in the United States did change. Within a few decades, newscasters, college graduates, and actors in film and television largely adhered to a rhotic standard—a standard that signified Americanness in large part by distinguishing itself from the speech of America's capital of immigration. Americans sound the way they do because New Yorkers sound the way they do.

A major vehicle of this change was radio. The most dramatic years of the rise of radio, 1931–1945, coincided with a period of political debate about immigration that continued to escalate even after the reforms in immigration policy discussed earlier. They also coincided with the Second World War, which secured the rapid triumph of radio as a medium, ensuring that the voices of radio newscasters were heard in every living room in America. A few factors had an out-sized effect on the sound of radio newscasting. Newspapers saw little future in the field, so they didn't buy radio stations, which it turns out they should have. (In an alternate universe, the biggest broadcaster in the United States isn't CBS, but the *New York Times*.) The people who worked in the new medium were therefore not members of the fourth estate's old guard, but, for the most part, inexperienced young-sters.[47] Normally individuals have little ability to move the tides of language, but in this case an individual had a decisive effect on the way news was reported over the airwaves, and by extension, the changes that real-world variants underwent, as they do, in response to airwave speech. That individual was Edward R. Murrow.

Murrow grew up in beautiful Washington State, where he imbibed the accent of the Pacific Northwest. He studied speech (ora-tory) at Washington State College, taking his B.A. in 1930, and then moved to New York City, as one does, to find his path in the world. From 1933 to 1935, he worked as the assistant secretary for the Emergency Committee in Aid of Displaced Foreign Scholars, which sought to help refugee scholars from Europe find places at American universities.[48] In 1935, he came aboard the Columbia Broadcasting System, a young radio broadcasting company based in New York City, as director of talks, a position that did not entail speaking on the air. Nonetheless, he soon had an influence on the station's news-casting as he ascended to a role that involved hiring other people as speakers. In 1937, he hired William Shirer, a Midwesterner who had been writing for the *Herald Tribune*. In 1939, he hired Eric Sevareid, another Midwesterner who had been working for the Paris office of the *New York Herald-Tribune*.[49]

Murrow wasn't, by any reports, a chauvinist about race or region; possibly he hired a fair number of Midwesterners because he felt a common affinity with them and because, as a Washingtonian, he didn't mind their rhotic speech. He went out of his way to promote the subordinates he took under his charge. For example, when Sevareid, who had first met Murrow in London after Murrow had started working in CBS's London office, had to give a voice audition to be considered as an announcer for CBS, Sevareid was so nervous that his hands shook: "listeners must have heard the paper rattling," he later recalled. The CBS brass indeed disliked the audition, but Murrow hired him anyway, saying of Sevareid's delivery, "I'll fix it."[50] Murrow's mentorship of Sevareid—and of other reporters, who became known as "Murrow Boys"—influenced the sound of news broadcasting for many decades. Sevareid later moved to television, where he continued to report for CBS until 1977. In his final evening news broadcast, he called Murrow "The man who invented me."[51]

But Murrow himself was the journalist who emerged from the war as the undisputed sultan of radio newscasting. He first sat before the microphone in 1938, when the speed of events when Nazi Germany annexed Austria obliged him to collaborate with Shirer, each in a different city, on reporting the news. He continued as a regular reporter for CBS, and did his most famous reporting just two years later, when, during the Blitz of 1940 and 1941, he reported to America from London. The war was still confined to Europe, and Americans, uncertain of whether to enter the war, concerned for the inhabitants of their former mother country, listened avidly to news of the bombings. Estimates suggest that the audience for Murrow's evening broadcast comprised some fifteen million Americans.[52] More than just numbers, however, he reported the bombings like nobody else.[53] Jeffrey Ian Cole conducts a careful study of the elements that gave Murrow's broadcasts literary potency, showing how, in one sample broadcast, Murrow incorporates a variety of figures and color details into a set of messages that goes beyond the mere paraphrase of events: "the common man battling a force over which he had little control; the democracy of an air-raid shelter; a metaphor using a common object, a cigarette, to represent a beacon in a darkened London." He also quotes Dixon Wecter, who wrote about radio for *The Atlantic Monthly*, as saying of Murrow's work that "the major premises of American democracy . . . can be detected in almost every broadcast."[54]

So when Murrow returned to the States in 1941—from his comments at the time, it seems that he wanted to help persuade Americans away from isolationist policies and felt he couldn't ethically take such an opinionated stance in his London reports—he returned as the country's most famous journalist. Radio had become the primary medium that Americans used to get their news. As Cole notes, the first radio newscast in the States, in 1920, reached perhaps 500 to 1,000 listeners; in 1941, newscasts about the attack on Pearl Harbor reached more than 100 million people. By 1942, more households owned a radio than owned almost any other appliance. And Americans looked to radio for entertainment as well as news. When *Fortune* magazine asked Americans which pastime they liked best, the most popular response was, "Listening to the radio." And here was Edward R. Murrow, back from the war, "lean, dark, and handsome" (in the *New Yorker's* words) and the owner of a baritone voice known in every living room in the country: "the only foreign correspondent," said one writer, "who could play a foreign correspondent in the movies and give the role all the glamour Hollywood wants."[55]

Variants on the ground can change in response to variants on the airwaves; this is a widely observed phenomenon. In Britain, for example, the longstanding use of Received Pronunciation (RP) on the radio and television has demonstrably changed regional variants, even though RP is an artificial accent. The very trait that ushered RP into standardization, that it was a distinctive class accent learned in elite schools, became dissociated by the fact of standardization, so that RP could give the impression of speech without a class or place of origin. (As Dick Leith notes, "its status as an accent has even been denied: if you speak RP, you speak English 'without an accent.' ")[56]

This is to say that Murrow's career holds linguistic significance because Murrow's success at CBS helped to ensure that "Network English" in the United States had a distinctly Murrovian sound. After the war, as Cole writes, "Murrow boys" who had trained in Europe, such as Cecil Brown, Winston Burdett, Charles Collingwood, Richard C. Hottelet, Larry LeSeur, Eric Sevareid, and Howard K. Smith, spread his manner through American radio and, before long, television. They also trained emerging voices, such as Walter Cronkite, Chet Huntley, Roger Mudd, Dan Rather, Harry Reasoner, David Schoenbrun, and Mike Wallace, who seemed to have the Murrow DNA. And Murrow, too, appeared regularly on television for decades.[57]

Few people read newspaper bylines, but we know the names of radio and television reporters. We hear their voices, see their faces, more often than we do the voices and faces of many of our friends. They share, or seem to share, those moments in our lives in which we feel especially like common people battling forces over which we have little control. Many radio journalists who had entered the war as small fry—American newspapers and press agencies, hoping to smother radio in the cradle, wouldn't even allow their reporters to speak on the air—found themselves returning home as celebrities. Moreover, their celebrity was profoundly interlinked with the war. For the American public, the positive resonance of the Western cadences of these reporters' speech, the way their regional identity linked up with emerging ideologies of American identity, "would have been massively strengthened," as Bonfiglio argues, "by their juxtapositions with the cultural signs of World War II. The drama, pathos, and unequivocal morality of that war could only have empowered that accent by association." In short, it's entirely reasonable, perhaps inevitable, that the speech of newscasters should become synonymous with the voice of authority, and even that a newscaster should gain the title of "the most trusted man in America," as Walter Cronkite famously did in the 1970s.[58]

During the war and for some time afterward, educated East Coast speech still held considerable prestige. President Franklin D. Roosevelt, who spoke a dainty that he acquired as a child in upper-class New York and honed at Groton and Harvard, was, after Murrow, the most important radio speaker of the wartime years.[59] In his famous "fireside chats," which reached a listening audience with a high point of almost 80 percent of American homes, as well as in his other radio speeches, he used a distinctly nonrhotic accent, along with Briticisms such as pronouncing *been* as "bean," *again* as "agayne," *against* as "agaynst," *either* as "eye-ther," and *neither* as "nye-ther."[60] Roosevelt combined this patrician diction with an idiom as plain and straightforward as Murrow's, showing that the elitist rationale of dainties was not incompatible with an egalitarian tone. (Roosevelt and Murrow set up a dinner meeting in 1941, which would have placed the foremost representatives of the nation's two forms of prestige pronunciation, the old dainty and the emerging network standard, in conversation over the same table. Unfortunately, the dinner meeting took place on December 7, which meant that, though Murrow still came, Roosevelt was away and busy throughout the evening.)[61]

Nevertheless, people working within the new standard for network English were already creating an ideological superstructure for it, as Bonfiglio notes. In 1943, James Bender, an Ohio native who taught speech at Queens College, and whom NBC had recently hired to teach diction to its reporters, published the authoritative-sounding *NBC Handbook of Pronunciation*, which supports a rhotic model of speech that Bender calls "General American." There, he makes the surprising claim that Americans have never accepted speech training that follows elite models: "Americans have always resented superimposition in matters dealing with standards of pronunciation. Government *académies*, designed to indicate 'correct' pronunciation, have not been tolerated." Instead, he says, Americans naturally feel that speech is best when it resembles, democratically, the speech of the most, which in the U.S. means the rhotic speech heard inland. "Thus," he adds, "a standard of pronunciation for the American broadcaster is reasonably based upon the speech heard and used by the radio audience that the broadcaster reaches."[62] Bender also links "General American" with the American West, which, while true if you're following the cardinal directions, is far too broad if you're describing regional variants, and which foreshadows how support for the new rhotic standard would programmatically align the American character with a romantic vision of the old western frontier.[63]

NEW YORK VALUES

The rationales that Harvard had used, in 1923, to pursue students who lived in regions away from the East Coast, emphasized populism and American identity. The "building up of a new group of men from the West and South, from good high schools in towns and small cities," explains a report by the Harvard committee assigned to study the admissions problem, would ensure that "the student body will be properly representative of all groups in our national life." The language of the report, as Bonfiglio notes, is a familiar (by now) form of populist discourse, where terms like *small-town* and *American* are used to stand in for *white Protestant*: "Of special note is the phrase 'country boys from the interior,' which indicates a protected internal area, a heartland insulated from the influence of coastal degeneration, where one would find, in the words of Columbia's dean, 'the average native American boy.'" The policy change that Harvard was proposing was on its face fairly radical, as it required the university to adopt the premise that the ideal Harvard boy would not live near the grounds of Harvard. He couldn't, since the ideal Harvard boy would be the ideal American boy, and the ideal American boy could no longer be seen to come from the cities of the East Coast.[64]

Again and again, as Bonfiglio notes, we find the same themes in rhetoric from this period that seeks to valorize the West as the true America. *Inhabitants of the interior are native-born Americans, whereas inhabitants of the East Coast are newcomers and outsiders. Earlier generations of immigrants assimilated quickly to American society, whereas the kinds of immigrants who are coming in now refuse to assimilate.* Harvard was not alone, but merely exemplary in marshalling this rhetoric. Lawrence Lowell, the president of Harvard during the admissions debate, said in a speech to the class of 1922, "During the earlier period of our country, and indeed to some extent so long as there was a broad area of frontier life to the westward, newcomers from other lands were easily assimilated ... now that our population has become vastly more dense, and huge numbers of strangers newly come from overseas are massed together in industrial centers, the problem of assimilation has become more difficult."[65] Or again, Charles Grandgent, the chair of the Harvard committee on admissions policy, published a paper in 1920 (he was a philologist) that praised the Midwest for retaining the postvocalic /r/ while other parts of the country, dissolutely following foreign fashions, abandoned it: "America has, in the main, followed about the same paths as the parent lands; but our enterprising Middle West, unwilling to abandon the r tradition, has developed and cherished an r-substitute, homely, to be sure, but vigorous and aggressive. What has the future in store? Will decay pursue its course; or will a reaction set in, restoring to the English-speaking world a real r of some kind, or a tolerable substitute?"[66] (It's merely a coincidence that the committee chair happened to be a scholar of language, but his contention that Midwestern speech is true American speech likely provided him with ready arguments for viewing Midwestern boys as true American boys.)

In this, Lowell and Grandgent were building on what was already a minor tradition. Consider Frederick Jackson Turner, a historian and bestselling author who made an early and influential argument that linked the American spirit with the spirit of the frontier, and also, in a 1911 essay, lamented the fall of the frontier spirit and the rise of a new population of immigrants—who came, he said, in "increasing measure from southern and eastern Europe."[67] According to these narratives, the values that best represented the American people were to be found far away from America's largest communities. Bonfiglio describes regional consciousness under this ideology as increasingly conflicted: "Simultaneously, New York was and was not, and Boston was and was not a proper locus of American power and identity."[68]

By the 1940s, these trends were affecting the attitudes of laymen toward assorted regional variants. In 1942, two language scholars conducted a study in which 2,700 persons from eight parts of the country listened to recordings of the speech of men from various regions. (More than one speaker represented a given region.) Listeners then rated the speakers and answered questions like, "Where do you think this type of speech is from?", "Do you like this type of pronunciation?", and "Would it be an advantage for you to have this type of pronunciation in your everyday life?"[69] In the study, the five speakers whom listeners most approved of used "General American" (which was by then a common term for Midwestern speech). Among the American accents, the two speakers from greater New York City received the most disapproval. (The authors characterize the speech of one as having "Yiddish Influence.") The authors expressed surprise at the low esteem that listeners accorded New York City speech, which, after all, had long represented education, sophistication, and economic might. They also observed that listeners from the New York area tended to give low rankings to speech from their own city, which was not the case for most other regions: "there is some tendency for subjects to prefer the local type of speech (except in the New York metropolitan area where the opposite is true)."[70]

In 1950, the linguist Allan Forbes Hubbell published an extensive study of speakers in New York City that records, for the first time, the efforts of some New Yorkers to suppress or reduce the nonrhoticity of their own speech. "Some speakers," he writes—"not very many— pronounce /r/ in the preconsonantal position as regularly and consistently as do speakers of General American." In others he finds "the complete absence of any pattern. Such speakers pronounce /r/ before a consonant or a pause and sometimes omit it, in a thoroughly haphazard fashion. In many cases this irregularity is a result of the conscious attempt, only partly successful, of originally 'r-less' speakers to pronounce the consonant because they feel that it is more 'correct' to do so."[71] Thus while New York City remained, like Boston, generally nonrhotic in its local variants, locals understood that feature to be a flaw that could be evaded by code-switching to rhotic speech. In 1962, a researcher found that informants in New York City were using rhotic and nonrhotic speech forms in roughly equal amounts.[72]

The problem for these speakers was that variant is treated as a brand of personality. Regional chauvinisms, combined with wider cultural discourses like the ones we have been tracing, mean that speakers of nonstandard variants risk being seen, not just as incorrect, not just as provincial, but as friendly and slow, or smart and dishonest, or some other assortment of traits beyond their control. When researchers ask us to evaluate the moral character of other people based on their variants, we recognize the question to reflect on a process that occurs in real life, which we wouldn't if they asked us to evaluate the moral character of others based on their heights. In a 1969 study, when young people listened to a range of ethnic and regional variants (the two overlap, of course) and evaluated the speakers based on a catalog of personal virtues—"upbringing, intelligent, friendly, educated, disposition, speech, trustworthy, ambitious, faith in God, talented, character, determination, honest, personality, considerate"—they accorded the top rankings to speakers of the network standard, preferring it over the accents of their home regions. (The speakers who ranked lowest overall were from New York City and Mississippi.)[73] The network standard can seem, to Americans, to be speech "without an accent," but it still manages to convey powerful suggestions about personal character.

Films often take advantage of these perceptions, sometimes in realistic and sometimes in absurd ways. In *Good Will Hunting* (1997), as Bonfiglio notes, the young men of working-class Boston use non-rhotic speech, while their peers at Harvard use rhotic speech. In *I Know What You Did Last Summer* (1997), set in Southport, North Carolina, the teens who plan to attend college use Standard American speech, while the teens who don't plan to go to college use speech dipped in regionalisms.[74] In *Captain America: The First Avenger* (2011) and its sequels in the Marvel franchise, Steve Rogers, a.k.a. Captain America, speaks Standard American English despite having grown up in Brooklyn in the 1930s. Captain America is a hero, not a "local color" character, not comic relief; his accent makes his hero status unambiguous, which in the films' storytelling is more important than another potential use of his accent: as yet another marker of the distance between the world he grew up in, the New York City of the years preceding the Second World War, and the contemporary world he now finds himself in. Well, if anyone is intelligent, friendly, trustworthy, faithful, determined, honest, and considerate, it's Captain America.[75]

A NEW YORK STATE OF MIND

Dainties took a few decades to fade entirely from finishing schools. In 1960, the nation welcomed a new First Lady, Jackie Kennedy, who spoke with a distinctive New York Dainty that she learned at Miss Porter's School. But the *sound* of dainties faded quickly from popular culture, while the variants of lower-class New York persist today in cinema and television, though in some cases the pronunciations being used are outdated by half a century. The stereotypical New York sound can be heard in Bugs Bunny cartoons, Woody Allen movies, Batman cartoons, and television procedurals like *Law & Order*, where, as Bonfiglio remarks, any character not dressed in a suit is likely to have a Noo Yawk accent.[76] It can also be heard in pop culture narratives with unexpected settings: a spaceship in a distant galaxy, a Tolkienesque fantasy world, medieval Saudi Arabia—places where we might expect not to find a New York City accent because in those settings New York City does not exist. All of this reflects the migration of the New York accent, together with the brand of personality that it's supposed to represent, into the realm of popular mythology: a New York City of the mind.

In 1998, two sociolinguists, Julia Dobrow and Calvin Gidney, conducted a classic study of variants in children's cartoons. Its lessons still hold very much true today.[77] In American television cartoons aimed at a young audience, they found, villains tend to have either foreign accents (British accents are especially popular) or New York accents. By contrast, the good guys almost always have Standard American diction. The received idea that this arrangement trades in, of course, is that Standard American speech is trustworthy and foreign speech is not. The New York accent, in its use as a standard villain accent, is arguably being treated as a subcategory of foreign speech (perhaps as a response to the city's immigrant population). The difference is that serious villains have true foreign accents, whereas villains with New York accents are used as comic relief. For example, the clumsy henchmen who work for a major villain might use a New York variant—with features like "dis" for *this* and "bakin'" for *baking*—that Dobrow and Gidney call "Italian-American gangster."[78]

If we extend our purview to animated movies, the pattern seems to be much the same. In *The Lion King* (1994), the ruler of the lions has a Standard American accent, while his brother, the villainous Scar, has a subtle English accent. In *Aladdin* (1992), the hero has a Standard American accent, the villain has an English accent, and the villain's comic henchbird, Iago the parrot, has a New York accent. (He was voiced by Gilbert Gottfried.) However, the rule that New York accents are comic accents provides a measure of flexibility, as Dobrow and Gidney note: a character on the side of the good guys can also have a New York accent, provided he is a funny character. In these cases, the character tends to be street-smart, a wisecracker, but also a little cowardly and unscrupulous. In *The Lion King*, one of the hero's sidekicks, a meercat named Timon, fits all of these attributes, to which he adds a New York wiseacre schtick bestowed by his voice actor, Nathan Lane. In the television show *Aladdin* (1994–95), a spin-off from the movie, Iago was promoted to the role of sidekick for the good guys. He was still a crook, but now he was a loveable crook. My favorite example of this motif is from the justly forgotten animated show *Beast Wars: Transformers* (1996–99). The show takes place on a planet far off in space, and none of the characters (they are robots who can transform into animals) seems to have ever heard of Earth. Nevertheless, one of the characters—only one of them—has an outrageous New York accent: he is Rattrap, a wiseacre whose animal form is a rat and whose catchphrase is, "We're all gonna die."[79] Rattrap's voice actor, Scott McNeil, grew up in Canada, so we know the accent was a deliberate choice.

GIVING IT TO THE MAN

This use of a New York accent onscreen—as a form of dialect comedy, a stock character's defining tic—is as old as the use of sound in film. The first "talkie," *The Jazz Singer* (1927), set in New York's Lower East Side, mixes sound dialogue with title cards. The protagonist uses the Californianized accent of the actor who plays him, Al Jolson, but the title cards, which give the dialogue of the protagonist's family and friends on the Lower East Side, use spelling and grammar that often make the dialogue into Jewish dialect comedy. ("A fine cantor you are going to be—smeshing synagogue windows yet!") The joke being made with the city variant (or rather, this particular city variant) is the same as that often made with the Cockney variant of London: Cockney speakers "should know better, since they did not have the excuse of living miles away from the center of power, culture, and fashion," and so its incorrectness is especially egregious.[80]

The most famous speaker of a lower-class New York variant in early film history is Groucho Marx, whose pronunciations, such as [bɜɪn] for *burn*, had not long before belonged to the upper-class variant of Teddy Roosevelt. The characters that Groucho played in his films were not just comic and quick-witted, but pointedly lower class and pointedly ethnic. In the 1937 film *A Day at the Races*, which addresses themes of racial conflict, the Marx brothers align themselves with African Americans against white elites; after all, according to racial ideologies of the time, as Jews, they too were people of color.[81]

Groucho's fast-talking persona helped to beget a cartoon character who is today the world's most famous user of the Teddy Roosevelt (and Groucho) accent, a style of pronunciation that is now outdated by more than half a century: Bugs Bunny.[82] Bugs got his start in the 1930s, when animators at Warner Bros. were scrambling to create competitors to Disney's popular stable of cartoon animals. Because Disney's characters embodied all-American values, Warner Bros. created a bunny character who was sly, cocky, and cool.[83] By the 1940s, Bugs had become, as the animators said, "a tough little stinker." The character's voice actor, the California native Mel Blanc, decided that someone who fit that description should properly be a New Yorker: "They wanted a tough little character," he said. "So, I thought maybe either someone who came from Brooklyn or the Bronx, which was the toughest talking area in the world. And

I thought, 'Why don't I put them both together?' "[84] In portraying Bugs as a quintessential New Yorker, Blanc borrowed verbal mannerisms from the low world of the streets ("What's up, Doc?"), as well as catchphrases from Groucho himself: "This means war!"[85] Sometimes Bugs even wielded his carrot like Groucho's cigar, tapping off imaginary ash.

The humor, with these characters and others who took up their manner, stems from the marginal position that the New York accent had come to represent. For if the New York accent meant comedy, then as now, because it was implicitly a "foreign" accent, it also evoked a narrative in which an underdog uses the American values of persistence and entrepreneurial guile to overcome, to make a fool of, his larger foes.[86] The Three Stooges, a comedy group that produced 190 short films for Columbia between 1934 and 1957, mixed the old New York sound with anarchic assaults against polite society. In the comedy duo Abbott and Costello, the straight man, Bud Abbott, uses a more standard accent even though he's the one who grew up in Brooklyn; Lou Costello, who grew up in New Jersey, uses what would have read as a purer New York sound, talking twice as fast as Abbott and using words like "de" (*the*) and "fo:st" (*first*).[87] And Rodney Dangerfield, who worked from the 1940s into the early 2000s, portrayed himself as the ultimate underdog ("I don't get no respect") but charmed the audience into rooting for his success.[88]

By such means, mainstream culture's tacit coding of New Yorkers as nonwhite, as non-American, enabled people to use New York speech patterns on the screen to address themes of cultural difference. "Groucho Marx's humor," as one historian writes, "stemmed from his self-conception as an outsider in his own country. He pointed out the hypocrisy of discrimination and the marginalization of ethnic immigrants and their families, who had to prove that they were as American as their Anglo-American neighbors."[89] In the case of Bugs Bunny, the same operations are in play, although the audience is doing more work to extract the meaning. Whereas Mickey Mouse talks (as the historian John Alberti writes) in a safe Standard American accent, a high falsetto voice that appeals to children (children and dogs both react to high-pitched voices as being especially aimed at them), Bugs has a greater appeal to adults, perhaps because he seems to be living in something closer to the adult world. Alberti relates Bugs, a trickster who uses wiles to defeat bigger foes, to trickster figures, like Brer Rabbit, who populate African American folk culture: "Bugs . . . remained a multi-ethnic hybrid, a cross between the trickster figure from West African folklore that had become a part of African American folklore and the smart street hustler associated with immigrant inner-city neighborhoods."[90] Bugs seems to hold a certain appeal for African American comedians, as well. The comedian Dave Chappelle, who has named Bugs Bunny among his inspirations, sometimes seems to be imitating Bugs's verbal style.[91] "Bugs Bunny was black," another comedian, Mystro Clark, has remarked: "for one he was cool. He never got flustered and he was always giving it to the man."[92]

IN NEW YORK, YOU CAN BE A NEW MAN

As the stock of New York City English continued to sink, films and television began to use it as a language of characters who felt they were being left behind and were insecure about it. The sitcom *All in the Family* (1971–79), which focused on the doings and sayings of Archie Bunker, a working-class bigot from Queens, featured a version of New York City English that must have seemed especially pronounced because it was a little anachronistic. The sitcom, which was one of the biggest television shows of the 1970s, based much of its comedy on mocking, through Archie's acerbic commentary, the social changes that accompanied the civil rights movement and the women's liberation movement, along with what Adam Gopnik calls, in a related context, "the sudden rise of the wide-eyed optimism of liberalism—the rhetoric of rights, personal growth, acceptance, and ostentatious tolerance."[93] The show's viewers seem to have seen in Archie what the show's producers intended for them to see: a sort of buffoonish King Lear character, empathetic in spite of his obvious flaws, bewildered and outraged by a world which, as he realizes, has left him behind.[94] The omnipresent sign of his having been left behind is his thick New York City English, which his own daughter and son-in-law do not share at all, and which is made ridiculous by his constant flow of malapropisms: "C'mon, youse two"; "You see that, you can't learn 'em nothin'"; "There ain't nothin a say, Florence"; "And then the topper of all, Edith—as the French used to say, the piece a resistance. I'm on the subway an I get a boin hole right there in my best comin-home-from-woik pants." Moreover, his use of the sliding vowel [ɔɪ] was outdated by decades (at least in the speech of middle-aged people): a language form as artificial as Received Pronunciation. Its prominent role in Archie's speech helped to sustain the vowel's place in the mythology of New York City—and likely deepened the insecurity of real New Yorkers over the way they sounded.

If a character who spoke New York City English registered this insecurity, her story was drama; if she didn't, her story was comedy. In *Funny Face* (1957), a magazine photographer takes photos of an elegant model posing with an abstract statue. The photographer encourages the model to adopt a thinker's pose: "You are in the Museum of Modern Art, Marion. Deep, Marion. Profound, Marion. You have come across this statue. It says something to you because you are intellectual, always thinking. What are you thinking?" She replies, in a *shocking* working-class accent, "I'm thinkin' this is takin' a lɔng tɔime, and I'll nevə be able to pick up Hærold's lɔndry. Boy, when Hærold doesn't get his lɔndry, disæstə." The joke is that the accent is incongruous with the elegance of the model and the gentility of her setting.

For precisely this reason, the line was written to maximize New York vowels: the /ə/ at the end of *never*, the /ɔ/ in *laundry*, the infamous New York /æ/ in *Harold* and *disaster*.[95]

By contrast, in *Working Girl* (1988), Tess, a secretary from Staten Island who wants a promotion to management, shows, by trying to abandon her accent, that she deserves not to be laughed at. At the start of the film, she tells her friend in a working-class accent, "No lunch. I got speech class." Her friend replies in the same accent, "Whaddaya need speech class foə? You tɔk fine." Here, of course, the joke is that the friend has demonstrated exactly why Tess needs speech class. Her accent is *incorrect*, at least according to the film's *Pygmalion* structure, and therefore it's holding Tess back. Later, Tess listens to recordings of her boss, an executive with polished Standard American English, and imitates her diction. "Dear Sister," says one recording, a letter dictation, "it's hard to believe, but it's been eight years since we said good-bye to Wellesley. But of course, we never really say good-bye. And on behalf of the Alumni Giving Fund, I'm writing to you to ask . . ." Tess pauses the recording and repeats the dictation in her boss's accent, focusing especially on the word *ask*, which in Tess's accent has the embarrassing New York /æ/: " 'Dear Sister, it's hard to believe, but it's been eight years since we said good-bye to Wellesley. But of course, we never really say good-bye. And on behalf of the Alumni Giving Fund, I'm writing to you to ask . . .' To ask . . . to ask . . . to ask. . . . I'm writing to you to ask. . . ."

DUNGEONS, DRAGONS, AND DIALECTS

The mythology of the city's language may be most apparent in works of fantasy. An especially famous fantastical mirror of New York City is Gotham City, a name born in the pages of DC Comics in 1941. (Of course, the name *Gotham* has been an alias of the city since the 19th century, when Washington Irving used it in a series of satirical essays about New Yorkers, taking the name from an English village whose inhabitants were supposed to be fools.) Gotham City is the home of Batman, who patrols the streets at night as a masked vigilante. In early comics, Batman lived in New York City; he moved to Gotham in 1941, under the theory that readers could more easily imagine it as their own city, but in practice Gotham has always been understood to be New York City under another name.[96] Gotham, like New York City, has five boroughs, and DC artists have consistently borrowed from the older buildings in Manhattan to create Gotham's brooding, Gothic architecture. (According to some depictions, a statue of "Lady Gotham" stands in the city's harbor.) One DC editor has called Gotham "a distillation of everything that's dark, moody, and frightening about New York. It's Hell's Kitchen. The Lower East Side. Bed Stuy. The South Bronx. Soho and Tribeca off the main thoroughfares at three in the morning."[97]

In all of his iterations, Batman speaks Standard American English. Well, it's to be expected; Bruce Wayne attended fancy prep schools and then the Ivy League. But in every iteration, the thugs, mooks, and henchmen who populate most of the city's criminal underclass use New York City features in their speech. So does the comedic villain Harley Quinn, whose most recognizable feature in television, films, and video games may be her singsong New York accent. In fact, the mythology that these speech features represent is strong enough to override the aesthetic demand of realism in versions of Gotham that differ from the norm. For example, Christopher Nolan, the director of the 2005 film *Batman Begins*, has said that he thinks of Gotham as a fictionalized Chicago.[98] Nonetheless, many of the thugs and henchmen in that film use nonrhotic speech, which is a feature of New York City, not Chicago. Or again, in the newest film franchise that includes Batman, the DC Extended Universe, Metropolis and Gotham are just across a bay from one another, visible from each other's shores. Nonetheless, Gotham has characters with New York accents and Metropolis does not. The difference between them simply comes down to mythology, or our cultural imagination of the place. Metropolis has always been depicted as more optimistic, more all-American, than Gotham. Frank Miller, a famous comic book writer and illustrator, phrased the distinction this way: "Metropolis is New York in the daytime; Gotham City is New York at night."[99]

But it's in the realm of *pure* fantasy—magic lamps, enchanted woods, galaxies far, far away—that we find the clearest distillation of the mythology of New York City speech. For these works have no reason, on the grounds of setting or plot, to distinguish a character as a New York City type. The speech is an act of pure characterization. As we have seen, *Aladdin* is set in the antique Middle East, and *Beast Wars* is set on a planet with no human habitation, yet both see fit to distinguish particular characters from everyone else via a New York accent. In a more recent film, *Guardians of the Galaxy* (2014), which follows the adventures of a band of misfits on a spaceship in a distant sector of our galaxy, one character has a New York accent: Rocket Raccoon, a talking raccoon from the planet Halfworld. He has a New York accent because he's shrewd, unscrupulous, and mouthy, not because he has ever been near Earth (he hasn't). Only one member of his team is (half-) human, and that character, the film's protagonist, speaks Standard American English.[100]

Did you know that C-3PO was originally going to have a New York accent? When George Lucas wrote the early scripts for *Star Wars*, he expected that C-3PO would have "the cadences of a Bronx used-car dealer." Only after the English actor Anthony Daniels, who delivered lines at the table read in a placeholder role, delivered a compelling interpretation of the robot sidekick, did Lucas rewrite the character as "a fussy English butler." (Actually, both Lucas and Daniels dragged their feet for a while, as Daniels disliked space operas and Lucas really thought the car-dealer robot idea had legs.)[101]

While the idea of the protocol droid as a New Yorker may seem odd at first, it's worth dwelling for a moment on what might have been—and on why it would have been that way. After all, George Lucas deals not in realism but in archetype, and with more success than anyone else in the business. To start with, C-3PO is a *funny sidekick*. He's a good guy, but not a hero; indeed, he's something of a coward, which is a handy source of internal conflict throughout his storyline, and which remains an aspect of his character in the Anthony Daniels rendition: no stiff upper lip for this butler. He's also part of a comedy duo, with the sensible R2-D2 playing the straight man and C-3PO playing the clown.

If you read through an early script (I consulted one titled "The Star Wars" and dated 1974, three years before *Star Wars* hit theaters), you find a version of C-3PO that makes sense as a brash New Yorker. Here, the two droids, identified as Artoo and Threepio, are not servants of Princess Leia, but rather "construction robots." They slide into the main storyline rather haphazardly: they start out as mechanics on an Imperial space fortress, flee in an escape pod when the fortress comes under attack, and bump into Luke, Leia, and company after touching down on a planet's surface. They join the resistance simply because the resistance finds droids useful and droids don't have loyalty. Artoo talks in this version, by the way, and his conversations with Threepio—they fight constantly, but they need each other, like all comic duos—are full of insults and accusations:

> THREEPIO: I don't care what you do, but I'm getting out. All the power's out. Those explosions are coming from the reactor section. This is the end. Abandon ship.
>
> ARTWO: Our work—we can't leave! It's desertion. It's not possible. It's not possible.

THREEPIO: Your programming is so limited. My first order is preservation. You stay. I'm going to eject before the whole thing goes up.[102]

In this version of the characters, Threepio shows more pragmatism and self-preservation than does Artoo, who cares more about fulfilling the directives given to him from above. And while this Threepio says a few lines that we know from the movie, in this narrative, the lines appear in a new light. For example, he introduces himself to a new acquaintance as he does in *Star Wars*: "I'm Seethreepio, Human-Cyborg Relations. Your kindness is greatly appreciated."[103] But while Anthony Daniels delivers this line straight—albeit with a smug propriety that we might laugh at—this version of the character is supposed, I think, to deliver the line with irony: because he's pretending to a diplomatic role that he doesn't really have; because he's being far more polite, in this moment, than he really is; and because he's speaking with a thick "Bronx" accent that presumably undercuts the decorum: "Soitanly. Ah'm Seethreepio, yuman-cybɔːg relations. Yeh kindness is greatly appreciated."[104] In fact, he says the line several times over—whenever he meets a new person. It's a comic riff, a callback joke that he has with himself. (*Third base!*)

For me, the most jarring instance of New York City English as a fantasy variant doesn't come from the *Star Wars* drafts, but rather from a fantasy roleplaying game. *World of Warcraft*, which first launched in 2004, is a massive multiplayer online game where users roleplay as orcs, dwarves, paladins, elves, and other creatures in a Tolkienesque fantasy landscape. Here's the thing: in *World of Warcraft*, goblins tend toward New York accents. One prominent goblin, Gazlowe, speaks perfect New York henchman: "We got work to do, buddy!" "You can get anything done for a price." "So they blew themselves up, you say? Now that's occupational commitment! Anyway, ya done good, kid. Take these items, it's the least I can do to repay ya." (An official character description likens Gazlowe to a cab driver: "If Azeroth was New York City, Gazlowe would be a cabby. He's a wise cracking smart-guy, whose only real concerns are besting the Gnomes in an invention and design war. Gazlowe is cranky and abrasive, but means well deep down.")[105]

In a Tolkienesque world, what kind of fantasy race suggests a New York accent? In *World of Warcraft*, goblins are swindlers, traders, and con men; they are simultaneously big spenders, and hoarders, of wealth. The first reference for players is likely the game's official wiki, which states:

> Goblins are small humanoids, crafty and shrewd, bearing an overwhelming interest in commerce and a strong curiosity about mechanical things. Goblin society is fragmented, defined chiefly by commerce and trade. The ultimate schemers and con artists, goblins are always in search of a better deal. . . . Their mission in the world is to create incredible new inventions, accrue the resulting wealth, and cause as much subtle mischief as possible along the way.[106]

I sent this text, along with some audio clips of Warcraft goblins speaking, to a colleague who works in linguistics and asked for his thoughts. The next time we met, he said with an apology that he didn't listen to the clips because, after reading the description, he was afraid that the clips would be anti-Semitic. I was taken off guard—and chagrined—because I hadn't intended to reference something like that. I don't think the goblin variant references Jewish speech patterns. But it does reference New York speech patterns, and in popular culture the stereotypes that New York Speech patterns reference, in turn, rely on a history of distrust toward the Jewish and immigrant populations of New York City. The idea that fantasy races can reflect stereotypes about real-world ethnic and cultural groups is not new;

in Tolkien, critics have often remarked, hobbits seem to represent the Irish, dwarves the Scots, and humans the English. In *World of Warcraft*, for better or for worse, New Yorkers have taken their place in this modern mythology.

HELLO! THIS IS LIBERTY SPEAKING

This chapter has discussed the historical development of New York speech as an artifact of our collective imagination, with the city's speech changing from—potentially—the prestige pronunciation of the United States to a form of pronunciation that defines American English only by way of contrast. Those changes have affected both the choices of individual New Yorkers in the management of their speech and wider shifts in the patterning of New York City variants. They have also affected the biases with which Americans, including New Yorkers, listen to speakers who sound like New York.[107] Although no variant in existence can be said to be "sloppy" or "careless," those terms, along with "fast," "rude," and "very little schooling," belong to the words that listeners from around the United States use to characterize New York speech, antitheses to American values like friendliness and education.[108]

Still, as a few famous instances suggest, in times of external danger, American values and New York values have been found to be encouragingly compatible. Bugs Bunny first appeared onscreen in 1938, but it was in 1941, when the U.S. government asked Warner Bros. to create a short cartoon promoting defense bonds to show in movie theaters, that the character really took off. Bugs's war-bond short gives the "tough little stinker" a foe that outscales him more than any other he's faced, namely the Nazi regime. Nevertheless, the audience recognizes that he is at his best precisely when the going gets tough; and, as Bugs suggests via a series of allusive costume changes, the "urban" traits that define him as a character—a head for enterprise, a pragmatic willingness to work every angle, a penchant for show business, an eternal position of fighting up from below—are thoroughly American.

Audiences responded powerfully to the image of the tough little New Yorker fighting for their side. An animator from the golden age of Warner Bros., Bob Clampett, has remarked that, for Americans during the Second World War, Bugs became "a symbol of America's resistance to Hitler and the fascist powers . . . we were in a battle for our lives, and it is most difficult now to comprehend the tremendous emotional impact Bugs Bunny exerted on the audience then.'"[109] Nor was Bugs the only New Yorker to be conscripted, onscreen, to bring the city's mythos to the defense of the nation. In *Casablanca* (1942), Humphrey Bogart plays yet another tough guy with a New York accent, and, while speaking to a Nazi officer, he gives a shout-out to his hometown: "Well, there are certain sections of New York, Major, that I wouldn't advise you to try to invade." The story goes that when audiences in New York City heard this line, they gave it thundering applause.

Of course, New York *has* been invaded—first by the Dutch, and then by the British. For American victors of the Revolutionary War, the city was, militarily, the birthplace of a new country, and newcomers from every part of the Earth have come to America through New York. As we will see in the next chapter, each new group to call New York home has shaped the city in ways that are still present when we read a subway map or give someone directions.

Chapter 3

On and Off the Map

MIRANDA
O brave new world,
That has such people in 't!

PROSPERO
'Tis new to thee.

—William Shakespeare, The Tempest (c. 1611)[1]

The map is not the territory, as the saying goes, but the map is a meaningful landscape in its own right. Place names, in particular, tie the territory to human history, as they provide a view into the feelings, values, and agendas of the people who confer those names; reflect the ways in which the territory gives shape to people's experiences; and accumulate, over time, deep banks of cultural meaning, so that an address on Fifth Avenue can mean something entirely different to locals than an address on Tenth Avenue. This chapter examines the names that settlers have written and rewritten over the territory that became New York City, starting from the days of Dutch exploration of the region.

If the Dutch had never set foot in the region, New York would most likely be known simply as *York*. In 1664, when the English took over possession of New Amsterdam, they renamed the colony in honor of the Duke of York—King Charles's second son, also styled the Duke of Albany, and the proprietor of the colony from his home in London. The compound *New York* was unusual, however; at the time, the term *New* rarely appeared in place names in English. That habit of naming belonged to the Dutch, who set *Nieuw Amsterdam* on a colonial map that included, in the same region, *Nieuw Amersfoort, Nieuw Dorp, Nieuw Haarlem,* and *Nieuw Naderland,* and farther afield, *Nieuw Holland, Nieuw Zealand,* and another *Nieuw Amsterdam* (this time in Guyana). New York is *New* York only as a loan translation of *Nieuw* Amsterdam, a surprising and somewhat touching tribute to the colony's former holders.[2] But this style of naming, so unusual for a British colony, caught on in British North America—influenced perhaps by the Spanish, who often used the same style for their American holdings, such as *Nuevo México,* but also perhaps by the growing prominence of "New-York" as a center of British commerce, migration, and military power: a testament to the new land's wealth and possibility.

Over time, this style of naming became a defining feature of American toponymy. A glance across a map of the United States shows endless—and, to this reader, extravagant and optimistic—declarations of renewal: *Newark* (archaic for *new ark*), *New Bedford, New Brighton, New Britain, New Carlisle, New Chester, New Cumberland, New England, New Gloucester, New Hampshire, New Hanover, New Haven, New Ipswich, New Jersey, New Kent, New London, New Lyme, New Manchester, New Mexico, New Orleans, New Oxford, New Windsor.* If these names drew upon nostalgia for other places, the insistent *new* registered an emerging American character: a belief in starting over, a lust for competition, and a certain guileless audacity. (You have London? Fine, we'll make New London. It's sure to be even better.) Arguably, this practice helped to shape American identity, reinforcing a national sense of place in which anything could be new. *In New York, you can be a new man.*

Historians look to place names for insights into the history of a region's settlement; but more than that, place names assert ownership, legitimize histories, perpetuate local mythology, and even provide frameworks for living. Over New York City's history, population changes and historical events, large and small, wrote and rewrote the toponymic text of the city. This chapter examines the history of New York City through the names of its beauties, buildings, blocks, and boroughs.

THE COUNTREY OF MANNA-HATA

The word *Manna-hata* was first written in 1609, when Robert Juet, a sailor on Henry Hudson's exploration ship, recorded it in his journal. It began appearing on maps in 1610. Juet took down the name upon meeting with members of a local Lenape tribe, who, on the first day that Hudson's ship laid anchor in the area, approached in canoes in order to sell the crew tobacco.[3] The Lenape, who were by then accustomed to European travelers, "followed what archaeologists call a Late Woodland way of life," with agricultural villages anchoring an elaborate inter-clan culture and a seasonal cycle of "farming, fishing, foraging, and hunting."[4] Following a common practice among the land's first settlers, the Lenape often used place names that referred to natural features. Names also tended to comprise whole phrases; this was possible because Native American languages are *polysynthetic*, a term that describes the rules by which the speakers of a language can create words.[5] Polysynthetic languages allow speakers to combine multiple morphemes (the smallest units of language that carry meaning) in a word as well as modify those morphemes with inflections. Speakers can thus create individual words that encompass entire phrases or sentences: *place along the ocean; place beyond the pines; place of swans; where pipes are traded.*[6]

You may have heard that *Manhattan* is a Lenape name meaning "island of hills." In fact, *Manhattan* represents that name (or one like it; see later in this paragraph) transliterated into Dutch. Few of the Dutch explorers or settlers had any facility with Native American languages, and few of the Lenape, in turn, could speak European languages. (The Dutch referred to Native Americans as *wilden*, or "wild ones"; the Lenape called the Dutch *Swannekens*, or "salty people," likely referring to their seafaring ways.)[7] As a result, the names of Native American origin that Europeans set down on their maps represent, for the most part, transliterations of words in native languages into the phonology of European languages. *Hoboken* perhaps comes from the Delaware *hopokan*, or "tobacco pipe"; *Kisco*, from the Munsee *asiiskuw*, or "mud"; *Massapequa*, from the Southern Unami *mësipèk*, or "water from here and there"; *Rockaway*, from the Munsee *leekuwahkuy*, or "sandy land"; *Rahway*, from the Munsee *lxaweew*, or "it is forked." (The Munsee and the Unami belong to the Lenape people, who also call themselves the Delaware.) One scholar suggests that *Sing-Sing*, now the name of a famous prison, derives from the Munsee word *asunung*, or "place of stones."[8] This transliteration accounts for the impossible spelling of places like *Schaghticoke*, *Schenectady*, and *Schodack*, which implement the Dutch habit of clustering consonants.[9] It also helps to account for the difficulty, in some cases, of recovering the original word from before its transformation. For *Manhattan*, historians have proposed many possible derivations, including *mahatuoh*, or "the place for gathering bow wood"; *menatay*, or "island"; and *manahachtanienk*, or "place of general inebriation."[10] I hold with those who find the derivation *manna-hatta*—"hilly island" or "rocky island"—persuasive, not least because Manhattan really was a hilly, craggy place when the Dutch first laid anchor, a sloping terrain of marble, gneiss, and hard Manhattan schist. Only in the 19th century, determined to maximize the utility of its increasingly valuable real estate, did the city direct workers to dig down the sloping stone to the bedrock and cart away the hills in barrows. It took decades of backbreaking labor to flatten Manhattan.

For the seafaring Dutch, the island of Manhattan's easy access to the sea, along with its rich natural resources, made it an ideal site for a trading colony. They established a settlement in 1624, maintaining an uneasy relationship with the local Lenape. They left a lasting mark on the region's language of place. Famously, Wall Street takes its name from a fortification wall that the Dutch set up to keep out the English, who had a colony on the other side of Oyster Bay. But the words for natural features that the Dutch colonists embedded into the region's place names preserve an even richer, if subtler, image of their world, as Geoffrey Needler notes: *bush* (woods), *dorp* (village), *gat* (pass), *hoek* (corner), *kill* (channel), *kloof* (ravine), *vly* (marsh or creek), *wijk* (neighborhood or village).[11] In Manhattan, the Bowery neighborhood took its name from *bouwerij*, or "farm."[12] In Brooklyn, Bushwick began as *Boswijck*, or *village in the woods; Flatbush* as *Vlacke Bos*, a term referring again to woods; and *Red Hook* as *Roode Hoek*, referring to topography (*hoek* was the equivalent of *point*) and the rusty color of the local silt.[13] The word *vly* informed the name of the *Vly Market* or *Fly Market*, a public market that once operated in what is now Lower Manhattan; the term *flea market* derives from that one market's name.[14] In old drawings of New Amsterdam, we see the landscape that we now know as soaring canyons of glass and steel as a touchingly delicate scattering of footpaths, low houses, and windmills. The region's place names likewise capture a sensibility of Dutch pastoral: a world of villages, woods, and carefully managed waterways. (There's only one really funny line in Washington Irving's *Knickerbocker's History of New York*, but it *is* really funny. It's about the island of Manhattan as it was when the Dutch found it, which is to say as a rocky, brambly swamp: "The softness of the soil was wonderfully adapted to the driving of piles; the swamps and marshes around them afforded ample opportunities for the constructing of dykes and dams; the shallowness of the shore was peculiarly favorable to the building of docks; in a word, this spot abounded with all the requisites for the foundation of a great Dutch City.")[15]

The main commercial product of New Amsterdam—the beaver pelt, which traders sold as a staple commodity to the hat industry in Europe—also found its way into the region's names and symbols. Albany, once a fur-trading post and now the state capital, originally held the name *Beverwijck,* meaning "Beaver Village." Another post, located up the Schuylkill River, took the name Fort Beversrede, or *Beavers Quay.* Dutch settlers named Bever Straat in Manhattan, which is Beaver Street today. And Jamaica, Queens, takes its name from the word for *beaver* in Lenape, *yemacah*; the Dutch, who used the letter "j" to spell the sound /y/, transliterated the word as *Jameco.*[16] (This chain of derivation also gave a name to Jamaica Bay.) The beaver adorned the seal of New Netherland, and in 1686, the City of New York adopted a seal that likewise carries a beaver. Today, the beaver waves on the flag of New York State, an emblem of the enduring place of commerce in the region's history.[17]

In all, the sensibility that the Dutch colonists left on the region's map was pastoral and patriotic, an imprint of their homeland in a foreign wilderness. Many names on the map came directly from the Low Countries. Brooklyn, originally *Breuckelen,* likely takes its name from a town in the Utrecht province; Bloomingdale, originally *Bloemendaal,* from a village in North Holland; *Flushing,* from the Dutch village of Vlissingen. Harlem was originally *Nieuw Haarlem,* from a city near Bloemendaal. Staten Island, or *Staaten Eylandt,* was named in honor of the Estate General, the parliamentary assembly that governed the Netherlands.[18]

The Dutch sensibility was also more impressed by wealth than by military prowess. In Paris, street names often honor military figures or the dates of important battles. In New York City, place names are far more likely to honor the city's early landowners: Bleecker Street, Cortlandt Street, Leonard Street, Stuyvesant Street.[19] Bedloe's Island, now home (under a new name) to the Statue of Liberty, was a holding of the merchant Isaack Bedloo.[20] Rikers Island takes its name from Abram Rycher, who in 1664 secured a patent to build a farm there. (In the mid-19th century, the city bought the island and put it to public use, founding the now-infamous penitentiary in 1932.)[21] The Bronx takes its name from the landowner Jonas Bronck, a sea captain who, in 1639, bought 500 acres of land on which to raise a family; his descendants have long supported the theory that the odd specification *the* in the borough's name, "Borough of The Bronx," preserves the memory of the family, such that *going to the Bronx* meant *going to visit the Broncks*. (The other possibility is that the article *the* in *the Bronx* began as a reference to the Broncks, later Bronx, River.)

A smaller group of families than you might think gave their names to the streets of New York City. Until the early 19th century, as the historian Anne Raulin notes, Manhattan's real estate belonged to just a handful of families; nearly all of the city's streets named after humans refer to members of this small group. Some street names belong to sisters, wives, and daughters, as with Ann Street, Catherine Street, and Hester Street. Men sometimes gave first and last names to separate streets. (For example, William Street and Beekman Street both honor the same William Beekman.) Or again, a name might come from a formal title; Yonkers takes its name from *jonkheer*, a title meaning "young lord," which the area's landowner, one Adriaen der Donck, happened to hold.[22] In time, some of the street names honoring these families would be turned into numbers and letters. Nevertheless, the respect for wealth remained, even as wealth from landowning gave way, as the 19th century progressed, to wealth from industry.

HOSTILE TAKEOVERS

In 1664, after British warships made a show of force in the colony's harbor, the colony changed hands and New Amsterdam became New York.[23] After their hostile takeover, the English anglicized many of the colony's place names, changing the spelling and pronunciation to accord with English habits of language, and changed other place names to English names outright.[24] The Mauritius River, named for Prince Maurits of Holland, referred too obviously to the House of Orange, so the English renamed it the Hudson River—a diplomatic balance, as Hudson had been an English captain who had worked for the Dutch West India Company. Over time, Conijn Eylandt became Coney Island; Lange Eylandt became Long Island.[25] And Nieuw Haarlem changed its name to Lancaster, in honor of the brother of the Duke of York. (On paper, the change to Lancaster was official; the governor signed a patent in 1665 ratifying the new name. For reasons that have never been clear, everyone seems to have agreed to ignore the change, so that Lancastrians remain known as residents of Harlem today.)[26]

Many of the place names on the island's southern point preserve the ghosts of the city's old infrastructure. Broadway, which was the main road when the city was small enough to have a main road, used to be very broad indeed: more than forty feet across when the English drove carts down it. Bridge Street and Broad Street (the latter once bordered both edges of the Broad Canal) preserve the memory of the canals that the Dutch built in Lower Manhattan. Collect Pond, a freshwater pond in Lower Manhattan, was originally referred to as *de Kolck*, a Dutch word for pond. Mulberry Street, which received its name in 1767, and was later a main stem of Little Italy, denotes the mulberry trees that once stood in the area. Gold Street once looked over a "Golden Hill" (as a 1728 map has it) of starry yellow celandines.[27] (The map in Figure 3.1 shows the old green spaces of the island's southern point: farms, gardens, orchards.)

The English also created new place names that honored their rulers: Hanover Street (after the House of Hanover), Kings County, the Kingsbridge Road (later to become part of Broadway), Queens County, York County. Richmond County was named in honor of

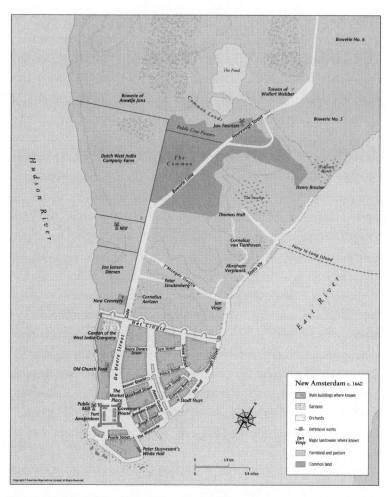

Figure 3.1   Map of New Amsterdam, circa 1660.

the king's illegitimate son, the Duke of Richmond. (Like residents of Harlem, residents of Richmond went their own way, continuing to call it by the old Dutch name, Staten Island.)[28] Governors Island is named for the royal governors who managed the city on behalf of Britain, to whom the island was given for private use. The city named

Essex Street, Norfolk Street, and Suffolk Street after counties in England; similarly, some of the new English landowners named their estates Greenwich and Chelsea, after districts in London.[29] Bowling Green, the site where Peter Minuit famously bartered for Manhattan with the Lenape, takes its name from a playing field in England for the game of lawn bowling.

The Anglophilic era of New York City's place names was soon to end, however. In 1774, New Yorkers poured out tea in New York Harbor in protest of the Tea Tax, just as Bostonians had done in Boston Harbor. Another reason for colonial unrest, less often discussed today, was the Royal Proclamation of 1763, which had confined Royal colonies to the east of the Appalachian range. Subsequent instructions from Parliament reaffirmed that the Crown forbade, "by the strongest prohibitions, all Settlement beyond the limits therein described as the boundary of the Indian hunting Ground"—an effort to protect the territory and sovereignty of indigenous peoples, and thereby to establish peace in the east.[30] Colonial Americans were ambitious, and they had their eye on lands west of the Appalachians.[31] In 1776, they declared independence at a gathering in Philadelphia, then the largest city in the colonies and a center of politics and culture; during the war that followed, New York City held, militarily, an opposing position, as Britain made the port city its chief base of naval operations.[32]

To briefly summarize our nation's foundational moment, a war about which thousands of books have been written: the British lost. On November 25, 1783, General George Washington rode into New York City alongside the English governor of New York. At 1:00 p.m., a cannon fired to signal the dismissal of British troops, who rowed out on longboats to ships waiting in the harbor. Over the next few years, some 60,000 Loyalist civilians left the new country, half of them settling in the British province of Nova Scotia.[33] Tribes of the Iroquois Confederacy numbering tens of thousands of members also moved north to lands that the Crown still protected, some of them eventually settling in the Grand River Valley to become the Six Nations of the Grand River. Their migration out of the American Northeast opened up more lands for colonists to settle and name, but ironically would help to halt the nation's northward expansion at the 49th parallel.

For a time, New York City was the federal capital of the young republic.[34] President Washington lived and worked there (his address was 3 Cherry Street), and Congress met and passed laws in what is now Federal Hall on Wall Street. The city celebrated independence by bestowing place names in honor of the Revolutionary War and its heroes. Starting in the 1770s (and continuing for centuries), New Yorkers named local sites for major figures in the Revolution, including Hamilton Terrace, Place, and Heights; Lafayette Street and Square, and Plaza Lafayette; Montgomery Street; Washington Street, Square, Park, Place, Mews, and Heights, as well as the George Washington Bridge and Fort Washington Park and Avenue. Steuben County, outside the city, honors Friedrich Wilhelm von Steuben, who oversaw the training of the Patriot army. Lexington Avenue is named for the Battle of Lexington. William Pitt, the British prime minister, had advocated on behalf of the American colonies, though he supported the British side during the Revolution. His name remains on New York City's Pitt Street because the Patriots regarded him as a friend. (He also gave his name to Pittsburgh.)[35]

Independence from Britain also left existing streets in need of renaming, as Raulin notes: King Street changed to Pine Street; Prince Street, to Rose Street; George Street, to Spruce Street; and Little Queen Street, to Cedar Street. (The pattern here—naming streets after trees—comes from Philadelphia, which at the time was regarded as the greatest city in the colonies. New Yorkers were trying to grab some of that Philadelphia magic.) Other new street names included Beaver Street (formerly Princess Street), Liberty Street (formerly Crown Street), Market Street (formerly George Street), Stone Street (formerly Duke Street), and William Street (formerly King George Street).[36] Kings County remains Kings County to this day, but we refer most often to the borough of Brooklyn, which has coterminous borders with Kings County.

LORDS OF THE SOIL

Looking beyond place names in New York City to place names in New York State at large offers a glimpse of American settlers' hopes and plans for the new world following independence. For in the decades following their break from the motherland, Americans made a national project of building a lexicon sufficiently lofty to match their ambitions. In New York State, as elsewhere, they adorned the landscape with grand names from the Bible or classical antiquity: Babylon, Ithaca, Jerusalem, Mount Sinai, Rome, Syracuse, Troy. They also turned with fresh enthusiasm to Native American names, as Native Americans were one feature the new world had that Britain did not. The fantasy that settlers wrote upon Native Americans provided settlers with a classic myth that belonged to the United States alone: the American landscape was paradise and Native Americans were its noble savages, an Edenic ideal custom-made for the Enlightenment.[37] In the years following the Revolution, place names deriving from indigenous languages populated European-American maps of New York State: Allegany County, Erie County, Ontario County, Oswego County, Niagara County.

Washington Irving, who lived in the Hudson Valley, admired the valedictory poetry belonging to this style of naming. In 1839, Irving argued in the *Knickerbocker* that New York State and New York City should also take on indigenous names, with the state changing its name to *Ontario* and the city to *Manhattan*. (An alternative, he said, would be to call the city *Manhatta* and make *Manhattan* an adjective.) The practice of using place names like Rome and Ithaca, he said, smacked of an effort to borrow glory, an equivalent to dressing in fancy secondhand clothes: "the whole catalogue of ancient worthies is shaken out from the back of Lempriere's Classical Dictionary, and a side region of wild country sprinkled over with the names of the heroes, poets, and sages of antiquity, jumbled into the most whimsical juxtaposition." Restoring the "original Indian names of places," he said, "would have the merit of originality, and of belonging to the country; and they would remain as reliques of the native lords of the soil, when every other vestige had disappeared." That disappearance must have seemed to be close at hand: in 1800, fewer than 550 Native Americans were living on Long Island and coastal New Jersey, according to the historian T. J. C. Brasser.[38]

With independence in hand, settlers were freed up to pursue imperial ambitions. A letter that John Adams wrote on the occasion of Congress declaring independence shows that he was already thinking of the new republic as a vast territory: "I am apt to believe that it will be celebrated, by succeeding Generations . . . from one End of this Continent to the other from this Time forward forever more."[39] In fact, it was around the time of independence that New York State received the nickname *the Empire State*. Theories about the phrase's origin vary; we do have on record a 1785 letter from Washington to New York City's local government that said, "I pray . . . that your state (at present the Seat of the Empire) may set such examples of wisdom of liberality, as shall have a tendency to strengthen and give permanency to the Union at home—and respectability to it abroad."[40] Thus it seems likely, since empires rely on overseas holdings, that the nickname refers to the region's strength as a maritime center. The Dutch, with their powerful trading empire, and the British, with their famous navy, had shown the importance of water to political and economic imperialism.

THE MATRIX OF MAN

In 1811, New York City's commissioners unveiled an ambitious plan to set down the streets of the growing city in a rectangular matrix. The plan's origins lay in the lands of Trinity Church—a major city landowner since the early 18th century—which developed its holdings around Wall Street in a pattern of rectangular lots. Some nearby landowners followed suit.[41] In the late 18th century, the city hired surveyors to map the inhabited parts of Manhattan as well as the uninhabited "Common Lands." When these maps divided portions of the Common Lands into lots to be sold at auction, most of the lots had a rectangular shape, as each needed to have access to the lone common road.[42] The plan was ambitious because, even as the map projected a regular grid, the Common Lands were still wild and forbidding, a landscape of sloping hills, thickets, and mosquito-infested swamps. (One of the surveyors died of yellow fever from a mosquito bite.)[43] In order to build their rectilinear city, New Yorkers would have to beat back, pare down, and rationalize their hilly island.

The gridiron street system represented man's domination of nature in more ways than one. The right-angled intersections that the 1811 commission had signed off on wouldn't work if the streets had to curve to accommodate Manhattan's natural hills. But more to the point, the city government understood that flat terrain has more value than uneven terrain, because it has a larger usable surface area. (One commissioner, Gouverneur Morris—Morrisania, in the Bronx, takes its name from his family—said the commission was mindful "that a city is to be composed principally of the habitations of men, and that strait sided and right-angled Houses are the most cheap to build, and the most convenient to live in.")[44] The prospect of raising the value of the city's real estate was a strong enough motivation for the city to dedicate immense labor and expense to leveling the terrain. All told, laying the famous grid up to 155th Street required six decades of hard labor: workers dug up tree stumps, excavated earth, hacked at rocks and natural cement with chisels and pickaxes, installed culverts to drain off water, drilled holes in stone, and planted gunpowder charges.[45] Although some American cities had already adopted grid layouts, among them Philadelphia and Washington, Manhattan's natural surface presented a challenge that made the commissioners' plan extraordinary in the scope of its ambition. As one critic later wrote, "nothing had ever been attempted that equaled in brutality the grid stencil to be clamped over the cliff-and-ravine studded shelf."[46]

The work of leveling the island also obliged workers to fill in the many watery areas—especially in the 1840s, when a need to produce more usable real estate in Lower Manhattan led to the elimination of water sources. Several place names in Manhattan preserve a record of the island's swampy, watery past. Spring Street was named for a freshwater spring that has since been covered over. The water in the area that is now Canal Street used to be a danger to public health: a tide of polluted runoff from Collect Pond that New Yorkers tried, by building a canal, to divert away from the city. Street names also preserve a record of the waterfront and its importance, although this area has been maintained. Front Street, Moore Street, and Water Street are conventional names for streets by a waterfront; New Yorkers borrowed them, once again, from Philadelphia.[47]

If you're in the city, head uptown and take a walk around Central Park. Famously, the park is the brainchild of Calvert Vaux and Frederick Law Olmsted, who between 1856 and 1863 supervised the creation of an 843-acre park, groomed with native flora, that they had campaigned to build as the "lungs" of the city.[48] Everywhere you look in Central Park, you can see hills of stone sloping above the lawn: gneiss, mostly, along with veins of granite and some boulders that wandering ice sheets left behind during the last ice age. (You can see scratches from those same ice sheets on top of the gneiss hills.) This is the rock that laborers dug away elsewhere in order to lay down straight, level streets. Even the space of the park, which can seem so hilly when you walk around it, is much flatter than it was before Olmsted developed it. He blasted away terrain to create "an open, 'natural' look along English pastoral lines over the craggy nature that actually existed on the site."[49] Even so, the contrast between the hills left standing in the park and the level surrounding streets testifies to the tremendous labor that went into making Manhattan a grid city.

Inspiration for the practice of numbering streets came, once again, from the crowning city of the colonies, Philadelphia, where numbered streets run north to south and named streets run east to west. New York City uses numbers for both, with *avenues* running parallel with the Hudson River and *streets* running perpendicular. (A further nicety is the separation of *east* and *west* streets, with Fifth Avenue as the dividing line. Nobody remembers why this was done, although Raulin suggests it was an imitation of London, where many place names include cardinal directions.)[50] The numbering system marched steadily northward until the early 20th century, when Manhattan ran out of wild space. Meanwhile, developers in the Bronx had kept up the numbering of cross-streets from across the river in Manhattan, from East 132nd Street onward. (The sitcom *30 Rock*, in a crosses-the-line-twice joke about the MTA, pretends the numbers go on infinitely: "The train's going express for no reason. Next stop, One Millionth Street and Central Park Jogger Memorial Highway.")[51]

Today, Manhattan has 214 numbered streets, which connect to more than 2,800 intersections, every one of which, it sometimes seems, holds a distinct meaning in the New York imaginary.[52] The city's literature abounds with references to the street grid that highlight its ability to signify. In the musical *Avenue Q* (2003), the grid is a ruler that measures the distance between aspiration and reality: the protagonist, fresh out of college and looking for an apartment, finds the rents too high on Avenue A; he goes down the alphabet until he finds a place he can afford on Avenue Q. In *Rent* (1996), it's a pick-up line: "They say I have the best ass below 14th street. Is it true?" In *A Chorus Line* (1975), it shows the prestige of a plastic surgeon: "Grab a cab, c'mon/ See the wizard on/ Park and 73 for/ Tits and ass!" On *Seinfeld* (1998), it's the basis for a mystical experience: "I'm on 1st and 1st," says a very lost Kramer. "How can the same street intersect with itself? I must be at the nexus of the universe!" Given time and a rich enough culture, even the barest, most descriptionless place names— a numbered grid—will be overlaid with myth. The urban jungle grew into the empty spaces where cliffs and forests once were—electric with color, stinging with smells, and heavy with emotional humidity.

FAKE IT 'TIL YOU MAKE IT

The romance of money was one of the first myths to establish itself on the new grid. And small wonder; the very purpose of the grid was to make it easier for the city to divide land into monetizable parcels.[53] (Perhaps it's the case for every great city. In 1791, William Blake wrote of London, "I wander thro' each charter'd street, / Near where the charter'd Thames does flow"—with *chartered* referring to the division of land into monetizable parcels of real estate.)[54] Fifth Avenue, which began, "in 1811, as a line on the commissioners' map," became the index of a city expanding northward: "to Thirteenth Street by 1824, to Twenty-First Street by 1830, to Forty-Second Street in 1837. It had reached as far as One Hundred Twentieth Street by 1838."[55] Because monied New Yorkers followed the street northward, Fifth Avenue became, early on, a byword for wealth. The descendants of John Jacob Astor, an immigrant who made his fortune in the fur trade, built their piles here, while their wives fought ferocious battles with calling-cards over who got to be called "Mrs. Astor."[56] By the late 19th century, Fifth Avenue had the nickname *Millionaires' Row*.

Wealthy neighbors raise property values, but so can the right name, if you're willing to improve the truth a little. Consider the example of Greenland, which is icier than Iceland but adopted a pastoral name in order to attract settlers. This is what happened to Park Avenue, a stretch of Fourth Avenue above 43rd Street that for decades had been known as Railroad Alley.[57] When the city conferred the new name in 1888, the area had no park to speak of. It did, however, have a railroad, which had been set up on Fourth Avenue because the land was too poor in quality for anything else. (The avenue sits over a seam of hard Manhattan schist, which made the work of cutting out space for foundations forbiddingly expensive. Developers raised buildings on nearby Lexington Avenue instead.) The locomotives gave off smoke and noise, and railway accidents were common, which discouraged people who could help it from living there. Into the 1880s, most of the housing on what would become Park Avenue consisted of tenements crowded with Irish immigrants.[58]

Two things happened to make Railroad Alley more appealing to wealthy buyers. One was the application of aspirational realtors' language. In 1880, a landowner named Egbert Viele successfully campaigned to have a portion of Eleventh Avenue renamed *West End Avenue*, a change that aimed to lift real estate values by glamouring the shabby district with the aura of London's posh West End.[59] He started a trend: soon, place names started appearing across Upper Manhattan—*Fairview, Morningside, Overlook, Sylvan, Terrace View*— that presented a pastoral image at odds with what was then the reality of these properties: hard-to-reach, swampy terrain.[60] The rechristening of Park Avenue was part of this trend.

The other change, and this was doubtless more consequential, was the building of Grand Central Depot, whose soaring architecture imitates the great railway stations of London. When the station opened in 1871, New Yorkers jeered at the ambitious name *Grand Central*: what was so *central* about a site way out in the sticks of

Fourth Avenue, in an area "basically uninhabitable and too far from the real city"? But the new station made the area, a portion of 42nd Street patchy with bogs, woods, and train yards, newly accessible both to commuters who worked in "the real city" and to developers who recognized that the future of high-end real estate lay uptown. Over the next few decades, developers cleared away the bogs and forests, set up well-groomed lines of trees up along Fourth Avenue, and replaced the tenements with tall apartment buildings. By the early 20th century, the volume of traffic was so high that Grand Central Station had to be replaced with a larger building.[61] By the 1920s, the avenue's apartment buildings were sufficiently grand as to have made a Manhattan icon of a form of conspicuous consumption still familiar today: doormen, who stood watch in gloves, braids, and tassels meant to evoke the livery of servants in old England.[62]

HOW THE OTHER HALF LIVES

Let's go back down the island's length from the top, and with it down Manhattan's economic scale. Above 57th Street, those who couldn't afford even Lower Manhattan built squatter communities on undeveloped land. They tended crops and animals among wooden shacks, and sometimes found work building roads.[63] The squatter communities kept one step ahead of the city's growth uptown, as wealthy urbanites moved northward to get away from the crowds and smells of the city's older districts. (One count reckoned that in 1864, some 20,000 squatters made a home on the island.)[64]

In Lower Manhattan, the city's slaughterhouses set up on the shores of Collect Pond, since the marshy terrain around the pond was deemed unfit for habitation. By the early 19th century, the area stank with slaughterhouse runoff. Even after the city government drained the land and filled in the pond with earth, the ground remained damp and the air, people thought, very dubious. People who dared live in the area were those with few options, mostly immigrants, the poor, and freed slaves—but New York City had a great abundance of such people, and the area, now known as Five Points, was soon the most desperately crowded neighborhood in the city.[65] Not far away, the streets that bore ferry traffic from the East River, in particular those on a hook of land on the river called Corlears Hook, housed the majority of the city's brothels. The rise of sex districts in the city was connected, like so much else in the city's history, to the value of real estate. Districts with an overabundance of poor residents had problems with late rent payments, but also had housing that was valued too low to make selling the property worthwhile. Landlords countenanced brothels—indeed, encouraged them—because brothels paid higher rents and paid on time.[66]

Nicknames for the city's seedy districts slipped into the city's mythology. For example, you may have heard that we get the word *hooker* from Corlears Hook; I am here to reinforce that claim. Both the historical narrative and the word's documented history are persuasive. In 1839, *the Hook*, as locals often called the neighborhood, held "thirty-two houses of assignation and eighty-seven brothels"— this according to a guidebook published that year, which attests, at the very least, to the reputation the neighborhood had made for itself.[67] (Corlears Hook was named for a Dutch settler, Jacobus van Corlaer.) In 1859, we find the first dictionary definition of *hooker* as *sex worker*, which appears in a New York City glossary of underworld slang: "HOOKER. A resident of the Hook, i.e., a strumpet, a sailor's trull. So called from the number of houses of ill-fame frequented by sailors at the Hook (i.e., Corlear's Hook) in the city of New York."[68] (The specification "a sailor's trull" may be a useful collateral detail; the brothels of the city grouped near the East River ferries and shipyards.)[69] In 1835, we find the first casual use of the word, reported in a New York City newspaper: "a female prisoner is quoted as telling a magistrate that 'he called me a hooker,' the magistrate asks a wit-ness 'what did you call her a hooker for,' and the witness answers, 'Cause she allers hangs round the hook, your honner'"—referring to Corlears Hook.[70] (I tend to imagine that the witness meant the term in the racy sense, and pretended to the court that he did not.)

Or again, consider Five Points, so called after the bladed inter-section of Anthony, Cross, and Orange Streets in Lower Manhattan. As the city's most infamous slum, the neighborhood of Five Points became a popular subject for newspaper crime stories and dime novel melodramas. The writer who made Five Points infamous across the English-speaking world was Charles Dickens, who in 1841 toured the slum, a police escort at his side, and wrote a horrifying account of his experience in his travelogue, *American Notes*: "See how the rot-ten beams are tumbling down, and how the patched and broken win-dows seem to scowl dimly, like eyes that have been hurt in drunken frays."[71] The general tone of this passage belongs, horror aside, to a guidebook and certainly readers received it as such. Before long, New Yorkers from wealthy neighborhoods were touring Five Points, as Dickens had, "with a police escort, to marvel at its poverty and gawk at its displays of vice." This may, indeed, have been the origin of the word *slumming*.[72]

The slang for a troublemaker from Five Points was *Bowery b'hoy*. Bowery Street, which crossed the eastern section of Five Points, once ran through farmland (hence Dutch *bouwerij, farm*). By the 1830s, however, the Bowery had become a term describing a seedy district of tenements, crowding, and crime. For New Yorkers, a *Bowery b'hoy* (the spelling suggests an Irish burr) was a sporting lad given to drink and foolery—pugnacious, patriotic, and suspicious of immigrants despite being the offspring of immigrants himself. The b'hoy's unof-ficial uniform included a top hat, a vest and gaudy cravat, and thick boots—of which the latter were supposed to be useful at a moment's notice if the wearer was summoned to a fire, volunteer fire companies being much celebrated in that world.[73] By the way, this is where the word *buff*, as in *fanboy*, comes from. Volunteer firefighters in New York City used to wear buff-colored uniforms; for a long time, Webster's Dictionary defined *buff* as "an enthusiast about going to fires," then expanded the definition to include enthusiasts of all kinds.[74]

In short, the parceling of the city into districts, along with the crowding together of social and economic classes, led from the naming of places to the power of places to name. *Bowery b'hoys, hookers, Tsars of the Tenderloin; little nifties from the fifties, innocent and sweet; sexy ladies from the eighties, who are indiscreet.*

Farther up the island, tanneries also set up at the banks of the Harlem River—once the *Great Kill*—which flowed out to the Hudson River from a confluence of streams at what is today Tenth Avenue and 40th Street. As with Collect Pond, tanneries used the river to dump runoff, and as with Collect Pond, the resulting pollution made housing in the area, which swelled in the mid-19th century as the city's population surged, undesirable except to poor immigrants. By the 1880s, the area had acquired the menacing nickname *Hell's Kitchen*, perhaps a reference to local vice industries and gang activity: if the hottest part of Hell is the kitchen, then the most dangerous part of town is Hell's Kitchen. Later, when midtown real estate became valuable enough to make middle-class housing a better investment than houses of vice, developers tried, with mixed results, to replace the nickname with *Clinton* (after a park named for Governor DeWitt Clinton). The city government uses the name Clinton, but movies, comics, and local businesses often use the juicier name Hell's Kitchen.[75]

Police officers sometimes sought assignments in the city's vice districts because local businesses would bribe them to look the other way. A group of precincts that included, and surrounded, Hell's Kitchen, stretching west to the theater district, acquired the nickname *the Tenderloin*, based on the joke that an officer taking payoffs could dine on expensive tenderloin steaks. (Wags called officers in these precincts "Tsars of the Tenderloin.")[76] In 1894, a police captain named Max Schmittberger testified to a committee scrutinizing police corruption that officers took "advantage of any opportunity that presented itself to make money out of their respective precincts." Schmittberger himself worked in the Tenderloin district and participated in payoff schemes. "He testified that policy shops [gambling dens] in his district paid twenty dollars a month, liquor dealers about eighty, pool rooms two hundred dollars, and 'disorderly houses' anywhere from ten to five hundred dollars, depending on their quality and clientele. He personally earned nearly four hundred dollars each month from the vice industries in his precinct. Regular patrolmen involved in collecting the monthly 'dues' each earned approximately one hundred dollars of blackmail money per month."[77]

Uptown, the areas that became known as "good" and "bad" parts of town followed patterns of development and displacement. Above 59th Street, the land to the west side of Central Park was hillier than the land to the east side; for this reason, the east side was flattened and developed before the west side was. (Indeed, the west side remains the hilliest part of Manhattan. Washington Heights, named after a fortification that stood on the site during the Revolutionary War, is the highest elevation on the island, at 265 feet above the water line.)[78] Starting in the 1830s, when anti-abolition riots broke out in Five Points, African Americans began fleeing in large numbers from Five Points to the Upper West Side, a trend that persisted into the decades following the Civil War.[79] The neighborhood of Harlem became the heart of the city's African American communities, growing as people of color fled north from the Southern states during the Great Migration. In the 20th and 21st centuries, the city renamed many streets in the district to celebrate African American heroes, such as Frederick Douglass, Harriet Tubman, Malcolm X, and Martin Luther King, Jr.[80]

BRIGHT LIGHTS, BIG CITY

Broadway was never meant to be as its nicknames later described it: the Main Stem, the Canyon of Heroes, the Great White Way. The commissioners' plan snipped the stem at 23rd Street, where it was called Bloomingdale Road. If the plan had been faithfully executed, the city would have built over the road after that point. But New Yorkers kept tramping up and down Bloomingdale Road, extending it ever further uptown.[81] In 1866, the city changed tack and decided to turn Broadway into a wide public walk like the Avenue des Champs Elysées; anticipating this use, the city named the branch of Broadway between 59th and 108th Streets *the Boulevard*.[82]

Pictures from this period show what City Hall imagined for *the Boulevard*: pedestrians strolling two asphalt paths on either side of a grassy mall, delicately shaded by well-groomed elms. But once again, New Yorkers persisted in putting the street to the uses they felt most appropriate, namely entertainment and commercial enterprises; by the 1880s, the plan for a Parisian Broadway had been quietly dropped. In 1889, the city named the growing stem "Broadway," overwriting the names of the other roads that made up its length: "Bloomingdale, Kingsbridge, Middle, Old Harlem, and East Post Roads."[83]

Broadway's diagonal cant created "bowties"—paired triangular blocks—as it crossed the city's straight grid. The city called these tri-angles *squares*, in imitation of London's square squares: *Union Square* (1815) after the union of streets at the site; *Madison Square* (1847) after President James Madison; *Herald Square* (as of 1908) after the *New York Herald*, a major newspaper that erected on the site a gorgeous building meant to be a landmark.[84] Other place names that follow the formula are *Cooper Square, Hanover Square, Lincoln*

Square, Mulry Square, Stuyvesant Square, Washington Square Park, and *Winston Churchill Square.*

Today, the most famous part of New York City by far is Times Square, a 20-block thoroughfare in which billboards, lights, and neon signs dominate every line of vision.[85] At the turn of the 20th century, this bowtie, then a modest ten blocks in length, was known as *Longacre Square,* a name that referenced a street in London that specialized in stables, horse sellers, and carriage makers. Longacre Square likewise anchored New York's equine trade, which in those years was a very big deal.[86] Since the city's colonial era, when gallants raced horses down St. Nicholas Avenue, horse racing had been for New Yorkers a sport that cut across classes as its more elite incarnation in Britain did not.[87] The American Jockey Club, founded in New York City in 1866, became a national powerhouse for the sport. (In the Bronx, Jerome Avenue, which divides East Bronx from West Bronx, is named for Leonard Jerome, who helped to open a racetrack for the American Jockey Club to hold events.)[88] Indeed, the city's most celebrated nickname, *the Big Apple,* comes from this part of its history. In the 1920s, horse racers in the eastern United States used the term "apple" as slang for the winner's purse. For these competitors, New York City was the big-time, with bigger crowds, greater glory, and bigger purses; the city therefore became "the big apple." One racing columnist in particular, John Fitz Gerald, popularized the usage as a way of deepening the sport's mythology: "The Big Apple. The dream of every lad that ever threw a leg over a thoroughbred and the goal of all horsemen. There's only one Big Apple. That's New York."[89]

During the 19th century, the city's commercial theater district had been creeping up Broadway, with theatrical companies moving north in pursuit of buildings with low rent. The theater district had the nickname *the Rialto,* after a similar locale in Venice. (New Yorkers, who in those years knew Shakespeare as we know Marvel movies, greeted each other with a line adapted from *The Merchant of Venice*: "What's new on the Rialto?")[90] In 1904, the operator of the city's first subway, the Interborough Rapid Transit Company (IRT), opened a station at Broadway and 42nd Street, an event that arrested the Rialto's northward flight. The subway made the theaters at 42nd Street so convenient to patrons as to make rising rents worthwhile. "By 1928, West 42nd Street was accessible to the furthest points of the city, with five subway lines, four elevated lines, five bus lines, eleven surface lines, and a ferry having stations, stops, and a terminal there. Such access gave West 42nd Street an incomparable advantage as a location for servicing three distinct groups of the metropolis: city residents, affluent suburbanites, and visitors."[91] Over time, the nickname for New York theater became simply *Broadway*, and 42nd Street became, lyrically, "the crossroads of the world."

At the news that the IRT would be opening a line on 42nd Street, the owner of the *New York Times*, Adolph Ochs, purchased a site nearby to erect a new building for the newspaper: 25 stories high, which was 23 stories taller than, and thus 23 stories better than, the Herald Building. When the Times Tower opened in 1904, the city changed the name of Longacre Square to *Times Square* in the newspaper's honor. By then, the district was the most eye-grabbing spot in the city; in the previous decade, electric lights had illuminated first marquees, then advertising signs, then street lamps, hotel entrances, and restaurant roof gardens, bathing evening crowds in a beguiling frenzy of color.[92] If artificial lighting "colonized the night," to quote one historian of urban culture, Times Square was the center of the empire: a new height of conspicuous consumption, drawing in pilgrims and sending out imitators.[93] Nicknames that emerged for the district and its various parts affirmed this status: *the Great White Way; Fun City; the 24-hour corner; the street that never sleeps*—an early seed of *the city that never sleeps*.[94]

WHEN THE WORLD CAME TO TOWN

The completion of the Erie Canal in 1825, which made New York City an even more appealing port of entry for steamships crossing the Atlantic, dramatically enlarged the city's immigrant population. By 1870, almost one million people were living in the city.[95] New Yorkers often lived in ethnically segregated enclaves—for protection; to hear familiar voices; because jobs often came from local ethnic networks, as when *padrones*, or employment agents, arranged for Italian immigrants to build tunnels and cart rubble for the growing subway system.[96] Both official and unofficial place names marked out these ethnic communities. By the late 19th century, *Hester Street* stood for the Jewish community, as *Harlem* did for African Americans. Residents of the Bronx could visit *Dutch Broadway* (Courtlandt Avenue), *Irish Fifth Avenue* (Alexander Avenue), or *Irishtown* (west Woodlawn).[97] In the 20th century, Puerto Ricans nicknamed the Lower East Side, which had a large Puerto Rican population, *Loisaida*; Dominicans shortened Washington Heights to *the Heights*. A little world coalesced on the map: *Chinatown, Little Fuzhou, Little Germany, Little Italy, Little Manila, Little Odessa, Little Poland, Little Sri Lanka, Little Syria, Italian Harlem, Spanish Harlem.*[98] (However, these nicknames did not necessarily correspond with local street names. For instance, as one historian notes, Chinatown has a single Chinese name on its municipal map—Kimlau Square, after the fighter pilot Benjamin Ralph Kimlau—largely because sustained restrictions on immigration from China meant that New York was relatively late to acquire a substantial Chinese population.)[99]

During this period, the motives that informed the naming of places changed from the exclusion of populations to the promotion of cultural diversity. As we have seen, Wall Street runs along the line of a wall that the Dutch raised to ward off the British; similarly, the Battery takes its name from artillery batteries that the Dutch set up to defend against the British. The Revolutionary War prompted a purge of British names from the city's streets. But by the late 19th century, Americans had come to see the British as glamorous stage villains rather than actual villains. Developers bestowed sites in New York City with British-sounding names, presumably in the hope of making them sound pricey and sophisticated: for example, on the Upper West Side, Central Park West, Convent Avenue, Lenox Avenue, Morningside Heights, Riverside Heights, the West End; in Brooklyn, Cambridge Street, Cumberland Street, Fort Greene, Kensington, Oxford Street, and Prospect Park South. Making money was more important than preserving ancient enmity.[100]

The 20th century found the city in a valedictory mood. The wars in Europe left America the world's foremost super-power; the city's history of attracting and cultivating talent from home and abroad had made New York City the greatest city in America.[101] These years saw a trend of endowing place names that honored immigrants and migrants who had helped to build the city, and by extension the communities those figures represented. Irish: *Blessed Edmund Rice Street*, named for a missionary who founded a Catholic teaching order; *Drumgoole Square*, for an immigrant who gave housing to the homeless; *Duffy Square*, for Father Francis Duffy, the chaplain of an "all-Irish division of the 165th infantry"; *John Lawe Street*, for an "immigrant who rose from bus cleaner to fourth international president of the Transport Workers Union"; *Kenmare Street*, after a town in Ireland that reared the mother of a prominent civil servant on the Lower East Side. Italian: *Mother Francis Xavier Cabrini Triangle* and *Father Demo Square*, named for immigrants who ministered to Italian American communities; *La Guardia Place*, for the first Italian mayor to serve the city; *Louis F. DeSalvio Corner*, for a political leader. Russian: *Louise Nevelson Plaza*, for the sculptor; *George Balanchine Way*, for the choreographer.[102]

African American (included in this list of place names honoring migrants because the city's African American communities drew in part on migration from the South): *Adam Clayton Powell Jr. Boulevard*, for an influential pastor and politician; *African Square*, for Harlem's African American community at large; *Alvin Ailey Place*, for the choreographer; *Langston Hughes Place*, for the author; *Malcolm X Boulevard, Malcolm X Plaza*, and *Marcus Garvey, Jr., Park*, for the political leaders. An exception to this use of names as monuments of the city's diverse history was Native American place names; these were rarely applied in the city, although they continued to be popular in New York State. (A 1911 book on Native American place names proposed that the contents would "help strengthen the custom, now considerably in vogue, of employing names of American Indian origin to designate villages and towns the outgrowth of the present day, estates and seats in the country or at the sea-shore, camps, hotels, cottages, vessels large and small, etc.")[103]

Historians have long noted that place names and monuments inform social memory.[104] The inscriptions on a map can help to shape the residents of the territory it describes. Even for a "gateway city," New York City is unusually rich in monuments and symbolic sites that honor the city's immigrant past: the Statue of Liberty (on *Liberty Island*, so named, for the statue, in 1956); *Ellis Island*, with its accompanying museum of immigration (named for a former owner, the colonial New Yorker Samuel Ellis); the statue *The Immigrants*, erected in the Battery in 1973; the statue of Christopher Columbus in Columbus Circle, which was erected in 1892 and which is the anchor point for official measures of distance from New York City. This in addition to sculptures honoring historical figures from all over the world, including Hans Christian Andersen, José Bonifácio de Andrada e Silva, Joan of Arc, Ludwig van Beethoven, Robert Burns, Confucius, Johann Wolfgang von Goethe, Golda Meir, Sir Walter Scott, William Shakespeare, and Lin Zexu.

The collective memory that gathers around such names and land-marks has taught New Yorkers to see themselves as part of an immi-grant past.[105] In the nineties, New York City's mayor, David Dinkins, liked to describe New York City using a metaphor that emphasized its multicultural character: "New York is not a melting pot, but a gorgeous mosaic," he said. "We have almost as many separate eth-nic identities in the city as the United Nations has member nations. Our religious and cultural institutions are multitudinous. I did not feel the need to scrub the unique qualities of each."[106] In one of my classes, when I mentioned the melting-pot metaphor for America, my students—most are New Yorkers—disagreed, instead offering a metaphor in the Dinkins model: "We're like a salad." They were delighted when I told them the origin of the phrase *E pluribus unum*.

ISLAND AT THE CENTER OF THE WORLD

A famous drawing by the artist Saul Steinberg, "View of the World from 9th Avenue" (1976), literalizes the joke that New Yorkers find only New York interesting: viewed from Manhattan, the world appears as a dramatically foreshortened map. The city blocks that line Ninth Avenue are alive with distinct detail: with storefronts, red-brick apartment buildings, fire-escape balconies, rooftop water towers, traffic lights, cars, mailboxes, sidewalk cellar doors, and stroll-ing New Yorkers. The city blocks that line Tenth Avenue are smaller but still detailed; then we see, receding rapidly from view (and in descending order of interest), horizontal strips that represent the Hudson River, "Jersey," the rest of the United States (a mostly empty rectangle; it's all flyover country), and the Pacific Ocean. China, Japan, and Russia are vague sleeping lumps on the horizon.[107]

If a map is a projection of its maker, as Steinberg implies, the portrait of New Yorkers that we gather from this map of the world is critical: their view of their city as the center of the world reduces their engagement with the world beyond their city. (Naturally, New Yorkers have taken the criticism as a compliment, which is why the drawing is reproduced so often.) But the fact of the matter is that, in a city with so many ties to the wider world, real insularity is impossible; and, more to the point, a sense of belonging in one's city turns out to be a useful gateway for those still learning how to articulate their sense of belonging in a new nation. In a 2002 study, researchers found that young people in New York City who were the children of immigrants tended to apply the term *American* in two senses: in reference to themselves, to distinguish themselves from parents who had less experience than they did with American customs; but also to describe a mainstream American culture that they feared would not accept them due to their skin color or ethnicity. In response to this complicated sense of belonging, the researchers said, they were "creating a vibrant youth culture that is neither 'immigrant' nor 'middle American,' but rather something new." That *something new* was simply New Yorker: when identifying themselves, they often "sidestepped [their] ambivalent understanding of the term 'American' by describing themselves as 'New Yorkers,'" a name that can signify as potently for every glittering chip in the city's mosaic.[108] So a new generation of Americans tentatively explores its birthright, in the process exploring the language of belonging, the power of naming, and the meaning of home—on an island that knows itself to be a world, lit by the lamp of the Mother of Exiles.

Confidence Man: I SEEN HIM FIRST, JOE
His Pal: LET'S TOSS FOR HIM

Chapter 4

Bootlegged Language

Hello, suckers!

—Texas Guinan

Looking back at the New York City of her youth, Edith Wharton wrote in 1934 that the old New York had become "as much a vanished city as Atlantis or the lowest layer of Schliemann's Troy."[1] The city's identity has long been defined by the creative destruction of speculative capitalism, the destructive creation of demolition and rebuilding brought about by some of the world's most valuable real estate, and a population endlessly renewed by migrants who move to the big city to make their fortunes—what the *New Yorker* has called the "open-hearted, glad-eyed, two-fisted, red-blooded, hustling, bustling, ready-for-a-big-time, whoop-her-up out-of-towner."[2] The city of yesteryear can seem, at times, like a lost civilization, a world whose relics survive only in the phantasmal form of stories.

The previous chapter examined how place names in New York City preserve stories of the past. This chapter considers how words that first appeared in New York City have survived the erosive forces of historical change to tell the stories of today. The historian Irving Allen argues that the most fruitful period for lasting slang to be coined in New York City was 1850 to 1950. This period coincided with "the modern industrial phase of American urbanization," which created new kinds of employment, new local characters, and new forms of mass communication.[3] While this phase of urbanization transformed many American cities, New York's growing role as a media center gave the new idioms it incubated a special reach, as locally produced songs, plays, newspapers, books, and (in time) radio and film helped to spread local speech across the nation.[4] This chapter digs deeper into one of the period's more treacherous lexicons, one that has unexpectedly flourished in the speech of the American mainstream: the slang of the criminal underworld.

This criminal "corruption" of mainstream American speech has much to tell us about changing conditions in the city. The modern institution of policing was established during the 19th century, leaving ghosts of that era in our language of law and order. The institutions of nightlife, with their attendant devilries, also expanded dramatically during these years. Beyond this, however, a need for methods of survival drove new parables and metaphors into the language of the city's underworld and then into colloquial speech at large—a transformation that highlights the capacity for slang to act as strategy in a world of distinctively modern dangers.[5]

DEFINING SLANG

For such a common form of language, slang is remarkably difficult to define. Slang is not distinctive in linguistic terms, only in social terms: it defines an in-group, usually one outside of the establishment. The linguist Michael Adams usefully describes slang as in-group language that lacks a professional purpose; hence, criminals on the job use *cant*, professionals and hobbyists use *jargon*, and "any other language that characterizes a group and identifies speakers with that group ends up slang by default."[6] I follow his lead in what follows, although with some necessary looseness; which term is correct for in-group language that civilians borrow from criminals in order to warn each other of threats, to show they are bored urbanites who have seen it all, to rework the city's sounds into art, or just to sound cool?

At first blush, slang would seem to be the opposite of durable language. After all, we tend to apply the term to words that are aggressively fashionable, which should imply that they will wear out with the arrival of the next fashion. And in fact, most slang, given a little time, vanishes utterly, reappearing only in the archives as an amusement for historians. But some slang remains in use as slang for decades, even centuries, never losing its raffish tone: *loaded*, for drunk, dates back in various forms to the Renaissance. And some slang manages to cross over into the sober flow of ordinary speech. The question of how this occurs is, at bottom, a question of how language moves between speakers. In practice, slang is impolite because polite people do not use it, and when a word enters regular use in polite company, it ceases to be slang. [7] It was with this reality in mind that Jonathan Lighter offered a definition of slang that emphasizes its impiety: "*Slang* denotes an informal, nonstandard, nontechnical vocabulary composed chiefly of novel-sounding synonyms (and near synonyms) for standard words and phrases; it is often associated with youthful, raffish, or undignified persons and groups; and it conveys often striking connotations of impertinence or irreverence, especially for established attitudes and values within the prevailing culture."[8] Of course, this kind of academic definition doesn't do justice to the spirit of slang. To put it more simply, the difference between slang and the merely colloquial may be that slang has a better memory of impolite company.[9]

In the United States, the language, like the populace, seems enamored of the national dream of shaking off a humble past. A great deal of language that we consider today to be colloquial but inoffensive—language that you can use at the dinner table with your girlfriend's parents—began as terms of honor among thieves. **Phony**, meaning counterfeit, may have arisen from a swindle involving a fake gold ring, as *fawney* (*fáinne*) is a term in Irish for *ring*. *To get the razzle-dazzle*, in the phrase's early use, was to be beguiled or distracted, especially during a swindle. *To get the rinky-dink* was to get swindled; later *rinky-dink* meant a sucker, and finally it came to mean something worthless.[10] In a similar transformation, *lemon* started as a term for *patsy* and came to mean an item sold to a patsy; possibly the term was a spin-off from *sucker*, meaning something like "this guy sucks lemons." *Bootleg* originated during Prohibition, when smugglers would hide bottles of alcohol inside boots. *Speakeasy*, for an illicit saloon, first appeared during the same period in New York City; H. L. Mencken suggests that the term was a spin-off from *speak-softly shop*, which in Britain and Ireland meant "a smuggler's house," where speaking softly served to maintain secrecy. *Shoo-in* started out meaning a horse certain to win a race, "as heard in the phrase 'to *shoo* a horse in,' the implication being that the other jockeys, by agreement, get behind a picked horse and chase him across the finish line."[11]

The normalization of these words has something to tell us about American life. But so do their low origins, for the very stigmatization of the subjects they named made those subjects prolific sites of language production. Scholars of language have long observed that sensitive subjects tend to acquire heavy clouds of verbiage, which grow as speakers try to keep ahead of stigma by coining new euphemisms or evasive slang. For this reason, identifying subjects that have amassed a large vocabulary can help to highlight the hot-button issues in a culture. (The historian Dick Leith suggests that "there are over 1000 words which in their history have denoted women and have also meant 'whore.'")[12] A variety of sensitive lines of business gave rise to the vocabularies that follow, ranging from sex work to swindling, but really they are unified in pursuit of a single goal. The word for this goal is incidentally our most famous borrowing from Dutch: the settlers of New Amsterdam left as part of their legacy to colonial New Yorkers a provincial coin, the *daler* (or *daalder*), that gave its name in the 18th century to the *dollar*, a regional denomination that became the basic unit of American currency.

The importance of currency to contemporary speakers can be seen in the enormous slang vocabulary around it.[13] Money generates words because it is a sensitive subject in both polite and impolite company, and also because we fetishize it, which gives rise to metaphors both disparaging (*chicken feed*) and plauditory (*honey*). More important, money generated *talk*—adding generative fuel to other lexical fields—because Americans are guaranteed the pursuit of happiness and a little coin is said to get you there faster. (A few times, I have asked students in the classroom to list slang words for money. Whenever I do this, they *smile*.) At bottom, this common pursuit among people on all sides of the law is the reason so much slang from this period persists today, much of it having been laundered into the legitimate coin of colloquial speech. In that sense, the story of the survival of the language of the old underworld is a story about legal entrepreneurs and extralegal entrepreneurs working together to build a city and forge the uncreated soul of a nation. Or at the very least, it's a story about New Yorkers trying to lay their hands on some scratch—not all of them honorably, but some of them quite memorably.

CRIMES OF MOBILITY

In the eyes of its critics and its admirers alike, the New York City of the 19th century was defined by the concept of mobility. People traveled into, out of, and around the city in such numbers that merely being in what visitors then called "Fun City" meant partaking in a festive crowd of the kind that small towns only experienced during carnivals and fairs. For city-dwellers, living in New York meant accepting that you would never know most of your neighbors, for mobility was also anonymity. Mobility and anonymity were common tropes in an emerging American literature; as the legal scholar Lawrence Friedman argues, 19th-century America was perhaps more mobile than any society before in history:

> It was a society of immigrants, but also a society of migrants— of restless, transient people who shuttled across the vast face of the landscape. Americans were also mobile in another sense— busily engaged in climbing, falling, and maneuvering through and about the many levels of social strata. It was a tumultuous society, a society in which people moved from East to West, from rags to riches and back, without formal barriers standing in the way. It was a society, moreover, that *believed* in mobility; mobility, after all, was the essence of "the American dream."[14]

Thus the Duke and the Dauphin, in Mark Twain's *Adventures of Huckleberry Finn* (1884), are able to work their swindles while voyaging down the Mississippi River, strangers in every town they stop at. Thus P. T. Barnum, in his 1855 autobiography, reminisces about the "sharp" tricks that the locals in his small hometown in Connecticut played on the peddlers who passed through. Even with this preparation, he reported, he found himself out of his depth when he arrived in New York City. The job advertisements that he pored over in the newspaper turned out to include a good share of swindles. ("Many is the wild goose chase which I had in pursuit of a situation so beautifully and temptingly set forth upon those 'wants,'" he recalled. "Fortunes equaling that of Croesus, and as plenty as blackberries, were dangling from many an advertisement . . . but when I had wended my way up flights of dark, rickety, greasy stairs, and through sombre, narrow passages, I found that my fortune depended firstly upon my advancing a certain sum of money, and secondly, upon my success in peddling a newly discovered patent life-pill.")[15] Swindling of any sort works best in a context where people move often from place to place, perpetually shedding familiarity, local knowledge, a paper trail, a past. Friedman argues, in fact, that such itinerancy set the basis for a distinctive genre of crime, newly prominent in the 19th century, that he describes as "crimes of mobility."

Any regular reader of print media would have known this genre of crime intimately. Newspapers loved frauds and swindlers, often featuring the word *swindler* in the headline. A common theme of these stories is the naïveté of victims: for example, an apprentice, while walking down Wall Street with a check in his hands, meets a man who offers to exchange the check for an easy-to-cash money order. The man sends the apprentice away with an order for what turns out to be ten guineas, or about 50 dollars, then goes to the bank and cashes the check for 370 dollars.[16] Another theme is false identity. A story from Philadelphia: "Yesterday afternoon, John Lewis Wagner, alias capt. John Miller, alias John Lewis, was apprehended. . . . This is supposed to be the same *gentleman* who has cut so many capers in New York and elsewhere."[17] From New York: "Be it known that the above elegant youth is no more or less than the notorious swindler *Robert Kennon . . .* now passing under the name of *Robert H. Norton. . . .*"[18] New York again, with the familiar headline, "A Swindler": "Some time since, a stranger of genteel appearance, calling himself *James Maxwell*, arrived in this city. . . ."[19]

The best stories featured flamboyantly lofty false identities. The Waldorf Hotel hosted, for a time, a dignitary who held court in the dining room as "Norman La Grange, the Lieutenant Colonel of the Queen's Guards"; when he skipped out without paying his bill, the hotel learned that "Norman La Grange" was just one of multiple false names he went by. (Another was "Lord Ashburton.") A self-described Russian count lifted $30,000 from the bank accounts of unwary New Yorkers. While dukes and dauphins might turn up anywhere out in the frontier, the press took for granted that the city was the swindler's native ground. To read the city papers anytime in the 19th century was to find constant evidence to support one New Yorker's complaint: "One cannot mingle much in society here without meeting some bewhiskered, mysterious individual who claims to be of noble birth."[20]

In 1849, this charismatic stranger received his modern name: *confidence man*. The term first appeared in print in a story in the *New York Herald* about the trial of one William Thompson, a swindler who plied his trade in Manhattan.[21] His tactic was to intercept a mark and ask, after friendly conversation, "Have you confidence in me to trust me with your watch until to-morrow?" There are no prizes for guessing whether he returned the next day. The *Herald* article makes it sound as though the "Confidence Man" had become, over the previous few months, something of a local institution, rather like the Naked Cowboy or Times Square Elmo. In any case, the press made such a commotion over the "Confidence Man" that the term became definitive of the genre, entering popular literature (Herman Melville titled an 1857 novel *The Confidence Man*) and even the clinical language of police reports. By 1922, writes Friedman, New York police arrested, in a single year, "377 men and thirteen women for 'confidence games.'"[22]

Con artists represented a remarkable array of conventional plots and stock characters in the theater of crime that the city's newspapers unfolded daily. One stock figure would throw snuff in a victim's face and flee, allowing his accomplice to pretend to help the victim while picking the victim's pockets. Another would knock over a victim in a crowd, then pilfer his watch while helping him to his feet. Another, always a woman, would lure a victim into an alleyway and pick his pockets; her partner, posing as her husband, would then arrive and shout that the victim had "seduced his wife," prompting the victim to run off before he realized he had lost his cash. Yet another took advantage of the city's maritime tradition; he would dress up as a sailor, present himself at the door of a house, and offer to sell the occupants fine silks and linens that had been smuggled off the ship—which were actually poor-quality fabrics. Another—a fake worshipper called a *groaner* who specialized in picking pockets in church—took advantage of the pious tradition of wearing one's "Sunday best"; he walk home with fine hats, watches, pocketbooks, and even Bibles.[23]

Figures of speech arose from the underworld—and often from reporting *about* the underworld—that consolidated the general wariness of the criminal connoisseur into vivid and memorable images. Some expressions mapped criminal activity directly onto the city (note that in this chapter, words and expressions that are first attested in New York City appear in bold). In the early 20th century, **third rail mob** was a New York term for a pickpocket crew that operated in the subways; **up and down Broadway** was the name of a dice con that swindlers performed in nightclubs; **up the river** ("in prison") once invoked Sing Sing prison, upriver from New York City. **Murderers' row**, slang for death row, originally referred to a set of cells in the Tombs jail in Lower Manhattan. Other expressions used the names of celebrated swindles as metonyms for swindling as a whole. A common scam in the 19th century involved gilding bricks made of cheap metal to give them the appearance of gold; by the 1880s, *to sell a gold brick* was a slang term meaning *to swindle*. Or again, in a scam reported in various forms, the swindler would stand upon a bridge, inform everyone he met that a new law demanded "a toll of one cent for foot passengers, two for horses and donkeys, and so forth," and collect his fees.[24] This would turn out to be only the second-best bridge scam that Americans would see. In 1901, a con artist from New Jersey was convicted of "selling" the Brooklyn Bridge, which of course he didn't own, to tourists who believed they would be allowed to set up a tollbooth. The scam inspired a phrase we still use today: "If you believe that, I have a bridge I'd like to sell you."[25]

FAITS DIVERS AND *FOUILLETONS*

As it happens, newspaper stories of urban crime, or rather crime stories that had a particular mixture of content, tone, and diction, were something new in the world. The French historian Michel Foucault famously analyzed the rise, in the early 19th century, of the *fait divers*, or true-crime story in the newspaper. This new genre was distinctive for its lurid prose and its mixture of ordinary urban settings with sensational urban crime; *faits divers* aimed to inspire "horror over the crime combined with a certain fascination for the criminal himself; a sympathetic identification with the victim tempered by a secret relief that the victim was someone else."[26] Foucault argues that this genre heralded "the birth of a literature of crime" in which readers vicariously experienced the underbelly of urban life.[27] While Foucault's analysis focuses on the newspapers of Paris, this genre of newspaper writing rapidly spread through other European cities and the cities of North America. As they say, bad news travels fast.

Publishers outside of France would have known about the success of the Parisian *fait divers* for two reasons: because newspapers in the 19th century often ran stories copied word for word from their competitors, leading to the rapid spread of popular pieces; and because of the international success in the literary marketplace of another, nearly identical French genre of writing—this one a genre of fiction.[28] For the rise of the *fait divers* overlapped in Paris with that of the *roman-feuilleton*, a genre of sensational crime fiction that began appearing in serial installments in newspapers. (The name means *serial novel*.) Crime fiction in the popular press closely resembled true-crime stories, adopting similar plotting, a similar prose style, and similar color details. Well before the mid-19th century, this style of writing was a familiar feature of the metropolitan press of New York City, where stories of true and fictional crime ran in the same pages and exploited the same techniques. (For example, in 1841, when the body of a young woman named Mary Rogers was found in the Hudson, the press devoted months of sensational articles to the fate of the "Beautiful Cigar Girl"—a description that could have featured in any crime fiction.)[29]

As it happens, these genres of popular literature—"one-day best-sellers," in Benedict Anderson's term for newspapers—also share a remarkable interest in slang.[30] For the same newspaper stories that ostensibly sought to warn the public about the dangers of the city's criminal element also kept the public up to date on the city's criminal argot. In the article that introduced the world to the confidence man William Thompson, the *New York Herald*, one of the city's most reliable sources of true-crime stories, reported that Thompson was "said to be a graduate of the college at Sing Sing"—a reference to Sing Sing prison, and a familiar expression in thieves' cant.[31] (As was usual for the *Herald*, the expression appeared without an explanation; the newspaper assumed that its readers would be current with underworld slang.) Or again, the *National Police Gazette*, a "sporting paper" that specialized in true-crime stories and news about boxing, not only used criminal argot to splash its stories with rich tones of magenta, mauve, and plum, but also ran first-person histories acquired, by interview, from prison inmates, placing their expressions on the page unmediated.

The authenticity that such expressions represented was a selling point of the *Gazette*, as its publisher, George Washington Matsell, recognized. In 1859, Matsell—who happened to be a former chief of the New York Police Department—published a "rogue's lexicon" of criminal argot in the city, which presented itself as an essential appendix to the paper.[32] Matsell's lexicon mingled definitions of the same raffish words that readers encountered in the pages of the *Herald*, the *Sun*, and his own paper with careful descriptions of how specific types of crime were carried out, no doubt drawing on his experience as an agent of the law. The descriptions of crime in the glossary testified to the authenticity of the argot, which in turn gave a feel of authenticity to the descriptions of crime in the newspaper. But as we have seen, the literary economy of true crime easily confederated nonfiction with fiction; Matsell's lexicon concludes with a fictional story of criminal life that purports to demonstrate how the argot works in action.

Or consider *The Mysteries and Miseries of New York* (1848), a massively bestselling novel that spawned a host of imitators. (The novel itself imitates a French bestseller of 1842, *The Mysteries of Paris.*) This novel, written by the newspaper journalist Ned Buntline, derived a good part of its prurient appeal from the claim that its stories of sin and sorrow were in fact nonfiction disguised as fiction. (Writes Buntline, "Not one scene of vice or horror is given in the following pages which has not been enacted over and over again in this city, nor is there one character which has not its counterpart in our very midst.")[33] One method by which Buntline sought to establish authenticity was by recording current slang from the city's streets; the characters use slang (or "flash language," as they call it) so often as to speak almost in dialect. Perhaps to drive home the importance of this feature, the author closes some installments of the narrative with glossaries of slang.

A remarkable amount of the underworld language in Buntline is ordinary, if colloquial, language today. In the narrative, quotation marks set off some terms that perhaps seemed too novel for the author's comfort: "ladies' man," "picked himself up," "a real bender," "see them through." Other terms lack quotation marks but are still clearly set off as slang, either in their usage or by appearing in the glossary: *beat* (a policeman's territory), *crib* (home), *cut and run* (to flee), *fence* (to sell stolen goods), *green* (naïve), *humbug* (fakery), *Jimmy* (a crowbar), *kick the bucket* (to die), *knock down and drag out* (a big fight), *lift* (steal), *OK*, *peepers* (eyes), *suited them to a T* (suited them perfectly), *street-walker* (prostitute), *spot* ("to recognize—to mark"), *spunk* (bravery), *square* (honest), *swag* (ill-gotten goods), *swig* (a gulp of alcohol), *tip* (to give), *tramp* (to walk).[34] The author clearly intended for the novel's language to be flashy, and most likely he embellished or invented outright some of the more outrageous forms of verbal display. But terms like those just cited certainly did exist, the proof of which is that they still exist today.

The best places to read this sort of thing were the metropolitan press and novels in the "city mystery" vein, but, in literary terms, there was no upper limit to the reach of criminal argot as an energizing device. Serious authors like Herman Melville and Charles Dickens sprinkled underworld slang into novels that sought to address the great themes of modern life. *The New Yorker*, a magazine that launched in 1925 with the aim of capturing the city's smart set, combined an educated colloquial voice with raffish slang and a keen interest in local wickedness. "The black-narcissus racket seems to have pretty well taken the place of the old fur-piece swindle," wrote a correspondent in 1929. "Men are the big buyers, but we know one woman who was taken in—paid a dollar for her bottle, and very nearly swooned when she finally uncorked her prize and smelled the contents, which seemed to be water flavored with something terrible."[35] Throughout the 1930s, the magazine breathlessly followed the doings of the nightclub owner Texas Guinan, who greeted customers with the catchphrase, "Hello, sucker!"[36]

Taken together, this literature makes clear how the informal idiom of crime was piped into the mainstream. The reading public loved fraud, at least when it was safely contained in newspaper stories about somebody else. In the city's popular literature, the *lexical field* of the criminal underworld, as a semanticist might put it, accumulated a deep bank of words that tended to circulate in the same pages: *artist* (a clever villain), *bender* (a drunken tear), *bogus* (a counterfeit coin; by extension, fake), **boodle** (fake money), *booze* (alcohol), *booby-hatch* (jail), **bouncer** (security professional), *brush* (to fool), *burnt out* ("worn-out roués"), *cave* (give in), *confidence man* (swindler), *cranky* (crazy), *graft* (criminal employment), *grafter* (swindler), *hawk* (swindler), *hog* (to fool), *humbug* (fakery), **john** (a prostitute's customer), *leak* (tell confidential information), **legit** (honest), *lushy* (intoxicated), **kitty** (a criminal's equipment), **madam** (brothel owner), *mark* (sucker), *nailed* (caught), **off-color** (shady), *pigeon* (informer), *played-out* (worn out), *pogy* (intoxicated), **pull** (personal influence),[37] *put away* (jailed), *queer* (counterfeit money), *scrapper* (a fighter), *sharp* (clever), *smoke* (to fool), **sport** (a gaming man), **spring** (abscond from jail), *squeal* (to snitch), *string* (to fool; now *string along*), *sucker* (mark), *sucked* (swindled), *sure thing* (a bet that cannot be lost), and *swindler* (con artist).

A ROGUE'S GALLERY

Why did the literary establishment insist on folding "flash language" into the literature of crime? One way to think about the uses of underworld slang in a body of literature aimed at the general reading public is to consider how slang might support the value such literature sought to give readers. In practice, these works offered a deliberately slippery blend of instruction and entertainment; they often promised explicitly to arm readers with guidance against the dangers of the city, but their thrilling plots and lurid details seem implicitly to be the real selling points. (Plausible deniability of this kind may have been most potent for yet another genre of underworld literature, pamphlets that promised to warn country folk of the dangers of the city: for example, *Tricks and Traps of New York City* (1857) or *The Snares of New York, Or Tricks and Traps of the Great Metropolis* (1879). Such works were still circulating in 1920, when the humorist Stephen Leacock published a satire of the genre: "The clergyman pounced upon him with a growl of a hyena, and bit a piece out of his ear. Yes, he did, reader. Just imagine a clergyman biting a boy in open daylight! Yet that happens in New York every minute.")[38]

In other words, the theatrics of instruction often justified the entertainment; but the reader learned much more about city life from the trappings of the story than from its explicit moral. The tone of the prose, along with the specialized names that flash language supplied, together taught by example an outlook, an attitude, a strategy for being out in the world: cynicism, knowingness, amusement at folly, a connoisseur's nuance in registering the urban environment.

If we were to categorize this discourse, we might start with its generous vocabulary of trickery: for example, *to get someone on a slow boat* (to defraud someone utterly); *to get taken* (to be cheated); *to get taken for a ride* (to be fooled or hoaxed); *gimmick* (a gadget used in a scam); *to put one over on someone* (to fool someone); **racket** (a scam or illegitimate line of business). Or again, we could move through a gallery of predatory, or perhaps just enterprising, street types, some of which terms have ameliorated into gentler meanings today: **Panhandling** started as a term for a con in which a beggar pretends to be disabled; *roughhousing*, as a term for violent mugging; *rubbernecking*, as a term for keeping a lookout while one's associate performs a swindle.

These are dubious situations, of course, but the literature provides readers with an ample script for responding to them. **Baloney**, perhaps a play on *blarney*, first appeared in the New York entertainment magazine *Variety* in 1922. **Hokum** started appearing in New York newspapers in the early 20th century, seeming, at first, to refer to flummery that plays on one's emotions.[39] **Poppycock,** or "nonsense," may derive from the Dutch compound *poppekak*, meaning "soft shit." In the 20th century, *phooey*, an expression of distaste or disbelief, crossed over to English-language literature from the Yiddish and German *pfui*. (The New York gossip columnist Walter Winchell helped to promote the word.)[40]

As we have seen, the subject of money had a capacious lexical field, from which here are some examples of New York origin: **boodle,** which often signified counterfeit or illicit money, comes from the Dutch *boedel,* or "belongings." **Kitty,** which, in addition to meaning a criminal's pack of equipment, refers to the pot while playing cards, likely comes from the Dutch *kit,* meaning "basket." (This also provided the phrase *kit and caboodle,* from *kit en boedel*—a term for the belongings of a bride who is moving to her new husband's house.) **Cheapskate,** or "miser," comes from the slang *skate,* for a shabby horse; *cheapskate* originally circulated in the context of horse racing, where it provided a grim assessment of a horse's odds of winning.[41] And the phrase **get-rich-quick** arose from fiction published, near the turn of the century, in *Cosmopolitan* magazine, which detailed the exploits of a swindler—or, as the title had it, an "American business buccaneer."[42]

As some of the examples just cited might suggest, speakers proficient in languages other than English contributed many loanwords to underworld slang. In New York City, the large community of Yiddish speakers contributed, for example, **kosher,** meaning (in an underworld context) trustworthy; **yentzer,** for a cheat; **spieler,** for a speculator; and **shyster,** which derives from the Yiddish and German word *scheiße,* or *shit.* The term *gun moll,* for a lady criminal, has nothing to do with firearms; *gun* comes from the Yiddish word *gonif,* or *thief.*[43] While the majority of words in the city's underworld argot were calqued from the English language or at least morphologically English, argot abounded with touches that reflected a polyglot city of immigrants: the slang word *coglione* ("a fool; a woman's dupe; a fop") is Italian for *asshole;* **fink,** for a snitch, "probably comes," the language historian David Maurer says, "from the German *Fink,* which can have a similar sense"; *katzenjammer,* for a hangover, likewise has a German counterpart; *spondulicks,* for money, adapts the Greek word *spondylikos,* referring to an antique unit of money.[44]

The Irish were a particularly visible immigrant community, having come to the city as one of the earliest major immigrant groups and established themselves in local institutions ranging from the theaters to the schools to City Hall. Like every cultural group, the Irish contributed rogues to the city's underworld, but they also went into policing in large numbers, a path that the city's many Irish politicians supported. In 1855, Irish immigrants made up 27 percent of the New York City Municipal Police.[45] The Irish did not get off easy for this prominence. Underworld slang branded police officers as *Paddy* and *Shamus* (presumably after *Seamus*); the vehicle for transporting prisoners was a *paddy wagon*, a term that is probably deliberately casual about whether the ethnic slur *paddy* refers to the police or the prisoners. Waggish expressions referred to the roadway as an *Irishman's sidewalk,* presumably because a drunken man's path might weave across the whole road, and the paving stones underfoot as *Irish confetti*.[46] Irish speakers—perhaps even speakers on both sides of the law—also contributed loanwords to underworld argot from the Irish language directly. *Bugaroch* came to mean *good-looking,* although in Irish *bagarach* means *threatening.* As we have already seen, *phony* (counterfeit) may come from the Irish *fawney* (*ring*); if this was the case, it may be that Irish police officers came up with the term, since the word **phony** first appears on the record in New York City, and since the ring scam that the word may refer to has never been particularly associated with Irish criminals. (Supporting this theory is that *fawney* is one of the Irish words known to many speakers, not only those fluent in Irish.)[47]

The language of policing shows vividly how both necessity and fancy can get caught up in the work of naming. As Allen argues, the reason that much of New York's historical slang dates from 1840 to 1950 was that this period gave rise to a great many new institutions in the city, which in turn demanded new names. Such was the case in the realm of policing. While police forces existed in the city almost from its beginning, the New York Police Department dates only to 1845, when the mayor established a large city police department after the model of the London Metropolitan Police Service. Our informal language of law and order came together in those years; used today, it offers a glimpse of the city from more than a century ago. The blue uniforms of the officers—adopted, in 1857, in imitation of the uniforms of the London Met—supplied *blue boys, blue coats,* and *men in blue. Billy club,* a term for an officer's truncheon, originated as slang in Victorian London—a waggish twist on *Billy,* which was slang for an "unclubbable man," or a man who could not get into a posh social club.[48] A *rogue's gallery* was an album containing pictures of criminals—the original facebook—that a police officer might carry on his beat.

But underworld slang from the period also preserves structures of feeling. With respect to the police, the overwhelming tone is combative—in contrast to firemen, for example, who seem never to have been called by derisive nicknames. In the 19th century, firemen were, at worst, *buffs,* a nickname coined for volunteers who were gung-ho about their work. Policemen were *bulls, flatfoots,* **pigs**, *shadows,* and *sparrow chasers*—all ominous or downright insulting names.[49] As in other domains of underworld language, these words provide glimpses of a mentality: a shared mental world, never fully coherent but meaningful in its recurring elements. (An unexpected element that resurfaces here reminds us of the ubiquity of Shakespeare in American popular culture: another nickname for a police officer was *Hamlet,* presumably because of their dark clothes. Slang for a brazen woman, by the way, was *Kate.*) The language of policing that the city's great era of slang produced points us not only to the new reasons for speech, but also the wariness and antagonism of the speakers. One slang term from the 1850s that has long since achieved mainstream innocuousness is **cop**, a shortened form of the earlier term *copper. Copper,* too, was a combative term in both its origins and its transformations; it derives from the slang verb *cop*, meaning *to grab*, and referred to both the officer and his truncheon.[50] (As it happens, *cop* is first recorded in Matsell's 1859 rogue's lexicon.)

THE USES OF SLANG

Why did so much slang from the 19th- and early 20th-century underworld survive to the present day—and not only survive, but join the mainstream? As we have seen, the literary circulation of underworld slang seems to have treated this language as the vehicle of an outlook, and this gives us a way to address this question by taking a wider view of the uses of this social form of language. Slang serves, of course, to separate initiates from non-initiates, to signal conversance with the latest fashions, to riff on cultural leitmotifs. But it also offers a taxonomy of noteworthy phenomena and a vocabulary for responding to them. In this, slang encapsulates, not exactly a *philosophy*, but certainly a *strategy* for getting along in that era.

The historian Robert Darnton has examined a similar dynamic in the old folktales of Europe. Focusing on French folktales, he shows that we can find in fairy tales strategies for living in a dangerous world. "Laudable as it may be to share your bread with beggars, you cannot trust everyone you meet along the road. Some strangers may turn into princes and good fairies; but others may be wolves and witches, and there is no sure way to tell them apart." In such a world of danger and uncertainty, we can best survive, these folktales suggest, by cultivating watchfulness, trickery, and readiness to leap through loopholes. The speakers who circulated these folktales handed down proverbs that promoted the same tactics: "Against the clever, the clever and a half"; "One must howl with the wolves."[51]

Slang, or at least the stories that incorporate slang, can participate in wisdom literature, although its guidance is more diffuse than that of folktales and proverbs. The "flash language" that Buntline and his contemporaries eagerly recorded portrays a world that is cruel, dangerous, and full of unreliable strangers. There are no wolves, witches, and bad fairies here; but there are thieves, grifters, gamblers, confidence men, pimps, and prostitutes, all of them ready to defraud the sucker or at least put him in moral peril. The newspapers, pamphlets, and penny literature that spun admonitory stories from this cloth may have designed such stories for prurient appeal, but they marketed them as a form of defense. (A typical opening for a newspaper story: "A new species of fraud has been introduced lately into this city, which it may be well the public should be guarded against.")[52] The victims in these stories may be figures of virtue, but their virtue gives them no sure protection, and they are often exaggeratedly ignorant and helpless: a widow, a blind man, a foolish apprentice. Meanwhile, the villains tend to seem helpful, charming, respectable, perhaps genteel. They play upon your confidence in your fellow men.

Perhaps the most resolute lesson, the most New York lesson, this vast literature extended to readers was: *don't be a sucker*. The word *sucker*, "or fool," didn't originate in New York—it is first attested in nearby Toronto—but within a few years of its origin, it became a local byword, a constant in the press and in popular fiction. Early on, speakers sometimes used the word as a general term of derision, much as English speakers had used the word *guy*; increasingly, however, it found use as a dark term of art describing anyone a crook could take advantage of. Writers applied the word to fraud at the card table, in the nightclub circuit, in the garment business, in the construction business, in the finance industry, in high society. They used it to make jokes that found predators everywhere in modern life (as with this quip in the *New York Herald*, which doubles the joke by playing on the term's origin in fishing: "Vassar girls believe in a fish diet as a good thing for the brain, and never miss hooking any sucker who falls in their way.")[53] Crime stories in the newspapers told readers of "sucker

fights" among gamblers, "sucker races" on the horse track, and under-
cover police officers who caught swindlers by playing the role of "the
'sucker.' "[54] The script that slang provides for responding to this lurk-
ing danger is a defensive script that places great emphasis on calling
fraud by its name. Hokum. Bunkum. Humbug. Poppycock. Phooey.

The emergence of the confidence man as a culture hero was an
extension of this survival impulse. Functionally, the confidence man
is a monster: a villain fashioned, like the witch in a fairy tale, to per-
sonify the mysteries and darker passions of the real world, the better
to teach the story's audience how to survive. Specifically, he personi-
fies dangers that came into full bloom in the Gilded Age—an era of
belief in mobility; of a financial marketplace whose unreliability ran
from the high sorcery of speculation to the mundane precarious-
ness of paper money; and of growing cities, where strangers took the
measure of strangers every day.[55] The confidence man has mastered
the art of being a stranger. Yet the popular literature surrounding the
confidence man also shows clear admiration, and not just because
Americans like competence and will forgive a fair amount of villainy
for its sake. In his own perverse way, the confidence man embodies
the egalitarian ideal of the self-made man: through wit and industry,
through hustling, the low can raise themselves high.[56]

A SUCKER BORN EVERY MINUTE

The skills of a con man are the skills of an advertiser, an entrepreneur,
an entertainer, as P.T. Barnum amply showed. Barnum, who moved
to New York City in his twenties, became the great wizard of an age
infatuated with humbug—which means "nonsense" but also served
as a term of art, meaning something that is neither definitively true
nor definitively false.[57] Barnum describes his excitement about his
first trip to "York" as a child: "I slept an hour or two towards morning,

dreaming of the great city with streets paved with gold, and many castles—in the air."[58] Barnum's American Museum drew enormous crowds to see his "humbugs" made of fraud and desire: for example, the Feejee Mermaid, which advertisements portrayed as a beautiful woman, but which in real life was visibly a dead monkey sewn onto a dead fish. He became a culture hero, a confidence man in legitimate dress; his success affirmed what Americans already knew: confidence games may be criminal, but they're also good business.

Barnum never actually said his famous catchphrase, "There's a sucker born every minute."[59] The phrase was in circulation in the late 19th century, but its messengers treated it, not as a celebrity's statement of character, but as a general proverb explaining the behavior of the marketplace. Still, Barnum's own writings about succeeding in business make clear that the line, in his America, between seeking out customers and seeking out suckers could be exceedingly fine. In *The Humbugs of the World* (1866), he documents, alongside hoaxes like "the Twenty-Seventh Street Ghost" (possibly conjured to scare off unwanted neighbors), predatory distortions of legitimate business: merchants who cut milk with water so as to move a greater volume of product; bakers who spike bread with alum so as to whiten their flour and disguise its poor quality; company presidents who acquire investments from speculators and then vanish with the capital. "Business is the ordinary means of living for nearly all of us," he writes, meaning that in the early republic the most conspicuous economic type was the self-made small businessman:

> And in what business is there not humbug? "There's cheating in all trades but ours," is the prompt reply from the boot-maker with his brown paper soles, the grocer with his floury sugar and chicoried coffee, the butcher with his mysterious sausages and queer veal, the dry goods man with his "damaged goods wet at the great fire" and his "selling at a ruinous loss," the stock-broker with his

brazen assurance that your company is bankrupt and your stock not worth a cent (if he wants to buy it,) the horse jockey with his black arts and spavined brutes, the milkman with his tin acquaria, the land agent with his nice new maps and beautiful descriptions of distant scenery, the newspaper man with his "immense circu-lation," the publisher with his "Great American Novel," the city auctioneer with his "Pictures by the Old Masters"—all and every one protest each his own innocence, and warn you against the deceits of the rest.[60]

As it happens, Barnum himself stayed generally within the bounds of legitimacy, only trespassing enough to tantalize the public. He put great effort into spreading rumors that his exhibits were hum-bugs, sometimes writing pseudonymous letters to the newspaper to accuse himself of fraud; however, this was largely because he under-stood that the public had few fascinations greater than humbug.[61] As with any cultural preoccupation, the public's eagerness to read about fraud and view it on exhibition had many layers: they wanted to fig-ure out the workings of a mystery; they wanted to safely experience the thrill of being scammed; and with the characteristic admiration that Americans have for competence, they wanted to appreciate a scam well done. When Barnum got hold of some half-dead buffa-loes, he advertised a "grand buffalo hunt" across the Hudson River in Hoboken, to be offered to the viewing public free of charge. (He did not charge money for subpar entertainment, although he made it pay off in other ways; "When people expect to get 'something for nothing' they are sure to be cheated," he remarked. In this case, he partnered with the ferry owner to share the fees from crossing the river.)[62] Writes the historian Neal Harris:

There were to be several shows, and by the time the first batch of spectators had seen the hunt, a second batch was passing them on the Hudson. The returnees called out from their boats that the hunt—a debacle in which the frightened animals fled to a nearby swamp—was the biggest humbug imaginable. Instead of being disappointed, however, the expectant audience, in the words of a witness, "instantly gave three cheers for the author of the humbug, whoever he might be."[63]

The imbrication of street-savvy slang into popular narratives of urban scheming plays out in Barnum's own memoir (1855). On the level of prose, Barnum's memoir belongs to the cloth of city mysteries and *faits divers* in that he uses slang regularly to assert authenticity, fill in local color, and convey a general attitude toward life: for instance, *cute tricks* (sharp tricks), *greenhorn* (novice), *humbug* (he proudly quotes a line calling him "the prince of humbugs"), *know the ropes* (know from experience), *licking* (losing a fight), *scheme* (devious plan), *sharp* (clever), *sharp trades* (clever trades), *sot* (fool), *straight-laced* (honest), *on the square* (honest), *sucked in* (fooled), *taken in* (fooled), and *wag* (practical joker). He also recites proverbs that suggest defining cultural motifs: the cautionary "wolf in sheep's clothing," the enterprising "you have to get up early in the morning to catch a weasel asleep," and the cynical "there's cheating in all trades but ours."[64] The marketplace had created conditions that gave buyers reason to beware, but it also gave entrepreneurs both inside and outside the law new pathways to, and images of, success. In his self-help proverbs, Barnum does not identify with a wolf. But he does identify with a weasel.

In short, we can look to the modern folklore of popular literature about crime as a major tributary that carried slang from the underworld into the mainstream. True-crime stories, city mysteries, pamphlets on the evils of the city, the memoirs of cops and confidence men: this literature constituted a vast field of testimony to the inventiveness of urban extralegal entrepreneurs. Along the way, it gave readers a vocabulary for making money, identifying scams, and responding to dubious situations. "I see no reason for believing that Americans are unusually fertile in word-coinage," writes Kenneth Burke. "American slang was not developed out of some exceptional gift. It was developed out of the fact that new typical situations had arisen and people needed names for them. They had to 'size things up.' They had to console and strike, to promise and admonish. They had to describe for the purposes of forecasting. And 'slang' was the result."[65]

AMERICAN HUSTLE

In the early 20th century, one of the most popular boys' weeklies in England was *The Magnet*, which carried a running series of stories about a fictional school called Greyfriars. (Think Harry Potter without the magic.) When an American boy joined the cast—a New Yorker named Fisher T. Fish—the magazine's cover introduced him as "A 'Hustling' Junior at Greyfriars."[66] Fish doesn't *need* to turn every little thing into a moneymaking scheme; he's already wealthy beyond the dreams of avarice. ("My father's Vanderbilt K. Fish, the railroad king," he tells the others. "I guess you've heard of him!")[67] But he cooks up moneymaking schemes anyway, because he is an American and, as he constantly reminds the other students, because he is a New Yorker. The city taught him to hustle, it taught him to stay alert for tricks, and it stocked his vocabulary with demotic slang: "I guess," "O.K." (this term baffles a dean), "yup" and "nope" (these terms baffle the students), and "Jevver get left?"—meaning, loosely, *Were you ever out-hustled?*

This sense of the word *hustle*—to seize on business opportunities—is American in origin, which is why *The Magnet* sets it off, on Fish's introductory cover, as an exoticism.[68] The term, which originated in the 19th century, refers to entrepreneurial drive, which Barnum recommends for Americans of every class in his 1888 book, *The Art of Money-Getting*: "WHATEVER YOU DO, DO IT WITH ALL YOUR MIGHT. Work at it, if necessary, early and late, in season and out of season, not leaving a stone unturned, and never deferring for a single hour that which can be done just as well *now*."[69] For young people consuming popular media today, the word *hustle* needs no quotation marks; it represents a conventional, even clichéd, call to self-improvement through enterprise, albeit one that retains a frisson of rebelliousness from its origin in slang. (The hip-hop artist Young Jeezy, referring in an interview to "hustlers" in both legitimate and illegitimate business, demonstrates the easy ambiguity of the term: "I just think a hustler's ambition is that I never stop. I start off hustling and said I'll never stop hustling. An ambitious hustler is the one to hustle the hustlers. When I grew up, my heroes were hustlers. Now I'm their hero.")[70] But the word fits just as easily in the mouths of politicians, the memoirs of celebrities, the bourgeois discourse of self-help. John Cena, the family-friendly "All-American Face" of World Wrestling Entertainment, promotes the word on his official merchandise: "Hustle, loyalty, and respect."[71] Hustle is an all-American enterprise.

"By the 1950s," writes Irving Allen, "the classic city novel and similar literature had gone into near eclipse in favor of indoor and backyard suburban settings and unidentifiable locales."[72] The metropolitan press in New York City, along with the city's great houses of literary publishing, continued to coin and popularize new words, but never again at such a tremendous rate, and never again did slang make itself so essential to the general public. The New York City that we know today has changed so much from the city then as to be, in some respects, unrecognizable. (For example, Matsell's dictionary records slang terms that local thieves used for livestock, a reminder that in 1859, if you went up Fifth Avenue far enough, you'd hit farms and open land.)[73] Nonetheless, the lexicon of having and getting by any means possible has survived and even expanded. Today, we regularly use idioms that were minted in a gilded century of massive social change, suggesting that its opportunities and dangers—the imperative to hustle or be hustled—continue to make themselves felt in American life. As the next chapter will show, even the popular songs that have emerged from New York City's music industry partake in this tradition, joining language from the city streets with the metaphorical music of clinking coins.

Chapter 5

From Tin Pan Alley to Hip-Hop

Assist me, Muse American, to tell
A tale so good that it will also sell.
     —Franklin P. Adams, "Benjamin Franklin" (1931)

New York City is a great factory of language. Focusing on the city's music industry, this chapter examines language as artistic material that professionals polish according to the rules of their craft. On Broadway and off, lyricists expand the American Songbook. At musical workshops, rap battles, and hip-hop ciphers, writers sharpen sentences, search for collaborators, and throw their darlings into the den of peer review. In the pages of rhyme books, rappers hone individual voices that also speak on behalf of their communities. The result is a body of literature that is both colloquial and corporate, both puckish and pragmatic as the clink of coins. A fast-paced trading zone joins the city's sounds and its songs: the language of popular music influences the soundscape of the city, while elements from everyday speech end up in popular song.

TIN PAN ALLEY

In the late 19th century, music joined the era of mass commerce. Music publishers, who had once been genteel craftsmen, discovered the economic possibilities of mass production. Songwriters became entrepreneurs who sold songs to publishers by the piece, sometimes as often as a song per day. The music industry began to follow assembly-line techniques of mass production, assigning the different parts of a song's construction to different workers: lyricists, composers, arrangers, publishers, and "pluggers," or singing advertisers who would make a public showing of new songs on city sidewalks.[1] "Nowadays," a writer for the *New York Times* said in 1910, "the consumption of songs in America is as constant as the consumption of shoes, and the demand is similarly met by factory output."[2] During the same period, the music industry moved with other industries in embracing more assertive forms of advertising. Speakers began to use a new word, ***plug***, meaning to actively hawk a song or another product. They also created, in the music industry, a new meaning for the word *make*: to *make* a song didn't mean to write it, but to make it big, to make it a hit.[3] "What you sing and whistle," said a music scholar in 1930, "is hardly an accident. It is the result of a huge plot—involving thousands of dollars and thousands of organized agents—to make you hear, remember and purchase. The efforts of organized pluggery (I present that word to Webster) assail our ears wherever we go, because it is the business of this gentry to fill the air with music."[4]

The site of this transformation was New York City. The term *pluggery* never did enter Webster's Dictionary, but the word *plug* is a New York word, deriving from a Dutch word meaning *stopper* (and thus, presumably, the strenuous activity required to pound a stopper into a boat; to *plug* something is to work strenuously to promote it). By the 1890s, music publishing firms had made a definite capital of New York City, where publishers had easier access to show business. Around 1903, speakers began to refer to the popular music business using the term *Tin Pan Alley*, which refers, according to legend, to the clatter of piano music out of windows in New York City's music district, which was then a stretch of 28th Street between Sixth Avenue and Broadway.[5]

The fact that the popular music business was anchored, through the mid-20th century, in New York City—"By 1900," writes one historian, "it was a rare song that achieved mass sales and nationwide popularity after being published elsewhere"—profoundly affected the character of *the American Songbook*, in a term that we use to describe the most memorable popular songs from these years.[6] As music historians such as David Suisman and Ben Yagoda have shown in detail, the New York setting of the music industry shaped songwriting in many ways, not least by making the songs utterly American.[7] New York meant immigrants, outsiders, and entrepreneurs, and these figures not only observed the world of insiders as intimately as only an outsider can, but also endowed their songs with consummate New York values: irony, cosmopolitanism, and the founding American value by which members of different communities—and different languages, different faiths, different musical styles—come together to create a richer and more various whole. *E pluribus unum.*

HUSTLE ALL DAY

That the American Songbook reflects, in large part, the work of minority songwriters, especially those of Jewish descent, is well known. George and Ira Gershwin (born Jacob and Israel Gershowitz), Harold Arlen (born Hyman Arluck), and Yip Harburg (born Isidore Hochberg) were the children of Jewish immigrants from Eastern Europe. Dorothy Fields was the child of an immigrant from Poland (Lew Fields, born Moses Schoenfeld). Irving Berlin (born Israel Baline) immigrated from Siberia as a five-year-old boy. Andy Razaf (born Andreamenentania Razafinkeriefo) was African American and binational, having been born, after considerable palace intrigue, to an American diplomat's daughter and a Madagascar prince and then grown up in Harlem.[8] In this company, Cole Porter, a Midwestern WASP, represented a demographic exception rather than the rule. He was also gay; he made himself a pillar of good society's "four hundred" through dedicated effort and a special understanding with his wife.

From a simple industry perspective, the strong Jewish presence in Tin Pan Alley makes a lot of sense. Germans had long held a prominent role in the American music scene, "from the concert hall to the vaudeville stage," which opened doors in the industry for Americans of German descent, Jews and gentiles alike. As it happened, German Jews were also considerably active in the middle-class profession of salesman, selling everyday items like water filters, corsets, and neckties. Many new figures who entered music publishing in the late 19th century, the first generation to encounter the conditions that enabled songs to be mass-produced, had previously held jobs in sales. Their experience gave them a modern commercial orientation and a set of skills that worked brilliantly with the commercial arts: "This background in business and sales underpinned the whole of the popular song industry these men built, for they had apprehended that in some ways songs could be sold like soap."[9] In the early 20th century, as the demographics of immigration changed and New York Jews came increasingly from Eastern Europe, the composition of Tin Pan Alley changed as well, with members hailing increasingly from Russia rather than Germany, from the crowd of newcomers rather than the assimilated old guard, and from the working class rather than the middle class.[10]

The cultural attitudes of German Jews in New York, specifically, helped to shape the vision of America that emerged from Tin Pan Alley. One of the narratives about the difference between New York and Los Angeles is that the immigrants of Los Angeles were serious about assimilating, while the immigrants of New York were ironic about it.[11] Who can say whether this was true?

"ALL I HAD LEFT WAS A PENCIL"

The New York City upbringing of Tin Pan Alley's songwriters helped to prepare them to produce writing that was sharp, smart, swift, and sure. Consider the case of Ira Gershwin and Yip Harburg, who were classmates in high school in the Bronx. During the early decades of the 20th century, the city's board of education designed course content with a firm eye to the Americanization of a student body that it understood to be dangerously foreign.[12] The board's strategy for Americanizing students took the form, before all else, of a preoccupation throughout the curriculum with proper speech, with the idea that proper speech made proper Americans.[13] (Indeed, the board had a special division—the Bureau of Speech Improvement, discussed in chapter 2—that specialized in helping teachers to conduct speech training.) Thus public schools emphasized, for example, the recitation of poetry, which the board's curricular materials promoted with the view that recitation not only improves language, but also encourages virtues such as self-discipline and patriotism: that meter maketh man.[14] Harburg later remarked that he had liked school precisely for its emphasis on recitation: "I liked school because of the acting, the drama, and the recitation. Basically, I loved the English language, the poetry."[15]

As classmates, Harburg and Gershwin bonded over Gilbert and Sullivan. They started talking when Gershwin saw Harburg reading Gilbert's book of light verse; Gershwin started bringing Harburg to his home to listen to phonograph records of Gilbert and Sullivan shows. Together, they edited a column of comedy and light verse in the school newspaper, in imitation of Franklin P. Adams's column in *The New York World*, "The Conning Tower." Every large newspaper in the city ran light verse, as the historian Philip Furia notes— Adams's column in *The New-York Tribune*, C. L. Edson's column in *The Daily Mail*, Don Marquis's column in *The Evening Sun*—but "The

Conning Tower" was the most famous, a platform for brilliant writers like Robert Benchley, George S. Kaufman, Edna St. Vincent Millay, Dorothy Parker, James Thurber, and E. B. White. Harburg later said, "We were living in a time of literate revelry in the New York daily press—F.P.A., Russell Crouse, Don Marquis, Alexander Woollcott, Dorothy Parker, Bob Benchley. We wanted to be part of it."[16] Every writer starts out by writing unintentional parodies of those they admire, and for young writers of this time and place, the ones to emulate were the urbane wits in the press. After Harburg and Gershwin entered college together at the College of the City of New York (now the City College of New York), they edited a similar column for the college newspaper.

Gershwin, who grew up in the middle class, felt secure enough in his future to drop out of college and head right into the music industry, following the path of his brother, the composer George Gershwin. (George had left high school at fifteen to pursue a career in music, breaking in as a plugger for a music publisher.) Harburg, who grew up in poverty, working outside of school hours in a garment factory with his sister and parents, was more cautious.[17] After finishing college and serving an obligatory stint in the military, he started a career in the secure, respectable electrical appliance business, writing light verse on the side to submit to "The Conning Tower"—but not, as his business partner made him pledge in writing, during work hours. Then the stock market crash of 1929 wiped out his business: as he later said, "All I had left was a pencil."[18] His old friend Ira Gershwin loaned him some money and helped him start working as a lyric writer, the rare career in which a pencil was all that one needed.[19] It turned out to be a perfect match of man and métier. Harburg was a monster of productivity—and a reliable producer of the hits that kept Tin Pan Alley running.[20] He produced more than 530 songs over the course of his career, some 150 of them with his frequent collaborator, the composer Harold Arlen.[21]

ELEGANT PUZZLES

What does it take to write lyrics for popular songs reliably? For a start, it takes knowledge of the rules that structure a song. Despite the association of song with freedom and release—*wine, women, and song*, as we say in the traditional list of Dionysian pleasures—most great songwriters are not Dionysians, but Apollonians: dedicated students of rationality, order, and rules. Indeed, some songwriters, like Stephen Sondheim, are crossword addicts, which makes sense given that both lyric writing and crossword puzzling are problem-solving tasks that entail working with patterns, navigating structural constraints, and balancing rules with aesthetic effects. Sondheim, who has described writing lyrics as "an elegant kind of puzzle," even created crossword puzzles for *New York Magazine,* and introduced the cryptic crossword to the United States.[22] For his part, Ira Gershwin remarked in an interview that he learned his craft in part by playing with strict poetic forms as a teenager, drawing on the emphasis on poetry in his school's curriculum: "In my late teens, I fooled around with French verse forms, such as the triolet, villanelle, and especially the rondeau—with its opening phrase taking on new meanings when repeated."[23] As we will see, a song's refrain, too, often works by taking on new meanings when repeated. And Harburg described the difference between lyrics and music as the difference between thought and feeling: "Words make you think thoughts, make you think a thought. Music makes you feel a feeling. But a song makes you feel a thought. Together, they stand ready to soothe not only the savage breast, but the stubborn mind."[24] For him, lyrics were the work of the head, music the work of the heart.

The rules that structured a pop song in the early 20th century were remarkably similar to the rules that structure a pop song today. They were also different from the rules that had structured pop songs in the 19th century. The older tradition had favored long verses and short choruses, using the long verses to tell a story. The new culture of advertising, the assertive pluggery that didn't just inform the public about a product, but encouraged them to buy it, changed the format of commercial music, shortening the verses and making the chorus the most important part of a song.[25] After all, if a song is an advertisement for itself, the chorus is the jingle. Examples abound of songwriters in the early 20th century commenting that a song's "ultimate success or failure" relied on the chorus; Suisman quotes one who adds that the goal, therefore, "is to get to the chorus, or refrain, as quickly as possible."[26]

The stanzas of a song must follow a specific sequence. Usually, that sequence is A-A-B-A, where A is a version of the chorus and B is the bridge, which is a section of the song that switches up the melody and beat.[27] Pop songs still follow this sequence today. Because a pop song was, as a rule, brief—the basic structure is almost always just 32 bars in length, though it may be repeated several times to accommodate more lyrics and instrumental riffs—lyricists found it useful to work new meanings into the chorus and refrain as they repeated, in order to achieve a larger dramatic arc within the short length. Ira Gershwin reported that his hardest chore while composing a song was to get the title phrase, which was also the refrain, right; having accomplished this, he would then move straight "to the last line" of the song, in an effort "to work the title in again; with a twist, if possible."[28]

Finally, songwriting has special constraints that written poetry does not have: a consequence, first, of the fact that a song needs to *sing* well, and second, of the fact that a singer delivers a song in linear time. A poet can choose all sorts of vowels and consonants with which to make effects like alliteration, assonance, and consonance; but a lyricist will seek to favor open vowels and pleasing consonants, because, as William Zinsser puts it, the "words must 'sing.'" He adds, "Not all consonants are bad for singers—'l' is mellifluous, 'r' is resonant, and 'v' is forever good for 'love.' But the harsh consonants tighten the throat, and lyricists try to avoid them."[29] And a song, unlike a poem, usually works better if the language and syntax are pared down, enabling the listener to understand the lines as they are delivered in time; a song must be, as Sondheim says, "underwritten."[30] A composer who worked with Dorothy Fields described her earliest efforts at songwriting as "prose," by which he seems to have meant, not unrhymed lines, but "not music."[31]

TOO DARN HOT, LIKE MY MAN COLE PORTER SAID

The wit and invention that Tin Pan Alley lyricists gave their lyrics helped to elevate their music as art. The language they chose made it a distinctively American art. For the songs of Tin Pan Alley drew overwhelmingly upon the language, the poetry, of the American vernacular. Ira Gershwin plucked his titles, he said, "from thin air, figuratively and literally . . . by listening to the argot in everyday conversation."[32] And their interest in the vernacular extended not only to slang, but also to the vernacular in the sense of everyday life—which was also, for them, life in the pluralistic, multicultural trading zone of New York City.

Thus Cole Porter, for example, traditionally recognized as the most white-shoe of the Tin Pan Alley lyricists, filled his songs with slang and phrases of recent coinage: *you're the top; I get a kick out of you; anything goes; how long has this been going on; who cares; I hit the ceiling; my one and only; I've got a crush on you.* Porter wrote a world of top hats, champagne, jaded romance, and ennui, but his speakers still know the slang of the city's sidewalks, nightclubs, and speakeasies. Indeed, in songs like "Anything Goes" (1934), he composed in the vernacular dance time of the foxtrot, which had spread throughout the city after being innovated on the dancing floors of "colored clubs."

Or again, as Zinsser notes, Gershwin worked sometimes with African American Vernacular English: in his most famous song, the line is not "I've got rhythm," but rather "I got rhythm."[33]

For songwriters like the composer Harold Arlen, a cantor's son who played the piano for the Cotton Club, and Dorothy Fields, who worked as a songwriter for the Cotton Club together with her frequent collaborator, the composer Jimmy McHugh, the city life closest at hand included the voices and music of black New Yorkers, whose migration to the city had swelled during the same years as that of Eastern Europeans.[34] The first hit songs that Fields wrote with McHugh, "I Can't Give You Anything but Love" (1928), "Exactly Like You" (1930), and "On the Sunny Side of the Street" (1930), use slang and colloquial phrases from Harlem, the Jewish neighborhood of Hester Street, and further into the city: *I've been blue; I used to walk in the shade with those blues on parade; it's tough to be broke, kid; you know darned well; grab your hat, baby*; and (with Fields's signature internal rhyme) *Gee, I'd like to see you looking swell, baby*.[35] In this, they extended an important historical relationship between Jewish and African American artists that has been the subject of much critical discussion.[36] For the white nightclubbers who treated the Cotton Club, which featured black performers but only admitted white patrons, as a safely contained form of slumming, hearing these sounds may have felt like a way to get in touch with an "authentic" New York City. For Jewish and African American audiences, both understood to be people of color, hearing familiar phrases, verbal and musical, in the city's department stores, in the cinema, on the radio, in popular nightclubs, may have felt a little like arriving—though perhaps also with a bitter sense of self-estrangement as their music climbed higher in the world than they could expect to.

Lyricists often took their language from the vernacular and commercial language of the city. Irving Berlin read the term "heatwave" in a newspaper and turned it into a sultry hook: "She started a heatwave by letting her seat wave." Porter took a slang expression of distaste, "you're getting under my skin," and turned it into an expression of love: "I've got you under my skin." Ira Gershwin folded the underworld slang *low-down* into *sweet and low*, a phrase from English poetry: "Grab a cab and go down, to where the band is playing, where milk and honey flow down, where everyone is saying, blow that sweet and low-down!" As Zinsser notes, Gershwin also drew on the punchy new language of advertising—*cleanable, peelable, refillable, kissable*—for the hook of "Embraceable You."[37]

WHIMSY AND HUMOR

Each songwriter brought his or her own twist to the form. Lorenz Hart grounded Richard Rodgers's dreamy melodies with sober lyrics. Cole Porter created an effect of jaded sophistication via knowing allusions and little twists that added humor to his underlying themes of romance and sadness. (One of his speakers, ordering a drink, says, "Make it for one who's due to join the disillusioned few; make it for one of love's new refugees.")[38] Yip Harburg, by his own account, couldn't believe in a song unless he sprinkled it with stardust. The Gershwins combined George's Dionysian phrasing with Ira's neat Apollonian wit. George usually wrote first, and his rapid, changeful musical phrasing left Ira with the challenge of finding verbal shapes to fit; Ira likened writing lyrics for him to crafting a mosaic. Other songwriters called Ira "The Jeweler."[39]

From the vantage point of almost a century later, the wit and irony of this era's pop lyrics marks them as belonging to a different time. Ira Gershwin described the requirements set upon a good lyricist as follows: "Given a fondness for music, a feeling for rhyme, a sense of whimsy and humor, an eye for the balanced sentence, an ear for the current phrase, and the ability to imagine oneself as a performer trying to put over the number in progress—given all this, I would still say it takes four or five years collaborating with knowledgeable composers to become a well-rounded lyricist."[40] The point he makes of *whimsy and humor* is notable, given that these virtues are no longer requirements for writing popular music. Pop music still operates as a factory system—"the song machine," as John Seabrook calls it—but New York City has long since ceased to be its factory floor. (A notable exception is hip-hop music, which is as witty and referential as ever.) Now the writers of the songs one hears on the Top 40 are, quite often, Swedes like Max Martin, who synthesize American genres like rock and R&B in interesting ways and who seem to possess an uncanny ability to get to the sweet-sour taste of pure pop.[41] But contemporary pop seems to lack the chattering-class literariness of the urbanite and the irony of the outsider.

My favorite wit among the writers of the American Songbook is Dorothy Fields. Fields, too, came into songwriting by way of literary puzzles: she submitted light verse to "The Conning Tower," and her earliest lyrics, as she discussed with charming frankness later in her career, ripped off Hart's and Gershwin's intricate rhymes.[42] But she used that literary impulse to find the poetic possibilities of plain United States language. Fields preferred hooks that make concrete declarative statements: *lovely to look at, on the sunny side of the street, close as pages in a book, I'm in the mood for love, I feel a song coming on, I can't give you anything but love, if my friends could see me now.*[43] As one critic notes, Oscar Hammerstein, writing with Jerome Kern, wrote a song that praised loftily "All the Things You Are." Fields, writing with the same composer, focused the same emotion in a specific, imperishable detail: "The Way You Look Tonight."[44] She is emotionally fluent in the floating abstractions of love and romance, but tethers them to an idiom as concrete and pragmatic as the clink of coins. It is this quality, together with her sense of humor, that gives her songs an *urbane* sensibility, a sense that the speaker can handle herself in a world of mobs, marks, and masks:

> I dream too much, but if I dream too much
> I only dream to touch your heart again.
>
> ("I Dream Too Much," 1935)

> A fine romance! With no quarrels!
> With no insults, and all morals!
> I've never mussed the crease in your blue serge pants,
> I never get the chance,
> This is a fine romance.
>
> ("A Fine Romance," 1936)

> True love should have the thrills that a healthy crime has!
>
> ("A Fine Romance," 1936)

> You couldn't be cuter
> Plus that you couldn't be smarter
> Plus that intelligent face
> You have a disgraceful charm for me.
>
> ("You Couldn't Be Cuter," 1938)

> I'll buy it,
> Moonlight, romance,
> Cool quiet
> And someone to hold.

> I'll grab it,
> Marriage, babies,
> I'll buy it,
> I'm finally sold.
>
> ("I'll Buy It," 1957)

The minute you walked in the joint
I could see you were a man of distinction
A real big spender
Good looking, so refined
Say wouldn't you like to know
What's going on in my mind

("Big Spender," 1966)

OF THEE I SING

The values and experiences that enabled Tin Pan Alley songwriters to write so brilliantly about city life did not prevent them from writing songs that also spoke directly to the self-understanding of the nation at large. On the contrary, they wrote songs that listeners across the country embraced as timeless expressions of mainstream American culture: "You're a Grand Old Flag" (1906); "Take Me Out to the Ballgame" (1908); "God Bless America" (1918/38); "Swanee" (1919); "Ol' Man River" (1927); "On the Sunny Side of the Street" (1930); "Brother, Can You Spare a Dime?" (1932); "Easter Parade" (1933); "Pick Yourself Up" (1936); "Louisiana" (1936); "Over the Rainbow" (1940); "Happy Holiday" (1942); "White Christmas" (1942); "Oklahoma" (1943). (Interesting note: the writer of "Take Me Out to the Ballgame," the vaudevillian Jack Norworth, drafted out the lyrics while sitting in a New York City subway car.)[45]

These writers wrote brilliantly on American themes in part because they sometimes felt that they stood outside of the American mainstream looking in. The writers of Tin Pan Alley, most of them immigrants, the children of immigrants, or members of other marginalized groups waiting to be welcomed into the mainstream, had special occasion to reflect on the meaning of democracy, the iconography of patriotism, the signs of belonging to the mainstream, the symbols of an emerging popular culture, the uses of nostalgia, the beauty of America's ideals, and the distance between America's ideals and its reality.

Consider the making of Yip Harburg's "Brother, Can You Spare a Dime?," which first appeared in the 1932 revue *Americana*. He later explained that the hook of the song, which, in one critic's words, "became the anthem of the Great Depression," was a phrase that he had been hearing on every sidewalk of the city. He deliberately chose not to build from the phrase an isolated tale of hard luck, but rather an allegory about every American who had invested sweat, pennies, and faith in the American Dream:

> The prevailing greeting at that time, on every block you passed, by some poor guy coming up, was: "Can you spare a dime?" Or: "Can you spare something for a cup of coffee?". . . "Brother, can you spare a dime?" finally hit on every block, on every street. I thought that would be a beautiful title. If I could only work it out by telling people, through the song, it isn't just a man asking for a dime. . . . I wanted a song that would express his indignation over having worked hard in the system only to be discarded when the system had no use for him.[46]

Or consider Harburg's greatest hit, "Over the Rainbow" (1939). This song has entered the American mythos as decidedly as "Take Me Out to the Ball Game." (In 2001, the National Endowment for the Arts voted it the best song of the 20th century.) Harburg later said that throughout his work (with the composer Harold Arlen) on the songs for *The Wizard of Oz*, he was thinking about Roosevelt's New Deal specifically, and more generally about Americans' desire for their own country to be self-assured, generous, and lavish with freedoms of mind, spirit, and opportunity. Harburg meant the lyrics of "Over the Rainbow" to ruminate, he said, on the *pursuit* part of *the pursuit of happiness*. In Harburg's view, the term *pursuit* is not a caveat or a qualification, but rather the key to an important idea, namely that, though we recognize that we may not live to see our hopes and ideals fully realized, pursuing those hopes and ideals anyway is what makes for a better, more perfect world:

> I don't know what happiness is and I don't think anybody knows what happiness is, nor did the founding fathers of our constitution tell you that they are making a land and a constitution that will give you happiness. They say, "Life, liberty, and the *pursuit* of happiness." Pursuit is the secret word in the meaning of life. It's the pursuit of something that the spirit inside tells you that somewhere, as exemplified by the rainbow, that it isn't just this little bit of arid earth that we're on, but there is a liaison, a bridge . . . between our little planet, our little earth that we're on and the heaven of your imagination. Because this is where heaven is—it's in here. . . . It's within you.[47]

"I have a job to do," Harburg said of his profession. "I am a blacksmith or a carpenter, excepting that I do it instead of with nails, I do it with words. And that's my job."[48] But he also worked as though his pop-culture carpentry had the reach and responsibility of high art; and in this he was much in agreement with his peers. A comment that *Scribner's Magazine* made in 1899 about vaudeville, a popular form of theater that fed directly into Tin Pan Alley, seems to me to capture the ethos of the best commercial art of this era: "The vaudeville theater belongs to the era of the department store and the short story. It may be a kind of lunch-counter art, but then art is so vague and lunch is so real."[49]

GOODBYE TO ALL THAT

The song machine of Tin Pan Alley penetrated many sectors of the commercial arts. During the industry's heyday, the same lyricists and composers who wrote for music publishers and nightclubs also wrote for Broadway shows and, starting in the 1930s, for Hollywood films. The tight connection, early on, between Broadway and Hollywood resulted partly from the Great Depression, which slashed the work available on Broadway and sent professionals fleeing to the less prestigious, but more remunerative, world of film. (This marked the start of the bicoastal commuter culture between New York City and Los Angeles.)[50] But it also resulted from the desire of Hollywood studios to pinch talent from the language factories of New York City. In addition to the offices of music publishers, studios also looted the offices of magazines: Robert Benchley, George S. Kaufman, Charles Lederer, Dorothy Parker, and S. J. Perelman were among the many writers who, after training at New York publications like *Vanity Fair, Time,* and *The New Yorker,* were lured out west to write scripts for Paramount and MGM. The literary tastes of this community help to account for the intricate wordplay in many Hollywood films of this period, including *The Front Page* (1931), *Monkey Business* (1931), *Horse Feathers* (1932), and *His Girl Friday* (1940).

In time, Los Angeles cultivated screenwriting hothouses of its own. New York City's chattering class ceased to be shapers of language in popular film, just as its songwriters gradually ceased to be the shapers of pop music. The Broadway musical kept going strong, of course, and within its arena, figures like Stephen Sondheim extended the traditions of Fields and the Gershwins across the second half of the 20th century. Sondheim, as one observer noted, has "lived most of his life in a 10-by-30-block morsel of Manhattan," and many of the musicals for which he wrote lyrics (*West Side Story, Company, Merrily We Roll Along*) are love letters to New York City.[51] Linked directly to the old world of musicals through the composer Oscar Hammerstein, who took the ten-year-old Sondheim under his wing, Sondheim continued the tradition of the 32-bar song; the tradition of urbane polish, favoring not just perfect rhymes, but also devices like alliteration, assonance, consonance, parallelism, repetition, and reversal; and the tradition of treating art as craft, writing songs with the aid of careful lists and schema.[52] And he upheld the old guard's appreciation of comedy, frivolity, and wit. ("To some, there is a chasm between 'light' and 'serious,'" he once wrote; "to me they differ only in style, not in substance. I put Phyllis McGinley right up there with Keats and Shelley.")[53]

Sondheim cut his teeth in the profession by working, in his twenties, as a lyricist on *West Side Story*, which taught him the value of having collaborators: "I have to work *with* someone," he later said, "someone who can help me out of writing holes, someone to feed me suggestions when my invention flags, someone I can feed in return."[54] Indeed, collaboration is the rule on Broadway, where a lyricist will typically collaborate with a composer, director, librettist, performers, and producer, at a minimum. In part for this reason, Broadway has a rich and venerable workshop culture. The music-publishing organization Broadcast Music, Inc. (BMI) runs a legendary three-year workshop that many of Broadway's most notable creators have attended; the American Society of Composers, Authors, and Publishers (ASCAP) offers a rich array of workshops to its members; New York University has a workshop-based musical-theater MFA program.[55] These institutions testify to New York's role as a laboratory of creative and expressive language.

The value of these institutions, says Greg Pliska, a musical-theater composer who has set the Bard's words to music for Shakespeare in the Park, does not lie in the craft they teach or the credentials they confer: "A constant thing in the arts, especially the commercial arts, is a need to be commercially successful in order to survive. There is no indication that having an MFA means you'll produce a hit." The real value of workshops, he suggests, lies in the people you meet at them: "I think that what everybody with a hit has done has found a collaborative team with whom they can succeed. A great place to find that team is in a workshop." A good workshop allows you to meet collaborators, test your styles in each other's company, and develop a shared vocabulary for working together—the challenge being, as with any institution, to avoid getting trapped in the hermetic discourse of the profession and keep your ears tuned to the wider world. Slang that only has meaning within a profession is jargon, and no singable, sellable song ever took its hook from jargon, though a hundred thousand have taken their hooks from slang. "Musical theater grabs the vernacular," Pliska says. "Not just everyday language, but the vernacular. All the Latin music in Cole Porter. The foxtrot. You speak to people where they are."[56]

I, TOO, SING AMERICA

In the later decades of the 20th century, hip-hop music, which originated in New York City, overtook other musical genres—among them, other homegrown American genres such as blues, country, rhythm and blues, jazz, rock, and the musical—as the musical form of greatest influence over American language and popular culture writ large. It is to this young genre, and its vernacular commitment to convert the language and experiences of ordinary people into art, that we now turn.

Hip-hop culture has been entrepreneurial from the very start. It has also, from the very start, been tied to the people and politics of New York City. Its origins in the 1970s accompanied a boom in immigration to the city from the Caribbean, where DJs at dance parties spun records featuring ska, reggae, or African American popular music, talking between songs in a patter that blended music commentary with rhyming boasts.[57] The date that historians usually give for the birth of hip-hop is August 11, 1973, when the siblings Clive and Cindy Campbell, teenaged immigrants from Jamaica living in the West Bronx, held a neighborhood party in their apartment building with the aim of raising money to help Cindy buy clothes for the new school year. While Clive Campbell spun records under the stage name DJ Kool Herc, his friend Coke La Rock, acting as MC (master of ceremonies), engaged the audience with rhymed braggadocio, a mode of performance that later became known as *rapping*. Within a few years, such parties nurtured a thriving subculture where DJs and MCs joined forces with *b-boys* and *b-girls* who showed off during passages in the music that were called "the breaks."[58]

In the 1970s and 1980s, DJs, MCs, rappers, producers, breakdancers, and other bearers of hip-hop culture set up parties in private homes, rented rooms, community centers, and city parks; tapped into city streetlights (on occasion) for electricity to power their equipment; cut and sold their own records; competed for cash prizes in churches and school gymnasiums; and performed for money in the streets and subways.[59] *Hustling*, or earning income independently of dominant social and commercial institutions, was integral to hip-hop culture from the start. The slang and lyrics of hip-hop reflected this commitment. Phrases like *crossing over, keeping it real, selling out*, and *sticking to the rawness* registered the moral peril of choosing mainstream success over the perceived authenticity of street entrepreneurship.[60] At the same time, rap embodied a dream of improving one's station in life via language itself, via the wit, elegance, and distinctiveness of one's way with words. You could talk your way out of trouble, the dream suggested: write your way out of dismal circumstances.

In time the counterculture of hip-hop was appropriated by the very commercial forces that it opposed. Hip-hop culture moves merchandise, produced and trademarked by huge corporations, that ranges from music to cars to clothing to consumer electronics to films to food to jewelry to liquor to luxury goods.[61] In 1994, when Snoop Dogg's song "Gin and Juice" went gold, Seagram's Gin, which the song mentions, rose in sales to 4 million cases from 3.3 million cases per year, and the Seagram Company added a new label to the bottles highlighting the drink's use in gin and juice.[62] Although hip-hop artists and audiences register (and often moralize) a difference between local entrepreneurship and corporate sponsorship, between working with record labels and selling one's own mixtapes, at both ends of this scale hip-hop is a thoroughly commercial art—and a global one at that, having spread beyond New York City to Atlanta, Los Angeles, Philadelphia, and around the world.

LISTENING TO THEY WALKMAN TALKIN' THE NEW YORK FUCKING SLANG

Like the songwriters of Tin Pan Alley, the writers of hip-hop often built their songs around the sounds of the city's speech. Because hip-hop foregrounds the idiolects of specific singers, these sounds could come down to local accent features. In "Who Shot Ya" (1994), The Notorious B.I.G. rhymes *quarter, slaughter,* and *daughter,* which sounds much better with his New York accent than it would without.[63] Salt-N-Pepa, a hip-hop group from Brooklyn and Queens who were most active during the 1980s and 1990s, signaled their New York heritage in part by using a glottal stop for medial /t/. ("Just who do you think you are / Puttin' [puːin] your cheap two cents in / Don't you got nothin' to do than worry 'bout my friends?") Nicki Minaj, a 21st-century rapper who grew up in Queens, uses an accent feature from New York that is both a recent development and specific, in New York, to women's speech: in front of the vowels /i/ and

/u/, she replaces the sound /d/ with the sound /dz/, so that *didn't* becomes *dzidn't* (or, with a glottal stop, *dziːn't*).[64]

Rap also registered the sounds of city speech through slang and colloquial language: *he looks like a sucker; you're a sucker sucker dude for thinking you're slick; these are the breaks; I wasn't salty; I guess they frontin'; I'd be geeked when she'd come around; she was really the realest, before she got into showbiz; live it up, shucks; let it all hang out; we can rock it; I'm gonna mess around and funk you up; I'm cold as ice.*

> Don't push me 'cause I'm close to the edge
> I'm trying not to lose my head
> It's like a jungle sometimes
> It makes me wonder how I keep from goin' under.[65]

Though they drew as surely as the lyrics of the American Songbook on the low, graceful music of colloquial speech, rap lyrics were inclined to criticize the American way rather than long for a place in it. The New York in which the pioneers of hip-hop hustled for a living was gutted, defunded, relocated to make room for Robert Moses parkways, contested by gangs and a hostile police force, with musicians left to steal electricity from streetlights for their equipment while elite cultural institutions that staged Wagner and Mozart could raise the prices of the most expensive tickets again and again without losing any sales.[66] The music publishers that sold the hits of Tin Pan Alley were at once extensions of the songwriters' communities and mainstream institutions. The record companies that signed most hip-hop artists were proudly, defiantly separate from mainstream record companies.

For this reason, hip-hop music places emphasis on creating lineages for itself from prior black American musical traditions, as the music historian Joanna Demers has argued. In particular, *sampling*, or the reuse of recorded passages from older songs in new songs, has enabled hip-hop musicians to reference forebears in blues, funk, jazz, rhythm and blues, and soul, among other musical traditions.[67] (The "East Coast" style of hip-hop, meaning the music of New York City and its surrounding regions as against the "West Coast" style of Los Angeles and its surrounding regions, is notable for sampling in high volumes.) More than this, however, sampling, like the wordplay of the best MCs, traffics in clever contrast and layering. It belongs to hip-hop's preferred modes of irony.

LYRICS ARE FABRICS, BEAT IS THE LINING

Meticulous as hip-hop lyrics can be, we have no definitive academic format for transcribing them. The New York rapper Tupac Shakur used the couplet as his basic unit for a bar; other rappers use the more conventional four beats as the length of a bar; and others use still other measures.[68] Like a poem from the age of manuscript, when every copy had to be made by hand, the lyrics of a given rap, as the rap reappears in liner notes, books, magazines, and lyric websites, "might be written dozens of different ways," the literary scholar Adam Bradley writes: "different line breaks, different punctuation, even different words." Rap is a striking holdover from manuscript culture, as authors typically write their lyrics in physical notebooks called *rhyme books* or *books of rhyme*.[69] These objects appear in music videos, films about rap gods, and, of course, lyrics.[70] Nas describes "writin' in my book of rhymes, all the words past the margin." Mos Def claims to write "lyrics so visual / They rent my rhyme books at your nearest home video."[71]

The formal intricacies that a rapper must work with are formidable, and include working within the constraints of measure (usually 4/4 time), meter (a beat is the equivalent of a metrical foot), and rhyme scheme (a stanza is usually sixteen bars); working within the architecture of song structure, which sometimes follows the pop-music sequence of A-A-B-A; arranging the sequence of vowels and consonants so that the speaker can deliver them quickly and cleanly, and without drawing constant breaths; making thoughtful use of—and thoughtful rhyming patterns with—end rhymes, internal rhymes, perfect rhymes, slant rhymes, monosyllabic rhymes, poly-syllabic rhymes, rhymes created by a distinctive accent or pronun-ciation, and other rhyme forms that have distinctive effects; paring down the language and syntax when necessary (as with lyric writing for a pop song), so as to keep any one part of the song—the rhymes, the lyrics, the hook, the beat—from overwhelming the others; and keeping the words to the beat while allowing for "calculated rhythmic surprise." Rap music valorizes not universal lyrics that anyone might sing, but lyrics whose rhythm and personality mark one individual rapper and no other. In the words of the hip-hop historian William Jelani Cobb, *flow*, the aesthetic quality that rappers enshrine as a Holy Grail, is "an individual time signature, the rapper's own idiosyncratic approach to the use of time."[72]

WITTY UNPREDICTABLE TALENT AND NATURAL GAME

Wit and cleverness, twists and knowing allusions, inform hip-hop as they do other New York varieties of art. One part of wit, surprise, may appear in the rhythmic performance of a song. Wit can also present itself through wordplay. In rap lyrics, wordplay might parody nurs-ery rhymes, advertising messages, or political catchphrases in order to suggest new dimensions of those commonplaces. It might recon-textualize low language in order to suggest a mastery of low worlds ("Skip the bull 'cause we matadors").[73] It might extend the tradition of the ritual boast ("I'm more amazing than Grace is when I say shit

/ You should say 'Amen' after my name, kid").[74] It might simply play and tease ("Don't you know how you do the voodoo that you do so well").[75] Wordplay refreshes language; it also enables writers to frame their subjects in new ways. "It's one thing to say, 'I sell bricks, I sell bricks,'" the New York–born rapper Pusha T, using slang from the drug trade, once told an interviewer. "But when you saying 'Trunk like Aspen / Looking like a million muthafuckin' crushed aspirins,' dog, we getting back to the colors."[76]

But the language of rap is not merely startling as a form of wit. Often, it is startling in the sense that profane language (which abounds in rap lyrics) is startling, aiming to speak straightforwardly; to grab the attention; to offend; to use every part of language; to communicate anger, alienation, and revolt. Rap music references crime, drugs, poverty, sex, violence, and weapons more than most other musical forms do, and writers often draw on informal idioms from these domains (*dirty, dough, feel on, gear, heat, hot, paper, pop*, and so forth). Writers may also use calculatedly aggressive slang (*bomb* or *burn* for graffiti tagging; *rope* for a necklace; *spitting* for writing or rapping; *slay* for "impress"; and, as compliments, *bad, ill, sick*, and sometimes *motherfucker*). These idioms serve, in part, as deliberate provocations, what Umberto Eco calls (in another context) "semiotic guerilla warfare."[77] They reinforce the idea of power from below through the performance of speech from below. The New York rapper Jay-Z, who used to sell drugs, uses slang, wordplay, and a mixture of "high" and "low" subjects to describe his criminal past as an extension of American domestic and foreign policy agendas:

> Can't you tell that I came from the dope game
> Blame Reagan for making me into a monster
> Blame Oliver North and *Iran-Contra*
> *I ran contra*band that they sponsored
> Before this rhyming stuff we was in concert.[78]

More than a witty gesture, Jay-Z's wordplay underlines his claim that he was acting in accordance with (unofficial) government agendas before he left drug dealing for rapping, which was therefore a more subversive career. *The system that you made was working when I was selling drugs; now that I'm rhyming, you don't like me.*

BATTLE RHYMES

A common type of peer-review workshop for hip-hop artists is known as a *cipher*, a term that is several decades old but does not (yet) appear in the Oxford English Dictionary. In a typical cipher, people gather in a group and improvise rhymes about the people, places, and situations around them.[79] "Much like the open mic," writes the sociologist Jooyoung Lee, "ciphers allow rappers to showcase their talents and evaluate one another."[80] They build on one another's leads, learn from example, practice their skills in front of knowledgeable judges, and expose themselves to bracing, sometimes blistering, criticism; they also find talented peers who may become future collaborators. The common practice of featuring in one's song one or more guest rappers who redirect the lyrics into their own flow is part collaboration and part competition in the spirit of the cipher battle.

The hustling ethic of hip-hop registers in the industry's professional affiliations, at once competitive and collaborative: MCs collaborate with producers, DJs, and other MCs, but they also openly, even theatrically, compete against their peers, as producers and DJs do in their turn. It registers in the pride that hip-hop artists take in mastering their trades, be those trades high or low. Raekwon, a member of New York's Wu-Tang Clan, suggests that hip-hop's profit motive, the art form's origins in economic lack, and its political commitments are entangled: "You can never get it no fresher, comin' up out of the projects, twenty years old, and you start rhymin', and that's how you make your money—by speaking your lingo. Rap, to me, is slang poetry. It answers your questions: why young kids is doin' bad, why they turn to drugs to get away from their misery. This is the shit we talk about—and how to escape it." The dream of success is also a dream of influence: only if you're heard do you have a voice. MC Lyte, a rapper from Brooklyn who released her first track at sixteen, told an interviewer, "When I was young, I was like, how else can a young black girl of my age be heard all around the world? I gotta rap."[81]

GIVE MY REGARDS TO BROADWAY

As hip-hop's triumph as an art form and style brought it into the center of popular culture, it was inevitable that American popular theater explore its voices. Let's close by considering the recent—and intergalactically famous—Broadway musical *Hamilton* (2015) as a convenient interlink between the lyrical traditions of Tin Pan Alley and hip-hop.

New York City native Lin-Manuel Miranda, who created *Hamilton* (when his name comes up in conversation among educators, it's conventional to include this exchange: "Did you know he used to be a substitute teacher?" "Yes, I know he used to be a substitute teacher"), seems to have recognized early on the parallel cultures of wordcraft in hip-hop and the traditional musical. In high school, Miranda directed a student performance of *West Side Story*; in 2009, when a producer asked him to create a Spanish translation of Sondheim's lyrics for a new bilingual version of *West Side Story*, the 29-year-old replied, "Sir, I think I was born to translate it."[82] He included some droll humor in his translation, as, for instance, in the song "I Feel Pretty," in which the female lead, Maria, delights in her lovability now that she feels loved. The original lyrics read:

Such a pretty face,
Such a pretty dress,
Such a pretty smile,
Such a pretty me!

In his Spanish translation, as Colleen Rua notes, Miranda maintained the waltz meter by paring down the passage to three lines:

Que bonita faz,
Que bonita atrás,
Que bonita forma de ser!

In English, the new lyrics read: *what a pretty face, what a pretty behind, what pretty poise!* By amending Maria's lines to include the word *atrás*—a quite formal term, it doesn't translate to *ass*—Miranda injected a dose of irony, of sweet and unexpected worldliness, into this most earnest and canonical of Broadway songs.[83] Why shouldn't Maria admire her figure?

Miranda's work as a playwright and lyricist has extended this rethinking of tradition. In the opening song of Miranda's 2009 hip-hop musical *In the Heights,* the protagonist quotes both Cole Porter ("too darn hot") and Duke Ellington ("take the 'A' train"), showing himself to be a fan of both Broadway and jazz—and claiming both as part of his musical lineage.[84] The context of the first citation—he refers to "my man Cole Porter"—references a Midwestern WASP in such a way as to draw him into the verbal world of communities of color.[85] *Hamilton,* a hip-hop musical about the American Revolution, likewise makes extensive use of sampling, borrowing, and referencing in order to shift the perceived ownership of history to ordinary people of all colors in stores, skyscrapers, and subways. When John Laurens, Hercules Mulligan, and the Marquis de Lafayette first introduce themselves, they begin their song with, "Showtime!

Showtime!"—the traditional phrase of breakdancers performing in the New York City subway. John Laurens describes himself as "in the place to be," borrowing a line from the 1986 song "South Bronx" that happens to be one of the more sampled passages in all of hip-hop.[86] In the second act of the musical, Thomas Jefferson makes a boast about his invincibility in rap battles—"Makes me wonder why I even bring the thunder"—that borrows from the 1982 classic "The Message" (*Makes me wonder how I keep from going under*).[87] The result, though members of hip-hop culture do not treat it as a major standalone work in their domain, is a show that celebrates the major works in a storytelling tradition that has often emphasized what historians call *history from below.*

The show's sampling is meant, in part, to be funny, an ironic juxtaposition of the genteel image of the 18th century and the hip, streetwise aesthetics of hip-hop. In the theater, the opening of the song "Ten Duel Commandments," which references the Brooklyn rapper Biggie Smalls's "Ten Crack Commandments" (1997), is a reliable laugh line. But sampling, with its concern for lineage and tradition-building, has more serious purposes in the show as well. The culture and music of hip-hop has often addressed the powers and duties of government (especially its power over, and duties toward, society's most vulnerable members).[88] The premise of a hip-hop musical about the birth of American government is a forthright extension of this tradition. In 2006, Nas, a celebrated rapper from Queens, explained the title of his album, *Hip-Hop Is Dead*, by referencing the concept of hip-hop as a political voice: "When I say 'hip-hop is dead,' basically America is dead. There is no political voice . . . I think hip-hop could help rebuild America, once hip-hoppers own hip-hop. We are our own politicians, our own government, we have something to say."[89]

Hamilton also borrows from other Broadway musicals, entwining its hip-hop lineage with a lineage in musical theater.[90] The score's use of repetitive motifs mimics that of *Les Misérables* (1980) and other musicals; King George, a comic-relief character who also serves as a villain, takes his cue from King Herod in *Jesus Christ Superstar* (1970). Miranda frequently cites his Broadway idol, Stephen Sondheim (whom he has called, in hip-hop patter, "The God MC Sondheezy").[91] For example, the score plays elaborately with the word "sir" and its rhymes, as do songs in Sondheim's *Sweeney Todd* (1979). But Miranda also seems to critique one of Sondheim's most famous rules for musical theater: namely, the insistence on "perfect" rhymes, or rhymes with a perfect identity in the rhyming phonemes (*fine* and *mine*, not *fine* and *time*).[92] Nonstop perfect rhymes are difficult to achieve in rap, since rap lyrics often use more rhymes than the English language accommodates in perfect form. In *Hamilton*, the villain King George, and only the villain King George, uses Sondheimian perfect rhymes in his singing. One of the messages seems to be: *I can do this. If I don't, it's because I choose not to.*

Describing the seed from which his show grew, a biography of Hamilton that he picked up in an airport, Miranda said that he found in the story unexpected parallels to his own experience: "I didn't know Hamilton was an immigrant, and I didn't know half of the traumas of his early life. And when he gets to New York, I was like, 'I know this guy.' I've met so many versions of this guy, and it's the guy who comes to this country and is like, 'I am going to work six jobs if you're only working one. I'm gonna make a life for myself here.' That's a familiar storyline to me, beginning with my father and so many people I grew up with in my neighborhood."[93] In his humble origins, his ambition, his combination of pragmatism and burning idealism, his drive toward literary and polemical expression, the wordsmith from the Caribbean "*embodies* hip-hop," Miranda said in 2009: "I think he embodies the word's ability to make a difference."[94]

Over the years, the song machine of New York City has changed its art dramatically, but its ethos very little. The shift from waltz to syncopated rhythms to spinning records with "breaks"; from the

American Songbook to the American underground; from department stores selling sheet music to hustlers moving their art in subways and on streaming services: throughout decades of change, the
city's popular art retained the pragmatic ethos of a commercial center, the ironic perspective of a community whose members are at
once insiders and outsiders, and the colloquialism of a nation that
esteemed new words and new phrases as an extension of its mythos
as a new world. The love of craft, the Apollonian discipline which can
help artists to work quickly and well, has been consistent, and so has
been a love of New York City itself: of its opportunities, its capacity for hope, and its responsiveness to change. In the next chapter,
we will see how New Yorkers have used language to create change
in their own lives and build affirming communities despite an education system that sometimes said their own speech was not correct
and a world that sometimes set limits, in part by prescribing language
use, on the kinds of people they could be.

Chapter 6

Code Switching

One day in *El Barrio* (New York City's East Harlem) in 1979 I asked a nine year old of Puerto Rican background what language she spoke with her brothers and sisters. "*Hablamos los dos.* We speak both," she answered casually, as if it was the most natural thing in the world to speak two languages and to alternate between them.

—Ana Celia Zentella (1997)[1]

The term *mother tongue* used to be derogatory. Your mother tongue is the language your mother speaks, and she speaks it because she has no proper education. You, however, went to school and learned Latin. Such was the case in 1500; today, since English has overtaken Latin as an international language, the sign of a good education is proficiency in Standard English. Even for native English speakers, this often entails learning to depart from a native accent or *variant* (the preferred term these days for *dialect*), both forms of speech that place the speaker in a region, an ethnicity, a class. Standard English, by contrast, is meant to signify (though it doesn't) a lack of loaded differences, a nowhere that extends its rule everywhere.

The accent that I use to teach at a public university is Standard American English. It's not required for the job, but it matches the accent of most of my colleagues; perhaps for them, as for me, losing differences in speech was an incidental side effect of schooling, as well as—just slightly—an aspirational attainment. Many of my students are from New York City, and I know, therefore, that they came through a school system that serves an incredibly diverse student population: in 2002, the children in New York City schools hailed from "more than 200 countries, speaking more than 120 languages."[2] But whatever other linguistic communities they can move in, in class and in their essays they use excellent Standard American. If I were being thoughtless, I might describe this by saying, in a stock phrase that is well-meaning but condescending, that my students are *competent speakers*. This chapter examines the public attitudes that have given such condescension a dark, warm place to feed and grow, as well as the actual linguistic phenomena that take place when speakers of multiple languages or variants move between worlds: to school or back home, with friends or with strangers, out in the public sphere or out of the closet in private circles.

As we will see, mistaken beliefs about how language works have often led educators and public officials to treat variants that differ from "school English"—for example, Puerto Rican English (PRE) and African American Vernacular English (AAVE)—as signs of "verbal deprivation." Until recently, even linguists did not bother studying some of the linguistic phenomena that arise where worlds collide, such as *contact languages* (new languages that arise when speakers of different languages have to communicate with one another, such as creoles and pidgins) and *multiple variant acquisition* (when a speaker learns more than one variant, often learning each under different social circumstances), because they believed these phenomena to be too primitive to follow universal rules of language. As it turns out, these forms of expression are not only as rich and sophisticated as other modes of language production, but also provide unique insights into cultural exchange in the mobile city.

THE BEST MINES OF THE NATION

Public education has deep roots in New York City, and its history reveals a lot about attitudes and practices around language. Under British rule, local children attended either private schools or free "charity schools" run by various churches. In 1787, a local anti-slavery society (of which Alexander Hamilton was a member) opened a free school in Lower Manhattan for children of color.[3] In 1801, a Quaker women's group opened a free school for girls and boys who couldn't enter charity schools because their parents didn't belong to a congregation. These schools became the seeds of the city's modern public-school system; over the years, the purview of public-school administrators expanded to preschools (or "infant schools"), then other "African schools," then evening schools for apprentices who worked during business hours.[4]

As New York became an immigrant city, the civic responsibilities of the public-school system turned toward helping to manage the offspring of the city's vast population of migrants and immigrants. By 1914, more than 75 percent of the city's children were the offspring of immigrants from Eastern and Southern Europe. Jewish children, specifically, comprised 46 percent of Manhattan's grade school students.[5] In the view of the city's officials, schools had an obligation to help drain off the dangers of these troublesome "races."[6] The city's board of education regarded Jewish students, in particular, as dangerous outsiders and potential smugglers of socialist ideology from Eastern Europe. The schools enforced policies aimed at cultural conformity, offering only non-kosher food and prohibiting students from wearing religious head coverings. Jewish families complained that the mostly Irish Catholic teachers treated Jewish students as instinctive criminals, a complaint that seems to have had merit given that the school board had officially "classified Jewish children as delinquent, backward, and 'unteachable.'"[7] During this period, the city's board of education laid heavy emphasis on Americanizing foreign students.

At every grade, the students were tasked with language work; but memorization and oral recitation, not reading and writing, were the primary skills assessed in their classes.[8] Lesson plans emphasized instruction in speech, via "consonant drills, vowel drills, foreign accent drills," the recitation of memorized texts, and exercises in reading aloud.[9] In the first year, students learned short poems and didactic plays, such as "Abraham Lincoln and the Little Bird," "The First Thanksgiving Day," and "Manner of Refusing or Accepting Anything Offered." They also memorized quotations that testified to American pride and productivity: "Let our object be our country, our whole country, and nothing but our country.—Daniel Webster"; "Commerce and industry are the best mines of the nation.—George Washington." By the sixth year, they were memorizing prose selections: the American's Creed; the Gettysburg Address; Lincoln's Second Inaugural; an "Old Athenian Oath" that promised obedience to civic duty. By the eighth year, they had moved up to Shakespeare's *Julius Caesar*, which was presented as part of this republican tradition. And every year, the students were re-assessed on their recitation of the Pledge of Allegiance.[10]

Another pamphlet that teachers received during this same period focuses entirely on methods of training students in proper American English. The pamphlet conflates racial traits and accent: an accent isn't the stresses and phonology of one language overlaid on another, but rather a result of bad personal habits coming down to biological race. An early section, titled "Characteristic Racial Errors," states, "Experience has shown that, because of the great intermingling of peoples in this country and the fact that the majority of them do not speak their native tongues correctly, we cannot definitely attribute peculiarities of accent to any one race, nor draw a definite line of demarcation." Nonetheless, the pamphlet goes on to describe the most distinctive faults of students belonging to specific "races"—for instance:

- "In general the Greek's articulation of English sounds is similar to that of the Latin Races, except that it is given with great rapidity of coordination; he speaks faster than they, too fast in fact to do justice to our Anglo-Saxon words";
- "Italians, Spaniards and Cubans have a characteristic languorous drawl. We notice, in their speech, an elision of syllables and consequent slurring, following the custom of the mother language. The final consonants, especially, are apt to be slurred or entirely omitted";
- "Russians find it extremely difficult to sound our h because of their peculiarly guttural explosion of breath."

And, for Russian Jews, the longest and most disdainful passage:

- "The greatest burden of our work in correcting foreign accent is among the people of Russian Jewish origin. Their speech in general is guttural, nasal and with a rising inflection at the end of phrases, sentences and emphatic words. . . . In speaking English the Jewish people find much difficulty with the vowels, giving them the wrong values, and, at the same time, showing a tendency to shorten them as: gaw *for* go; epple *for* apple; mit *for* meat. . . . There is a tendency to speak in disconnected phrases rather than in sentences, and to use the historical present in narrating descriptions. The latter is exemplified in the following sentence: "My vodder he goes vere lawyers iss und dey arrists de feller vat rubs (robs) him.""[11]

These are pretty bad ideas about language learning to present to schoolteachers. Aside from the egregious ethnic stereotyping, they're

factually wrong: biological race doesn't exist; a native speaker by definition speaks his language "correctly"; some of the accent features
described here are incorrect, and others, like disfavoring word-final
consonant clusters, are simply phonological rules rather than character flaws.[12] But the pamphlet testifies to the long history of the battle
between the front and back of the classroom, as well as the use of language as a weapon in that battle: here, between students who speak
nonstandard variants and teachers who speak "our Anglo-Saxon."

THE GREAT MIGRATION

In the early 20th century, African Americans—now entering the city
in unprecedented numbers as they fled poverty and oppression in
the South—joined Jews as a special problem class in the view of the
board of education. Their children, too, struggled under education
policies based on low resources and low expectations—problems
compounded, in the case of African Americans, by the challenges of
segregated schooling. (School segregation was illegal in New York
State as of 1900, but it continued in practice largely because children were assigned to schools based on where they lived.)[13] Starting
around 1945, the numbers of Puerto Ricans who migrated to the
U.S. mainland grew dramatically, with most of them moving to
New York City.[14] The new migrants tended to settle uptown, joining
historically black neighborhoods and creating what would become
known as "Spanish Harlem." As an interesting aside, the 1957 musical
West Side Story was originally going to be called *East Side Story*; it was
to be set in the Lower East Side and depict tensions among Jews and
Italian Catholics during the period that spans Easter and Passover.
Partly because of the visibility of Puerto Rican migrants at the time
the musical was being written, the creators decided to focus instead
on Puerto Ricans living on the city's West Side.[15]

The demographics of the city's public schools echoed these settlement patterns. In 1955, according to one study, 42 primary schools in New York City had student bodies that were at least 90 percent African American and Puerto Rican.[16] In 2010, at the average public school in the New York Metropolitan Area, 70 percent of the student body was Latino or African American.[17] Even today, the public schools in the New York metropolitan area have greater segregation than in any other region in the United States.[18] This is relevant to language learning because, as sociologists now emphasize, a student's peers, not his teachers, are the ones who really socialize him.

Language variants are like waterways: they flow, sometimes into each other. Perhaps the best metaphor comes from the geological concept of stream capture: two streams eat away at the rock that separates them until the wall is breached, and then they flow together in one direction or the other. Linguistically, we can identify this process of proximity and confluence in the relationship between Puerto Rican English and African American Vernacular English. Historically, Puerto Ricans and African Americans have shared neighborhoods in the city.[19] These two variants have flowed near and with each other in part due to spatial proximity, and in part due to shared cultural experiences. This shared New York history has affected the variant of Puerto Rican English even in parts of the country where Puerto Ricans are not in direct contact with African Americans.

As a notable New York City variant, Puerto Rican English dates to the years of growing migration to the city from Puerto Rico—an exodus known as the *Gran Migración*—that followed the Second World War. Though these migrants were mostly native speakers of Spanish, their children often spoke English as a native language.[20]

Predictably, Puerto Rican English takes some of its features from Spanish. One such feature is the ability to ask questions without inverting the word order in the sentence, which is a legal move in Spanish ("How he did that?").[21] Another feature concerns *prosodic rhythm,* or the way speakers manage stresses in speech. We produce speech in a flow of stressed and unstressed syllables. To hear them, try saying a sentence sarcastically; we indicate sarcasm by exaggerating stresses. Standard American English is *stress-timed*: speakers make unstressed syllables a little shorter than stressed syllables, and they tend to turn unstressed vowels into schwas. By contrast, Puerto Rican English, like Spanish, is *syllable-timed*: speakers give all syllables roughly the same length, and they voice and hear unstressed vowels. Observers say that stress-timed languages sound like Morse code, whereas syllable-timed languages sound like a machine gun.[22]

But other features of Puerto Rican English come from African American Vernacular English.[23] In 1974, the linguist Walt Wolfram investigated the presence of features from AAVE in second-generation Puerto Ricans in East Harlem. He identifies several variants in Puerto Rican English that come from "the assimilation of Black English features." For example, speakers of Puerto Rican English sometimes replace /θ/ with [f]; /maʊθ/, for *mouth,* can become /maʊf/. They replace some vowel glides, like /ay/ in *high* and *time,* with monophthongs, so that *time* sounds more like /tam/ than like /tɔɪm/ (the pronunciation in New York City English). They may use a form of negative called *negative inversion,* as in the sentence "Didn't nobody do it." They may use a verb form called "habitual *be,*" which means they distinguish actions that are habitual from actions that happen just once. (In Steven Pinker's example: "*He be working* means that he generally works, perhaps that he has a regular job; *He working* means only that he is working at the moment that the sentence is uttered.")[24]

Factors such as gender and age can affect how much a speaker of Puerto Rican English uses features of AAVE, as the linguistic ethnographer Ana Celia Zentella found while doing research in East Harlem in the 1980s.[25] Boys were more apt than girls to use AAVE features, because they spent more time in the wider city, for instance playing with African American friends in other neighborhoods, while girls, often tasked with keeping house, minding children, and running chores in the neighborhood, stayed closer to home, where speakers usually conversed in Spanish. As girls grew older, however, they used more AAVE features, a signal to hearers that they were becoming grown women of the world, "more influenced by community outsiders and more oriented to adult-style speech than their younger friends."[26]

Not that close contact is necessary for this kind of influence. Some AAVE speech characteristics, Wolfram found, were present in all speakers of PRE, "regardless of how extensive their contacts with blacks may be; other characteristics show up only in the speech of those Puerto Ricans who have extensive black contacts."[27] A 2006 study of Puerto Rican children and teenagers in North Philadelphia showed that the young people used features of AAVE even if they had rarely mingled with AAVE speakers.[28]

That Puerto Ricans make use of AAVE even when they do not mingle directly with African Americans shows the diversity of means by which one group may feel connections with another and express those connections through language. (A complicating factor, of course, is that membership in these groups overlaps considerably. Dominicans tend to identify as black, while most Cuban immigrants to the United States have been white; both groups identify as Hispanic, a term that in its current usage is more or less a creation of the U.S. census.)[29] In the United States, socioeconomic status is a profound component of identity, and on this count Puerto Ricans and African Americans in New York have had much in common; for several decades starting in the 1960s, when Puerto Ricans began to migrate in large numbers to New York City, they had the city's highest unemployment and poverty rates, which contributed to their living in poor areas like East Harlem. The experience of prejudice is another factor; as a scholar of New York's hip-hop culture writes, "low socioeconomic status initially ghettoizes Puerto Ricans together with

African Americans, and antiblack prejudice cements their relationship and blocks their mobility."[30]

One consequence of the structural prejudices long experienced by African Americans is that AAVE is a variant "particularly lacking in prestige."[31] In the New York public schools that Labov studied, teachers thought that students speaking AAVE were simply making errors. This led to considerable strife between teachers and students.[32] Toni Morrison once commented of the education system: "It's terrible to think that a child with five different present tenses comes to school to be faced with books that are less than his own language."[33] Though "less" is an inaccurate description—strictly, no language is *less* than another—the tense system of AAVE shows greater *complexity* than Standard American English. AAVE does have five present tenses, as the father-son scholars John and Russell Rickford note:

1. He runnin. (He is running.)
2. He *be* runnin. (He is usually running, or He will/would be running.)
3. He *be steady* runnin. (He is usually running in an intensive, sustained manner, or He will/would be running in an intensive, sustained manner.)
4. He *been* runnin. (He has been running—at some earlier point, but probably not now.)
(5) He *BEEN* runnin. (He has been running for a long time, and still is.)[34]

NUEVA YORK

These variants, as speakers use them in New York City, are as distinctively New York as the "New York City English" variant of *foəth floə, on line* (rather than *in line*), and *fuck off*. In recent decades, linguists have testified to the diversity of AAVE in different regions, and to the distinctiveness of the version of AAVE spoken in New York City.[35] For example, the New York version of AAVE uses a glottal stop for a medial /t/: *gettin'* becomes [gɛːɛn].[36] New York speakers in general, regardless of their ethnicity, use *metathesis*, or the switching around of sounds in certain words, for the word *ask*, which becomes *aks*; however, this has become a stereotype of AAVE specifically, not least because it's perceived as "incorrect." (Plenty of languages include this feature, including Standard American English: *iron* becomes *iorn*.)

Researchers say that Latino students in New York City high schools likewise see their own speech as distinctive: "not only do New York Latinos use a series of characteristic variants, but their speech is highly recognizable to New Yorkers."[37] These findings reinforce what linguists have long known: that variance goes all the way up to sentence structure and vocabulary, and all the way down to the pronunciation of individual sounds. For example, among other features, New York Latinos characteristically use *spirantization*, which is to say that they change plosives to fricatives (the /b/ sound in *candy bar* becomes /v/, so the word sounds like *candy var*); *lenition*, or the weakening of consonants, when they pronounce the sounds /d/ and /b/ (so the word *boyfriend* sounds like *boyfrien'*); and pronounce /l/, when it appears at the start of a word, as *non-velarized* (light) and *apical* (with the tip of the tongue).[38] Moreover, high school students may vary their use of these features depending on their social clique: skater, floater, hip-hop, geek.[39]

Even in the 1970s, when scholars' knowledge of AAVE was far more limited, Labov noticed that, among young people, adherence to AAVE was a measure of peer relationships—what he called "a fine-grained index of membership in the street culture." Speakers who used few features of AAVE were considered "lame," he reported, but their increased use of Standard American English offered them greater success in mainstream American culture.[40] For the young people in Labov's study—children and teenagers in Harlem—the peer culture that governed language organized itself in opposition to the school system, which, he said elsewhere, young people saw as "the particular possession and expression of the dominant white society."[41] The cultural pressure on young people was especially profound, because using the language of schooling might alienate their peers while failing to guarantee respect or success in mainstream American society.[42]

It is because New York City applies its own local pressures to language variants that, in 1973, the Center for Applied Linguistics in New York City recommended that bilingual teachers "understand the language and culture of both home and school." A teacher who knew Spanish might enter a school in East Harlem only to realize that the students had a "home language and culture" quite different from what the teacher spoke and understood. In a worst-case scenario, the teacher would come down hard on this different culture and the students would rebel.[43] Language splits in, and because of, the classroom.

SWITCHING CODES

The groups we join often define themselves in competition with other groups. (The formal term for this is *group contrast effects*. Contrast effects are remarkably arbitrary: for example, "Deaf Nicaraguans pride themselves on their punctuality, whereas hearing Nicaraguans . . . have a casual attitude toward time. It is exactly the opposite in the United States, where the hearing are generally punctual and the deaf have a more relaxed attitude toward time.") Children define themselves as *children, not adults*; boys define themselves as *boys, not girls*, and vice versa. (Many a liberal parent has been dismayed by the aggressive gender typing their children display: "Girls don't play with trucks," "Mommies do the cooking.")[44] But the fact of the matter is that people belong to more than one identity and often don't fit in the boxes they themselves create.

How do people with fluency in a nonstandard language variant navigate in and out of mainstream institutions? As we will see with the Department Store Study in the next chapter, speakers may alter their language performance according to various situations. The term that linguists use for this behavior is *code switching*. Young people may choose to use Standard American English in school and switch to PRE while hanging out with friends. They may use more features from PRE with some friends and fewer features with others. The classroom, the sports field, on the phone with the bank— each of these situations may require different calibrations of PRE. Indeed, Ana Celia Zentella argues that we should think of Puerto Rican English as a "bilingual/multidialectical repertoire": that is, a range of variants in English and Spanish, such as *Standard Puerto Rican Spanish, Popular Puerto Rican Spanish, Puerto Rican English, African American Vernacular English,* and *Standard NYC English,* that a speaker may switch between or among depending on context and conversation partners.[45]

There are three important things to know about code switching. First, it's deliberate. Zentella explained the reasons that Puerto Rican students might learn to feel self-conscious about their own variant and so acquire additional ones: "when the children of el bloque enter the schools, their oral bilingual skills are not seen as assets. They feel under attack because they speak Puerto Rican Spanish, because they speak Black English Vernacular (BEV), and because they mix these together."[46]

Second, code switching is incredibly nuanced; it goes all the way from the language chosen, through vocabulary and syntax, down to phonology and even syllabic rhythm. In the 1970s, a researcher who studied the use of syllabic rhythm among Puerto Rican teenagers found variations according to social context in their use of syllable-timed or stress-timed speech. He suggests that switching between syllable-timed speech and stress-timed speech itself constitutes code switching.[47]

Finally, code switching obeys universal laws of language. This came as a surprise to linguists, who for many years did not study code switching because they regarded it as a primitive, uneducated form of language. Only a few decades ago did they start to pay attention to it, and they found that, although code switching is deliberate, it obeys grammatical laws that are ingrained in the human brain, and therefore are not deliberate. For example, a famous 1980 article described two primary constraints that enable code switching in an utterance: first, a switch can only take place at a part of the sentence that does not break the laws of syntax for either language, which means that the syntactical structures of both languages should generally align with each other at the point of the switch. The phrase *a car *nuevo*, "a new car," would not work because saying "a car new" would break the rules of English and saying "*un nuevo carro*" would break the rules of Spanish. However, "*Siempre está* promising *cosas*," "He's always promising things," works because both languages have the same syntactical structure around the point of the switch. Second, a switch cannot happen, within a word, at a suffix or other morpheme that could not exist as a word on its own, such as -*ed*, -*ing*, and -*ified*: for example, *speak*emos*, "we speak," or *speak*amos*, "we will spoke."[48]

"NEW YORK CITY IS WRAPPED UP IN BEING LABEIJA"

As this book has mentioned previously, men and women often use different accents in New York City. The reason is likely that men and women are socialized differently and find themselves obliged to present themselves differently. In the 1970s, the linguist Robin Lakoff brought attention to the subtle ways in which women's speech differs from men's speech. One notable point was women's greater willingness to use color words (*cerise, mauve, periwinkle, puce*), apparently because men don't want to admit to knowing frivolous details that don't belong to the "real world" of men's work. Lakoff found that women learn to code-switch between women's speech styles and men's speech styles in order to moderate the downsides of each style: to use masculine speech is to be "unfeminine"; to "talk like a lady" is to be weak.[49]

But gender, as a category of identity, doesn't operate in a vacuum; it informs our sense of ourselves and our experience of the world in a complex interplay with other categories like ethnicity and sexuality.[50] The concept of "gay speech" is a myth, as speech pathologist Evan Bartlett Page told *Out* magazine in 2006, but gay men may, as a form of in-group coding, adopt vocal patterns that we might see as code-switching into a feminine register: "elevated pitch, breathiness in quality, variable pitch contours, and the adoption of 'feminine characteristics' such as 'tag questioning,' in which statements are ended with a question ('The party's at ten, isn't it?')." Lesbians, on the other hand, may code-switch into a masculine register more often than straight women as a way of asserting their own sense of gender identity, the communication scholar Jimmie Manning told the magazine: "Lesbian women will often tell me that they may intentionally change their speaking patterns as a form of resistance. They don't want to sound girly or femme. They want to embrace that they're defying patriarchy."[51] And the ways in which gender and sexuality—as categories, as communities—act upon us can differ in keeping with factors like ethnicity and national culture: our culture sexualizes women of color more than white women, as in the case of Sofía Vergara; or again, French women supposedly consider themselves, among Europeans, to be especially feminine. Even one's city makes a difference, according to some. A New York choreographer who trained models in movement and posing once told a filmmaker that local girls were a challenge: "New York City women are a little bit harder than most women. Basically, I'm trying to bring their femininity back and bring some grace and poise."[52]

In short, when people code-switch, even for the purpose of claiming membership in one of their own groups, they often borrow from the repertoires of other groups: men, women, gay people, straight people, people of color, white people, adults, teenagers, and more. If we want to understand what people say, we have to understand these kinds of borrowings—and in a large cosmopolitan city like New York, there is so much to borrow from.

How does identity cross identity groups? In 1990, Jennie Livingston's documentary film *Paris Is Burning* introduced outsiders to the world of drag balls in New York City, where drag costume soirées first caught on in 1920s Harlem among queer communities of color.[53] Drag balls are competitions: participants compete in contests of dress, dance, and so forth in teams (and kinship groups) called *houses*, with *mothers* leading houses and *children* competing in them. (Pepper LaBeija, the mother of the House of LaBeija, boasted to the filmmaker, "The House of LaBeija is the legendary house above all of them. I have the most members. I'm the most popular. New York City is wrapped up in being LaBeija.") The film records a number of slang terms that occupy the leading edge of popular culture today, such as *voguing*, a dance form, named after the fashion magazine, which entails shifting between flowing movements and abstract poses, as though for a fashion spread; *shade*, or subtle insult; *reading*, or criticism; and *unbothered* (in the film, *not bothered*), or maintaining equanimity.[54] Such language indicates how far a subculture may run ahead of fashion.[55]

More important for our purposes is the prevalence of code switching in drag culture, which the linguist Rusty Barrett illuminates in a series of ethnographic studies of Latinx and African American drag queens. Barrett suggests that the speech of these performers makes use of so much code switching between registers—which include gay men's speech, African American Vernacular English, and (white) women's language—that it reads almost as "polyphonous" speech, or speech that brings together many different codes, even codes that seem to contradict each other, in a whole that is greater than the sum of its parts.[56] Together, these registers help to create a verbal identity for queer African American and Latinx men.[57] But if drag culture creates an in-group register of speech in part by referencing white women's speech, white women in turn have adopted words and cultural practices that first arose in Black or Latinx queer subcultures—as, for example, when Madonna's music video "Vogue" (1990) made the term *voguing* famous everywhere that MTV played.[58]

When I was growing up in the MTV Generation, I thought Madonna's "Vogue" video was about rich people playing with avant-garde fashion. But *Paris Is Burning* portrays people who, desperately poor but required to compete in labels in order to win drag competitions, had to beg, borrow, or steal their label clothes. In the age of mass media, the voices that carry farthest are often speaking an idiom they were the last to hear. Code switching, as a linguistic practice, is a legitimate and commonplace communicative strategy; but cultural borrowing can easily shade into appropriation, especially when the groups involved have such vast differences in power and economic resources.

In Livingston's documentary, Dorian Corey, the mother of a decades-old house in New York City, takes the role of explaining key terms, like *ball*. Corey defines these terms while speaking in a style that suggests not only a woman, but a woman *from New York City*: for example, *ball* has two syllables (*bɔall*), reflecting the tendency of New York women to stretch vowels into diphthongs. For people who transgress gender norms, Corey explains, honing one's skills at code switching, learning in minute detail how sounds suggest identity, can be not just a form of expression, but a matter of survival: "They give the society that they live in what they want to see, and they won't be questioned. Rather than having to go through prejudices about your life and your lifestyle, you can walk around comfortably, blending in with everybody else. You've erased all the mistakes, all the flaws, all the giveaways, to make your illusion perfect."[59]

TEACHER, TEACHER

We may find a valuable perspective on code switching in the concept of *interactional expertise*.[60] Interactional expertise is, essentially, being able to speak in the code of a group without being part of the group; it is the linguistic equivalent of *passing*. For example, journalists and historians who cover science may have interactional expertise in certain fields of science; they know the terminology, the important issues, the important figures, although they are not scientists themselves. Scholars have studied this phenomenon by way of experiments patterned after Turing Tests: people in one room sit at computer terminals, pretending to be someone else (men as women, people of color as white people); members of those groups (the ones who have "target expertise") at computers in another room try to guess whether they are speaking to a group member. What the researchers have found is that members of minority groups are very good at using the codes of majority groups, whereas members of majority groups are very, very bad at using the codes of minority groups. Marginalized groups have to be attuned to those in power in order to survive.

Scholars have also learned new details about the subtle ways in which in-group members communicate. One of my colleagues, a philosophy professor, participated in an interactional expertise game; his goal was to pass as a woman. He was the only member of his group to successfully pass. At the time, some women were in the news for experiencing toxic shock syndrome due to a specific brand of tampons, Rely. In the experiment, my colleague used the word *reliable* with a touch of irony. It may seem like a simple thing, but we communicate in very subtle ways. (I have to admit that I am really happy at how happy he was to pass as a woman.)[61]

One might even argue that schooling is an intensive process of acquiring interactional expertise: of acquiring not just knowledge, but also codes of belonging, whether the group one learns to emulate consists of rumpled physicists, slim-suited Ivy Leaguers, or even—as the New York City Board of Education once had it—Americans.[62] The efforts of the teacher at the front of the classroom to hand down authoritative principles are certainly less useful for this purpose than what students learn at the back of the classroom through teasing, role-play, clique alliances, and shared language games. The sociologist Judith Harris became famous for her argument that young people learn mostly from other young people, which is why, for example, the sons and daughters of immigrants who speak languages other than English may quickly attain not only the English proficiency of their peers but also their accent, while their parents may continue to speak with a different accent for the rest of their lives. The board of education was wrong to suppose that Americanization could be imposed from on high in the form of proper language; rather, students learned to be American by finding, down at the ground level of daily life, American communities they could call their own. Formal education is important in the classroom, but so is a healthy amount of misrule; adolescents learn to define themselves as a peer group in part by rebelling against the language of the teacher.[63]

When I discussed this with a friend who used to work as a high school teacher in a New Jersey suburb, he recalled that students often distanced themselves from teachers via language. Sometimes this verbal frontier entailed subtly undermining the language of the school as an institution. My friend's school required the students to call the teachers *Mister* or *Miss*, with no surname; in their delivery of *Mister*, he said, the students made sure their friends could *hear* their distance from what the teacher wanted: "They found a way to deliver the honorific and at the same time—I know this sounds paranoid—to undermine it. I read the undermining of the honorific as saying, 'I'm not going to learn your name.'" Or the frontier manifested as teenage slang, which the students treated in part as language designed to put distance between themselves and the teacher: "Sometimes they took joy in teaching me one of their words—but teaching it in such a way that subtle shades of meaning were being occluded or effaced."

Judith Harris's study of youthful learning includes an anecdote about a student who knew the value of speaking the right language for your group:

> A girl at my school was walking down the hall and remembered she forgot something.
>
> "Oh shoot!" she exclaimed.
>
> As she looked around and saw her friends she said, "I mean oh shit."[64]

MOTHER TONGUE

Code switching can be a vibrant source of linguistic creativity, and switching between codes requires a great deal of savvy in both. But for many children in New York City who speak languages other than English at home, the battle between prescriptivist approaches to language (which see language as grammatical rules to be learned) and descriptivist approaches to language (which see language as a natural phenomenon to be studied) is a source of unease at home as well as at school, as families hope that superior English will make for a better chance of success in their new country. The ability to code-switch has limited value to impress so long as one code holds domination. [65] One of my students wrote in a recent essay, "Where I'm from, we didn't call it prescriptivism. We called it success."[66] He continued:

My immediate family, whether they choose to accept the claim or not, have been staunch believers in the power of language for as long as they have been exposed to what they would laud as "English Proper." In fact, this phenomenon of self-deprecating reverence extends far beyond my family—it is a ubiquitous pattern among many Hispanic American circles who have been led and bred to believe that their Spanish *and* their English is socially inferior to the English of whiter America. Enter me, the third generation great grandson of monolingual migrants who dreamt in abstract shades of red, white, and blue until they reached the promising streets of NYC. I would never say my English is *perfect* but my manner of speech, the conscious linguistic choices I make have little to no resemblance to the variant spoken by my collective kin. It was important to my parents that I learn this lucrative language, so important that my native Spanish was all but sacrificed to hours of skimming dictionaries and repeatedly scribbling grammatically sound sentences. . . .

To be proficient in English proper, to "talk white" as I have often heard it said, is a sign of respect to you, your family, and the prospect of your success. Geoffrey Nunberg's *The Decline of Grammar* puts it in a more succinct perspective claiming, "Linguistic manners are like any others. People have always found it worthwhile to reflect on how best to behave, for the sake of at least individual enlightenment and improvement." So, to the elders of a Nuyorican household, we show respect through Spanish greetings and axioms, but to the rest of the world, we show our "manners" through cultural suppression and a snobbish adherence to rules created arbitrarily in history's passing. These linguistic manners have haunted me and many Nuyoricans who have been led to believe by both prescriptivist America and our hypnotized guardians that when it comes to speech, there is no room for change, flavor, or diversity, the three most crucial elements in Spanish New York. . . .

New York has been my home and the home of my family for the past few generations, and nothing will take from the fact that it has provided as much inspiration as the Puerto Rican mainland. I don't hate the English language; I don't hate grammar and usage rules I don't fully agree with; most importantly, I don't blame my parents for over highlighting my American "rights" to the ideal form of English. It is likely that I owe a large part of my success in my field to the culture of consistency and homogeneity with which I grew up. But, when I roam the streets of New York and hear the voices that do not sound like me coming from faces that look just like me, I am reminded that even in celebration of diversity and tolerance toward difference, society is still susceptible to the powers of purism. And so I ask, prescriptivist America: ¿Es mi inglés lo suficientemente bueno?

Chapter 7

A Voice Full of Money

FASHION PHOTOGRAPHER
You are in the Museum of Modern Art, Marion—deep, Marion, profound, Marion. You have come across this statue, and it says something to you because you are intellectual, always thinking. What are you thinking?
MODEL (New York City accent)
I'm thinkin' this is takin' a lɔng tɔime, and I'll nevə be able to pick up Hærold's lɔndry. Boy, when Hærold doesn't get his lɔndry, disæstə.
—Funny Face (1957)

In 1962, a linguist conducted a curious study in a set of New York City department stores. The results were so striking that researchers have been repeating the study regularly ever since, at intervals of about once a decade. The study, which involved a bemused shopper and helpful employees, found a clever way to use tiny, unassuming instances of speech to gain new insights into a subject that Americans don't like to face directly: namely, social class. Americans take pride in a national myth of equality, which has produced a distinctive form of prestige in which wealthy people take on working-class solidarity: the folksy oil baron, the television pundit who covers himself in aw-shucks normalcy, the politician whose appeal lies in the feeling that you could have a beer with him. Because the American Dream promises that one's rise is limited only by one's merit, honoring the spirit of that dream may seem a matter of pretending that only hard work stands between us and the company of down-home millionaires and stars who are, as the magazines promise, just like us. The writer John Steinbeck supposedly remarked that "Socialism never took root in America because the poor see themselves not as an exploited proletariat, but as temporarily embarrassed millionaires." Americans like to pretend they can't see class difference in practice and don't respect it in theory.

The *department store study*, as it came to be called, showed that Americans are more sensitive to class differences than they like to admit. It also showed that Americans register class as a product not just of category (the box you mark on the census), but also of context: a simple move from one space to another can change how speakers perform the little distinctions that mark this or that class. Indeed, the study suggested a picture of class as a repertoire of belonging, a measure of how we fit, or fail to fit, into social environments. In New York City, where clubs and shops a few streets from each other can serve clientele eight figures of income apart, the social environment can map onto the built environment in particularly subtle gradients. Real estate drives a lot of talk in this city. The department store study shows that real estate also changes the *way* we talk.

RETAIL PALACES

Europeans have castles; Americans, seeking their own pleasure pavilions, invented department stores. Department stores are our *retail palaces*: splendid ritual spaces through which we move as courtiers in the Court of Abundance. In New York City, department stores first appeared in the mid-19th century, a new take on dry-goods retailing that offered different kinds of goods in a single space: linens, carpeting, household furnishings, women's apparel.[1] By the end of the century, Broadway had a thriving department-store district, which New Yorkers called *The Ladies' Mile*. As custom flourished, department stores grew, adding features to encourage customers to linger: benches, galleries, dining spaces, fancy displays. At Saks Fifth Avenue, which first welcomed in the women of New York in 1924, shoppers could attend fashion shows, have their hair styled, or even hazard golf lessons inside.[2]

Retailers understood the value of spectacle for encouraging *window shopping*, a new term as of 1875, and thereby actual shopping. They sought increasingly to transform window displays into "artistic showcases," with high-end stores, like Saks, going so far as to hire famous artists like Alexander Archipenko to curate their displays.[3] Even the interior layout of different stores constituted a display of status, as one commentator noted: "Saks is the most spacious, especially on the upper floors, with the least amount of goods displayed. Many of the floors are carpeted, and on some of them, a receptionist is stationed to greet the customers. Klein's, at the other extreme, is a maze of annexes, sloping concrete floors, low ceilings; it has the maximum amount of goods displayed at the least possible expense."[4]

William Labov, who created the department store study as part of his program of research into the sociolinguistics of New York City, knew what he was doing when he chose the city's department stores as a crucible of class.[5] One reason that Saks had so few goods on display, and that a receptionist stood poised to intercept customers, is that Saks knew it was selling more than merchandise. In a luxury store, in a fine restaurant, in an elite hotel, the true commodities on offer are service and sensibility: the employees know what to do and how to do it. The employees also monitor visitors for signs of similar knowledge, and discourage those who don't have the moves right.[6] In short, department stores, in their theme-park thoroughness, cultivate social class as a *Gesamtkunstwerk*, or total work of art: on the level of merchandise, class as conspicuous consumption; on the level of décor, class as taste; on the level of customer service, class as a repertoire of signs of belonging. The three department stores that Labov chose for his study represented, at the time, the "top, middle, and bottom of the price and fashion scale": Saks Fifth Avenue; Macy's, the most famous middle-class department store in New York City; and S. Klein, a bargain basement.

A NATURAL EXPERIMENT

The study relied on what economists call a *natural experiment*. When a researcher conducts an experiment, they divide the population they're studying into at least two groups, a control group and an experimental group; the purpose is to introduce a difference to these otherwise identical groups (e.g., in a medical study one group receives a drug, one receives a placebo) and observe the effects of that difference. A natural experiment is an occurrence in real life that arbitrarily divides an otherwise identical population into at least two different groups. For example, a grading error on a military entrance exam might give passing grades to students who would otherwise fail, enabling researchers to measure the difference that military service made in the later civilian careers of the low-scoring applicants who got into the military compared with similarly low-scoring applicants who did not.[7]

In the case of New York City department stores, Labov realized that he had stumbled into a natural experiment when he noticed that the employees who worked at these stores—the counter girls, the stockboys, the uniformed young men who stood all day in the elevators and pressed buttons for the customers (this was the 1960s)—belonged to a socioeconomically homogeneous population. Regardless of where they worked, they had all grown up in the same economic class, lived in the same areas of the city, and belonged to the same income bracket.[8] The arbitrary divide in this experiment was what kind of department store someone worked at: a fancy store like Saks, or a frugal store like S. Klein. And arbitrary though it was, this was a divide that customers and employees alike understood to signify powerfully in the language of status. "From the point of view of Macy's employees," Labov comments, "a job in Klein's is well below the horizon. Working conditions and wages are generally considered to be worse, and the prestige of Klein's is very low indeed."[9] In short, the natural conditions of New York City department stores enabled Labov to control for the income and background of a population while comparing differences in status. It went without saying that the *customers* of these stores represented different prestige groups. The question was, would the *employees* behave like members of different prestige groups too?[10]

In the design of an experiment, it is important to choose an index of comparison that is both observable and measurable. In the department store study, Labov chose a single variable to measure the class consciousness of various speakers: the phoneme /r/, which you can hear, in a Standard American accent, at the end of the word *car*. Famously, as we have seen, the traditional New York City accent leaves this phoneme silent at the end of certain words or replaces it with a schwa: *Park Avenue* becomes *Paǝk Avenue*. By the time Labov arrived on the scene, pronouncing /r/ in the Standard American fashion was the prestige pronunciation. Moreover, as it happens, this variable in a person's speech displays *fine stratification*; that is, like a color card in a paint store, the pronunciation of /r/ registers subtle shades of difference. By observing the performance of this variable among the employees at Saks, Macy's, and S. Klein, Labov sought to measure how otherwise identical people respond to differences in social status.

The execution of the experiment had one last wrinkle. Labov wanted to prevent the possibility that the employees—the *participants*, as linguists now call the subjects they observe—would change their behavior because they knew a researcher was observing them. He wanted to chart the performance of /r/ as it appeared in the wild. For that reason, he gathered his entire data set in the guise of an ordinary customer. He would hail a participant—a counter girl, for example—and ask for the location of an item he knew to be on the fourth floor. "When the interviewer asked, 'Excuse me, where are the women's shoes?' the answer would normally be 'Fourth floor.' The interviewer then leaned forward and said, 'Excuse me?' He would usually then obtain another utterance, 'Fourth floor,' spoken in careful style under emphatic stress." The researcher thanked the girl, walked to where she couldn't see him, and scribbled information in a notebook: how she spoke, her apparent age, her apparent ethnic group. Then he found an elevator boy and asked again, "Excuse me, where are the women's shoes?" Eventually, Labov and his team recorded data for about 264 participants: 71 from S. Klein, 125 from Macy's, and 68 from Saks.[11] I like to think they also left a few store managers scrambling to find out what new item in stock accounted for the sudden rocketing popularity of women's shoes.[12]

LINGUISTIC INSECURITY

The results showed a remarkable sensitivity to status and prestige. Ordinarily, we might imagine that the dominant factors affecting a person's speech are demographic: her tax bracket, her cultural background, perhaps her ethnicity. But Labov's study showed that mere *association* with a prestigious environment can overcome these demographic factors.[13] Even though the participants had similar backgrounds, culturally and economically, they performed the /r/ variable with noticeable differences which correlated with the prestige of their environments. Employees at Saks tended to voice /r/

distinctly; employees at S. Klein rarely voiced /r/; and employees at Macy's fell somewhere in the middle.

In the test for careful speech ("Excuse me?"), Saks employees voiced /r/ as distinctly as they had in the test for casual speech. Macy's employees, however, voiced /r/ with greater emphasis in the test for careful speech, nearly matching the Saks employees. The researchers concluded that Macy's employees understood /r/ to be a desirable norm, but did not use it in their normal speech; when speaking with care, they moved toward the normative mark. S. Klein employees, too, shifted to a more emphatic voicing of /r/ when they spoke carefully, showing that they likewise subscribed to /r/ as a norm. In fact, the percentage of S. Klein employees who shifted, during this test, from r-less to r-ful pronunciation was the highest of the three stores.[14] In sociolinguistic terms, these employees displayed the greatest degree of *linguistic insecurity*. By contrast, Saks employees seemed to feel little need to change their pronunciation when speaking with care; after all, their casual pronunciation already hit the normative mark. They enjoyed high *linguistic security*.

As a term of art, *linguistic security* refers to the confidence that a speaker feels about her own accent and variant. Someone who feels her accent to be prestigious—a speaker of Received Pronunciation, or Parisian French—would be expected to have great confidence in her speech, and to change it very little when speaking with care or in a formal setting. Under those same conditions, a speaker who fears that her accent makes her sound like a rube, or a hick, or someone who never got out of the neighborhood, may well shift her speech in the direction of a prestige variant.

In 1962, when Labov conducted the study, postvocalic rhoticity was a relatively new prestige marker in New York City, having arisen only within the past twenty years. But New Yorkers felt profoundly the stigma that American culture attached to their nonrhotic speech. They told researchers (not in the context of the department store study) that other Americans looked down on them: "They think we're all murderers." "To be recognized as a New Yorker—that would be a terrible slap in the face." "Somehow, the way they say 'Are you a New Yorker?,' they don't care so much for it." And, although they were proud to be New Yorkers, they expressed the same prejudices toward New York speech, a formation all too common among stigmatized groups: "It's horrible." "Sloppy." "Terribly careless."[15]

Then as today, nonrhoticity was perhaps the best-known feature of New York City English. The only more famous sound is the vowel in "toity toid and toid," which was certainly long gone by 1962. In *Funny Face* (1957), nonrhoticity figures in a throwaway joke in which a magazine model opens her mouth and shatters the illusion of sophistication by revealing a New Yawk accent. (Her line, quoted at the beginning of this chapter, seems designed to include as many New York sounds as possible.) Even today, cultural images of nonrhotic New Yorkers are rarely flattering. For example—as Kara Becker, a prismatically attentive scholar of New York City English, points out—Urban Dictionary, a website for crowd-sourced slang, defines *New Yorkah*, in part, as follows: "Characterized by fake tans, backnee, valour jumpsuits, gold chains, suped-up cars with unnessecary [*sic*] spoilers. . . . This breed of American absolutely refuses to pronounce an 'er' sound if it appears at the end of a word."[16] Given portraits like these, who *wouldn't* have a little linguistic insecurity?

UPSTAIRS, DOWNSTAIRS

Since rhoticity had been a prestige marker in New York City for only two decades, the researchers expected to find that young participants used /r/ more readily than older ones. After all, many of our speech markers, including the voicing of /r/, are established in childhood. Twenty-year-olds would have been exposed to /r/'s prestige during that crucial time, while sixty-year-olds would not. The researchers were therefore puzzled to find a different result: dividing the participants into three age groups—15–30, 35–50, and 55–70—produced no differences of pronunciation.

As a point of comparison, consider the pattern of change in the American South, which also has a historically nonrhotic variant. In 1990, Becker notes, studies showed that rhoticity was "racing like wildfire" among Southern whites, having approached a complete transformation within one cycle of grandparent to grandchild. Among this population, age was the *only* social factor that affected rhoticity; the region and social class of the speakers made no difference.[17]

By contrast, in Labov's study, age didn't matter except—as he found when he subdivided the age groups by store location—as an appendix of prestige. *Overall*, the younger salespeople were not more inclined to use /r/—but at Saks, the younger salespeople used it almost entirely in both tests. Macy's and S. Klein did not show this result for their younger salespeople, which muddied the overall data. At Saks, the age distribution was like that of the South. At the other stores, it wasn't.

The full story appears to have been as follows: young people at Saks were fully aware that the "prestige pattern" of speech in New York City had drifted from that of New England, which does not voice /r/ , to that of the Midwest, which voices /r/. They adhered to this norm with more dedication than any other group. Older people at Saks maintained the older prestige pattern. By contrast, Labov suggested, at Macy's "a large number of younger speakers . . . are completely immersed in the New York City linguistic tradition. The stockboys, the young salesgirls, are not as yet fully aware of the prestige attached to r-pronunciation." Presumably these speakers would adopt the voicing of /r/ once they understood its relative status. Indeed, older participants at Macy's favored the newer prestige pronunciation; they had gained enough knowledge of the world to understand the phoneme's value, and their store was perhaps not quite upmarket enough to defend them from linguistic insecurity.[18] For this reason, the relationship between old and young speakers was flipped according to whether the speakers worked at Macy's or Saks. (At S. Klein, / r/ performance was equally low for all age groups.)

While Labov's study broke new ground in sociolinguistics, New Yorkers might take some of its lessons in stride. It confirms what New Yorkers already take as an axiom: that social identity ultimately comes down to real estate. Indeed, when Labov sifted the data for significant independent variables, one variable that proved surprisingly influential was *the floor that an employee worked on*. On average, an employee working on the ground floor of Saks displayed different linguistic behavior than an employee on the eighth floor. The reason, again, was the ladder of prestige. First, an employee's location on a specific floor was a marker, like his uniform, of his specific role, for example salesman or cashier; these roles demarcated another hierarchy within the overall prestige level of the store. More important, the interior of Saks was designed so that the ground floor would act as containment for ordinary shoppers wandering in "just to look" and the higher floors would sift out the cognoscenti.[19] It is a striking reminder of the extent to which New Yorkers sense and respond to the social meanings of real estate. The economic strata that divide New Yorkers are as high and steep as the canyons of the cityscape— and can be felt on as fine a level as the move from the ground floor to the eighth floor of Saks.

EMPIRICAL ON 34TH STREET

In later decades, researchers recreated Labov's famous study several times. Some of the questions that drove these follow-up studies were straightforward: has the speech of New Yorkers become more rhotic?

If their speech is indeed changing, how fast is the change in comparison with nonrhotic communities elsewhere? Does nonrhoticity carry the same meanings for New Yorkers today that it did in the past? The studies also responded to higher-order issues concerning the social study of language at large. Today, scholars tend to look more closely at gender and ethnicity than they did in the 1960s: men and women can adhere to different language norms; and ethnic minority variants, significant on their own, reinforce some aspects of majority language norms while challenging others.

The follow-up studies had to reckon with a few challenges of replication. Saks and Macy's still stand where they did in 1962, and they still hold the same positions as they did then on the scale of prestige, but every follow-up study has had to find a new replacement for S. Klein; the replacements keep going out of business, as S. Klein's location in Union Square did in 1975. May's Department Store, which stood on 14th Street, served as the replacement in 1986; in 2009, Loehmann's and Filene's Basement served together, since computer automation, and a concomitant drop in staffing at each store, made a combined survey of two stores necessary. All three of these stores held about the same position in the marketplace as S. Klein and stood in the same part of town. And, of course, every store that served as a replacement had to have a fourth floor.[20]

The other challenge of replication relates to a minor flaw in the study itself: the study's design obliges the interviewer to rely on guesswork for data about ethnicity and age. The exact demographic group that Labov surveyed can't be surveyed again in a replica study, since the demographics of New York's department store employees have changed. The workers in Labov's study were mostly white; by the time of a study in 2009, the workers at the working-class and middle-class department stores were mostly people of color. The researcher leading that study reconciled that change by arguing that the new population reflected the changing demographics of the Lower East

Side. In 1962, some two-thirds of the Lower East Side's population was white; today, the proportion is about one-third.[21]

But racial categories have changed, as well: for example, in 1962, it made sense to talk about "ethnic" whites, which is a vanishing category today. A 21st-century participant with ancestral roots in Ukraine might not identify herself as part of a minority ethnic group. On the other hand, a 21st-century researcher might find it pertinent to distinguish West Indians and Haitians from African Americans who have roots in the American South, and to distinguish Puerto Ricans, Cubans, and Dominicans among other Hispanics—all ethnic categories of political significance in contemporary New York. In short, when we trust in the good eyes of the researchers who conducted these studies, we must also acknowledge that what they looked for was, in part, a product of their cultural contexts. The department store studies are no less worthwhile for these caveats, but they are caveats worth noting.

The first follow-up study, which a New York University student named Joy Fowler performed in 1986, found the general distinctions from Labov's study still in place, although rhoticity had increased slightly across the board.[22] Fowler's study also reaffirmed the finding that young speakers were no more rhotic than older ones—with the exception, again, of Saks, where young speakers were the most rhotic.

In 2009, Patrick-André Mather, a linguist who studies creoles and contact languages, performed a second follow-up study, this time with an eye to seeing whether the distribution of /r/ had changed along with the city's demographics. Mather spoke with 169 employees, recording, for each, the variables of "store, occupation, floor within the store, sex, race, age, and foreign or regional accent," as well as the speaker's performance of /r/. Mather's attention to fine details led him to note features that hadn't appeared in earlier studies. For example, he noted that New Yorkers who don't use /r/ often replace /r/ with a schwa: *gorgeous* becomes *goəgis; fourth floor* becomes *foəth floə*. He also noted that white and black speakers tend to differ as

to *where* they use /r/: white speakers use it more often when saying *fourth*; black speakers more often when saying *floor*. Mather also
showed that, although black speakers display less rhoticity than white
speakers do, they adhere to the same patterns of speech differentia-
tion, store by store, as other New Yorkers, and they are participating
in the same general trend toward greater rhoticity. In other words,
black speakers in New York City are participating in some of the same
phonetic shifts that white New Yorkers are undergoing—another sign
that New York City's population is a unified speech community.[23]

In Mather's study, once again, the general distribution of /r/
remained consistent with Labov's study. The lower-class stores had
the lowest use of /r/; Saks had the highest; and Macy's was in the
middle. Once again, speakers at Macy's showed the greatest linguistic
insecurity, moving from /r/-less to /r/-ful pronunciation when they
repeated the phrase carefully. In the fifty years since Labov's study,
rhoticity had increased in Macy's and Saks alike: in Macy's, to 43 percent from 20 percent, and in Saks, to 54 percent from 29 percent. The
rate of change was still unusually slow, however, and the lower-status
stores showed little change in rhoticity since Labov's day. But one
significant development had taken place in the years since the previous studies. In 1962, older speakers at Macy's used /r/ more than
younger speakers did (39 percent versus 21 percent). In 1986, the
same pattern held. But in 2009, younger speakers at *all* of the stores
used /r/ more than older speakers did. This implies that, as of 2009,
young people from the lower-middle class were finally sensitive to
the Midwestern prestige model.[24]

SAY YES TO THE DRESS

Perhaps fittingly for the age of carefully curated virtual lives, the
Millennial update to this series of studies ditched Saks and Macy's in

favor of reality television. *Say Yes to the Dress* is a reality show that follows the adventures of the staff members at Kleinfeld Bridal, a bridal emporium on West 20th Street in Manhattan, as they help brides-to-be select wedding gowns. A colleague at my university, the very distinguished professor of linguistics Mark Aronoff, is a huge fan of the show, for one simple reason: the staff at Kleinfeld are New Yorkers, and many of them have classic New York accents. Recently, when I watched the show for the first time, I looked at my watch to see how much time would pass before I heard the word *goəgis* (*gorgeous*). I heard the word after forty-five seconds.

The appeal of *Say Yes to the Dress*, as with most reality shows, lies in the formula: comfort food with different seasoning but always the same ingredients. In every episode, the consultants help a group of brides who share some quality—they have big budgets, or theme weddings, or terrible families—try out dresses and show them off for friends and family. The episode ends with a scene from a wedding.

In 2013, two linguists at the University of Vermont, Maeve Eberhardt and Corine Downs, found a clever way to use the show as a new take on the department store study—which required, of course, figuring out how to use a single store to investigate a multifaceted question, namely, how the same New Yorkers behave in different contexts of social class.[25] The key was the bridal budget. On the show, brides walk into Kleinfeld with a predetermined budget—from as low as $1,000 to $40,000 or more.[26] (One bride spent nearly $200,000 on dresses for her wedding.) In their study, Eberhardt and Downs used budget as a measure of social class: the higher the budget, the closer to the eighth floor of Saks. If the bridal consultants changed their speech around wealthier customers, this would be a sign that proximity to class affected speech behavior. And though the single-store setting limited the stage that the researchers could observe, the television format provided a wealth of specific, recorded, rewindable linguistic information.

Eberhardt and Downs watched every extant episode of the show (showing that linguistic research can be fun!), recording every instance in which Kleinfeld's employees used /r/. In all, after watching 78 episodes spanning five seasons, they isolated 2,491 relevant *tokens*, or speech acts.[27] The results: many of the bridal consultants on *Say Yes to the Dress* do change their use of /r/ depending on the wealth of the client. In general, consultants use the most /r/ when advising brides with a budget over $8,000. With brides whose budget is between $3,500 and $7,500, they use less /r/; and with brides whose budget is under $3,000, they use the least /r/. Just as Labov's department store employees spoke differently depending on whether their clients were on the eighth floor of Saks, the consultants at Kleinfeld used "more prestigious" speech around richer clients.[28]

The biggest departure from the findings of earlier studies concerned the differences between white and black speakers. On the show, these differences diverged notably from what linguists expect when an interaction is not being recorded. Nonrhoticity is a well-known feature of African American Vernacular English—and regardless of whether AAVE or Standard English is being spoken, African American speakers often use less rhoticity than white speakers.[29] In the first three department store studies, African American speakers were less rhotic than their white counterparts (even as African American speakers followed the same overall patterns of stratification as everyone else). On the reality show, however, the consultants who are people of color (Keasha and Dianne) used the *most* rhotic speech of the consultants on the show.

In fact, on the reality show, the white consultants were *more* likely to use nonrhotic speech (which we can express as /r-0/) when their audience—the bride, her family—also used /r-0/. (One imagines they were trying to connect emotionally with the bridal family by sharing their speech patterns.) By contrast, Keasha and Dianne were even more likely to use /r-1/ when their audience used /r-0/. In the context of less prestigious speech, they used *more* prestigious speech. Even if they spoke the same variant in everyday life as their white colleagues, which is possible and even likely, this performance would stand out as unusual. The researchers suggest that Keasha and Dianne were mindful of the *real* audience of these interactions: the national television audience of the reality show. By avoiding the ethnic stereotype of using less rhotic, and therefore less prestigious, less "correct," speech, they quietly managed one of the invisible challenges that confront people from historically marginalized groups, who may feel the burden, on the air, of righting a history of sloppy representation.[30]

Because of the television format, the researchers could examine one final variable: whether the speaker was trying to connect emotionally to the listener. If you're selling bridal gowns, it makes sense to play on the customer's needs from two angles: on the one hand, their need for emotional support before a major life event, and on the other hand, their need for expert advice on a big-ticket purchase. Here is Debbie, one of the bridal consultants, speaking in the role of expert:

> **Debbie:** So I think we should try this one. It doesn't have the color [r-1] but you know what you have all this dimensional flower [r-1]. . . . You could actually see your [r-1] figure [r-1] through the tulle.

And here is Debbie, speaking to a bride whose sister recently died:

> **Debbie:** So that's why you have feelings about this dress. You want her [r-0] spirit in this dress.
> **Bride:** I do.
> **Debbie:** Okay. I understand [r-0] that . . .
> **Bride:** My—I'm counting my bridesmaids and it doesn't, nothing feels right—

Debbie: She's there [r-0] though.

Bride: So—

Debbie: Just remember [r-0] that. She is there [r-0] and she sees everything.[31]

As it turns out, the bridal consultants tended to use more rhotic speech when performing as experts, and to use less rhotic speech— to sound more like someone from the old neighborhood—when performing as confidants.[32]

I WOULDN'T CHANGE A THING

The department store studies presented a problem they could not, themselves, account for: although New Yorkers have been moving toward rhoticity, that move has been unusually slow. The researchers who performed the studies consistently remarked on how slow the rise of rhoticity has been compared with what developments in other language communities would lead them to expect.[33] Labov even suggested that the gains New Yorkers have made in rhoticity have mainly occurred in careful phrasing, which would mean that, even though they recognize the Standard American norm, they hold it at arm's length.[34]

In 2014, the sociolinguist Kara Becker conducted a study of rhoticity on the Lower East Side that sought to provide a fuller picture of /r/ constraints and /r/ change than the department store studies could.[35] Her study encompassed an ethnically diverse collection of speakers, whom she classified as Chinese, Puerto Rican, African American, Jewish, and (non-Jewish) white.[36] She found that all New Yorkers are subject to social constraints that vary the performance of rhoticity—for example, on the basis of gender, socioeconomic class, or age—and, further, that every ethnic group is subject to *similar* constraints, which affirms, once again, that New Yorkers belong to a unified language community. She also found that, counter to Labov's suggestion that New Yorkers are chiefly rhotic in careful utterances, New Yorkers' casual speech showed rhoticity across many ages and social classes.[37]

Becker identified the highest levels of rhoticity among women, members of the middle class, and young people. Ethnicity affected not just rhoticity, but also whether speakers' rhoticity was changing: speakers of Jewish, white, and Chinese descent were moving toward rhoticity, but speakers of African American and Puerto Rican descent were not. Yet there was an oddity: in 2014, the rate of rhoticity for African American speakers was far higher than the rates that Labov found in 1972. Yet *within* the 2014 study, young African American speakers used no more rhoticity than older ones, which *should* imply that African Americans are not becoming more rhotic over time.[38]

This contradiction mirrored more widespread contradictions. In 1966 and 1987, there was no sign that young speakers of any ethnicity used /r/ more than older ones—but follow-up studies have continued to show, snapshot by snapshot, that speakers are indeed becoming more rhotic. Linguists have long understood cases in which youth is a social factor predicting a vocal feature to mean that change is far along. But in New York City, even though young people in every social class are (as of 2012) more rhotic than their elders, the rate of change toward rhoticity is still remarkably slow. Southerners got on board with the standardized /r/; why haven't New Yorkers?

I (hɑːt) NY

Becker tackled this question in a 2009 study that examined seven lifelong residents of a single block on the Lower East Side—all white, all lower-middle-class, all middle-aged or older.[39] She led them through a wide-ranging interview that turned, on occasion, to matters of local life: *what restaurants in the neighborhood do you like? where do you order food from? how has rent changed in your years of living here? what games did you play on the street when you were a child? have you noticed any signs of gentrification? what other changes have you witnessed in the neighborhood over time?* When conversation turned to these "neighborhood topics," speakers often dropped their rhoticity in part or altogether—even the younger speakers of the group, even speakers who were fully rhotic the rest of the time.[40]

What was going on here? A good point of comparison might be a famous study of Martha's Vineyard that a little-known researcher conducted in the 1960s. (Actually, it was Labov's first study. The guy is a giant in the discipline.) Martha's Vineyard is a scenic island in New England with a small permanent population. During vacation season, hordes of tourists descend upon the little paradise, overwhelming the beaches, farmer's markets, and cute little stores with the chatter of the outside world. Martha's Vineyard was also a tourist haven in Labov's time, which meant that a researcher should expect any kind of local accent to be fading over time, since Vineyarders are constantly exposed to the standards of the wider world. But when Labov examined a set of Vineyarders who ranged in age from their thirties to their sixties, he found that the local accent was *strongest* in the youngest speakers. Labov theorized that these residents had grown up on the island, gone away to college, and returned home— and then exaggerated a stereotypical Vineyard accent in order to show that they were locals, not newcomers, or, God forbid, tourists.[41]

Residents of the Lower East Side likewise use the local accent to lay claim to a patch of earth and let the world know about its claim over them. Home sounds, as we might call the strongest features of that accent, take meaning from their stability in a world of change, as Becker notes: the constant turnover of residents in the early 20th century, when the Lower East Side provided cheap lodgings for working-class immigrants; the changing ethnic ratios of the decades following the Second World War, when growing numbers of Puerto Ricans, African Americans, and Asians joined the old population of working-class ethnic whites; the growing blight of the 1970s and 1980s, when real estate speculators let properties in the area rot as the city government sat idly by; the long tide of gentrification that started rising in the late 1980s, which brought in more people who seemed like outsiders than ever before.[42] Home sounds asserted that the speaker was *not* an outsider; he belonged to the history of the neighborhood, unlike his rhotic neighbors.

This helps to explain how the rise of /r/ in New York City has been so slow—even though movies and television barrage New Yorkers with the standard sound; even though an actor who uses /r-0/ can be expected to be playing a goon; even though the department store studies show that, as of 2012, young New Yorkers from every social class "know better." Indeed, many studies now chronicle cases of accent communities hanging on to "at least one or two features that sound local" against the pull of what one researcher calls "the leveling forces of increased dialect contact."[43] But they hang on only to the most prominent features, the ones that get splashed across tee shirts and bumper stickers. In Pittsburgh, for example, bits of writing that mimic how locals shorten certain vowels ("Git ahta tahn" for *Get out of town*) circulate in cartoons, headlines, and advertisements. The sound has been unusually slow to fade in daily speech.[44] The "Noo Yawk" accent has often been an object of derision, with popular culture casting its speakers as minor villains or comic relief. Becker's work suggests, however, that native New Yorkers have transfused the stigma with a "covert prestige."[45] *I'm from New York; can't you hear it?* It's a lot of weight for a little sound to carry.

A place is more than a patch of ground; as an artifact of culture, it is also a contour map of shared behaviors and sensations, among them sounds made meaningful by a sense of place. Because New Yorkers are slowly moving toward rhoticity, nonrhoticity, one of the most audible markers of New York City English against Standard American English, has emerged as a locus of meaning. Its preservation helps to maintain, for its speakers, a period set of an older city, a tiny island of indifference to a standardizing world. The sound makes tacit claims about who New Yorkers are, who they listen to (other New Yorkers), which classes hold their allegiance, and how deep their ties to the neighborhood run. And although its deliberate performance relies, to some extent, on reproducing working-class stereotypes, in its sincere uses it signifies authenticity, connection, respect, and resistance.[46] New York City produced a community of speakers with a distinctive sound, and by maintaining that sound, speakers help to produce the idea that is New York City.

THE TALK OF THE TOWN

Notes and Comment

One more issue of FUCK YOU/ A MAGAZINE OF THE ARTS to be puked out;
the *FLAMING COCK* issue. Orgasm. Hustle vectors. Total assault on the
culture. If the fuzz dont freak the Editor into the slams./---
Fuck You/ press will roar onward. The following are up and stomping
Fuck You/ publications: AMPHETAMINE-HEAD, poems, drawings, pukeouts,
                    rants & babble of the heroic pioneers
                         in the water soluble bensedrine
                                 movement.

      WARGASM,
  the poetry and insane babble
   of the Rev. Al Fowler

                              SUCK,
                         anonymous poems from the dicklicks

           Μαγεία
     magic & arcanics, a collection

                              GROPE,

                      erotic poems from the Greek, Egyptian,
                      Sanscrit, Latin, etc. in a bilingual edition.
(note: copies of 1st F.U./ Press pub. POEMS FOR MARILYN still available.)/--
also threatened: FUCK THEE/ a Quaker Journal/--- without having to suck
cock or lick ass the Editor & Editorial Board would like to snarf up an
Angel to freak us into FUCK YOU/ 6, the FLAMING COCK issue. (offset. more
durable paper. photos. larger printing. enormous pissoff.)/--- the Editorial
board was cornholing a young 8 year old boy the other night warming up for a
meeting & in walked, sparkle sparkle, Elin Paulson, who blew the lad into
a frenzy. The lad then went twat happy and El and he freaked to a 74 scene.
That's 69 with the 5 editorial board members watching. Later the Rev. Al
Fowler brought in some Flipamine Propene. It's now hip to trench arms with
razor and pack in the dope, so they slashed themselves and the Rev. Fowler
did the honors with his ivory trench-straw. Elephant Walks. Gobble scenes.
Hole Cons. Radiator whistle proved too much for Paulson so she split for
Nelson's to hustle some of his Chatanooga cock. No meeting held./--- well
well well, the Ed. and Ed. Board were spaced out at a peace demonstration
just recently(the big Cube rally) and the ass was unbelievable: fantastic
young high school BANE squack, old tired liberal squack, sweet crotched
college squack, Junion high school Concern Committee squack, Zionist-
Marxist perversion, foot-fetish twatgelt. A whole holocaust of funk-vectors.
/---   Adv.★ Adv.★ 1000's of satisfied customers!★ Adv.★ Adv.
                 TAYLOR MEAD, LTD., PERSONALIZED BLOWJOBS etc.
                      "No K-Y needed with T.M.
                         the mad salivator"
                         ★ Adv.★Adv.★ Adv.★

Epilogue

The film critic Robert Kolker has remarked that the Manhattan of films such as *Mean Streets* (1973), *Taxi Driver* (1976), and *After Hours* (1985) exemplifies "a New York-*ness*, a shared image and collective signifier of New York which has little to do with the city itself, but rather expresses what everyone, including many who live there, have decided New York should look like. . . ."[1] *And sound like*, he might have added. The city's mythology, the inexhaustible appetite with which the creators of films, books, and television shows inhale its clichés and stock scenes—the unreachable skyscrapers; grimy subway cars; psychedelic colored lights and billboards and video screens; yellow taxis; deafening intersections; pickup basketball games; bobbing waves of faces; shouting Italians; dark-suited detectives; Greek coffee cups; chess hustlers; hallucinatory nightclubs; muggers; preposterous loft apartments; office attire that, from film to film, may suggest either Coco Chanel or Lady Gaga; accents that graph against income in a general U-curve, with tough Noo Yawk syllables dominating at lower income levels, receding as income rises, and returning for the vulgar barons of Wall Street—such storytelling elements will always influence the ways in which real New Yorkers live out the meanings of their city and tell New York stories of their own. The likelihood that the most familiar features of New York speech will fade wholly while this mythology survives is small; but New York speech will continue to change as the city itself does, just as any living language, so long as it *is* living, must continue to undergo change.

A bird sings because it has a song. Famously, Robert De Niro improvised the lines in *Taxi Driver* in which, as Travis Bickle, he stands in front of a mirror and pretends to mouth off at an adversary: "You talkin' to me? You talkin' to me? You talkin' to me? Then who the hell else are you talkin' to? You talkin' to me? Well I'm the only one here. Who the fuck do you think you're talking to?"[2] The film's screenwriter, Paul Schrader, later lamented that, carefully choreographed as the weapons-brandishing scene was, the vulgar, incantatory words that go along with it are not his: "The bit that's not in the script, the only thing, is De Niro's dialogue; he improvised it, the whole thing about, 'Who you looking at? You looking at me? You're a fuck!' To me, that's the best thing in the movie. And I didn't write it."[3]

In the scene, Bickle seems to be taking inspiration for his posturing from movie heroes like John Wayne and Clint Eastwood; he has seized on the filmic myth of the heroic lone gunman, only to repeat the myth as farce.[4] Eastwood's Dirty Harry, a mumbling cowboy, speaks in soft, terse sentences; Bickle's mirror scene is faster, more confrontational, with more turn-taking, prompts, and repetition, and Schrader, who hails from the Midwest, perhaps could not have worked it up as smoothly as De Niro, who grew up in Lower Manhattan. I've looked at the original script for *Taxi Driver*, with De Niro's handwritten notes, and although he gives himself ample instructions on character emotions and stage business, nowhere does he write himself notes on dialect or accent.[5] The only note about dialogue that De Niro scribbled on the pages for the mirror scene is, "Mirror thing here?"[6] The rest he already knew how to say.

Tawkin Noo Yawk, above all, is making room for conversation. As this book went into production, sections of Manhattan lost electricity for an afternoon. New Yorkers, who knew the blackout was likely to be temporary, lit up social media with images and videos of unexpected beauty and goodwill: teams of good Samaritans directing traffic at intersections; Broadway performers bringing the show outside; a choir from Carnegie Hall, evacuated from their auditorium, lifting voices on the sidewalk in sacred song.[7] A deep crowd surrounded the singers, foot traffic pausing in pleasure but not surprise that the city's soundscape, still humming with laughter and chatter and the whine of passing buses, could erupt in such joyful harmony. As one New Yorker tweeted afterward about the resulting news coverage, "To those of you just learning that New Yorkers are actually nice people, go f*ck yourself."[8]

ACKNOWLEDGMENTS

I would like to thank my husband, Jeffrey, for his incredible patience, good humor, and insights into the subtleties of New York City and Long Island.

Mark Aronoff, a distinguished professor of linguistics at Stony Brook University, was an indispensable advisor throughout the project. Susan Brennan, a professor of psycholinguistics and cognitive science, also provided invaluable feedback. Deborah Tannen, Michael Newman, and Patrick-André Mather kindly talked with me about aspects of their research, and Greg Pliska graciously allowed me to interview him about the world of professional composers and lyricists. Kenneth Barrios gave me permission to quote a section of one of his essays.

I wish to thank Bill Shead, a Cree member of the Peguis First Nation, and Jon Parmenter, a professor of American history at Cornell University, for their insights into the history, languages, and cultures of North America's indigenous peoples.

Peter Manning and Susan Scheckel provided advice, support, humor, and keen editorial eyes; I remain eternally grateful to them.

Robert Crease, Catherine Keyworth, Karen Lloyd, Celia Marshik, Emily Parsons, Mike Rubenstein, Daniel R. Schwarz, Michelle Taylor, David Weinberger, and Jia Zhang offered advice on various aspects of the research. Barry McCrea helped me with Irish words.

Naomi Wolf and Chris Calhoun offered valuable insights at an early stage. Marilyn Marks and Ray Ollwerther provided essential guidance on one section of the manuscript.

My editors at Oxford University Press, Hallie Stebbins and Meredith Keffer, have guided this project since the beginning. I am grateful for their patience, guidance, and encouragement.

Thomas Lannon and other archivists at the New York Public Library have extended advice, support, and resources that could have provided for five or ten books in this narrow field. Michael Gilmore at the Harry Ransom Center at the University of Texas at Austin helped me to locate and work with important materials in film studies. David Ment of the New York City Municipal Archives guided me through treasure troves of information on the history of New York City's board of education and its language pedagogy.

My anonymous reviewers for Oxford University Press offered comments and suggestions that improved the manuscript as it took form. An anonymous subject-matter fact-checker for the press corrected errors and kindly noted West Coast idioms, like *freeway*, which I replaced with East Coast equivalents.

Some of the research for this book was carried out during fellowships at Cornell University and at the Harry Ransom Center at the University of Texas at Austin.

Lyric credits:

Blue Magic

Words and Music by Shawn Carter, Pharrell Williams, Denzil Foster, Thomas McElroy, Terry Ellis, Cindy Herron, Maxine Jones, Dawn Robinson and Bernhard Kaun

Copyright (c) 2007 EMI Blackwood Music Inc., Two Tuff—E—Nuff Publishing, USI A Music Publishing, Waters Of Nazareth Publishing and Carter Boys Music

All Rights on behalf of EMI Blackwood Music Inc. and Two Tuff—E—Nuff Publishing Administered by Sony/ATV Music Publishing LLC, 424 Church Street, Suite 1200, Nashville, TN 37219

All Rights on behalf of USI A Music Publishing Controlled and Administered by Universal Music Corp.

All Rights on behalf of Waters Of Nazareth Publishing Administered by Warner Geo Met Ric Music

All Rights on behalf of Carter Boys Music Administered by WC Music Corp.

International Copyright Secured All Rights Reserved

Reprinted by Permission of Hal Leonard LLC

I Dream Too Much

Words and Music by Dorothy Fields and Jerome Kern

Copyright (c) 1935 UNIVERSAL — POLYGRAM INTERNATIONAL PUBLISHING, INC.

Copyright Renewed, Extended Renewal Assigned to ALDI MUSIC and UNIVERSAL — POLYGRAM INTERNATIONAL PUBLISHING, INC.

Print Rights for ALDI MUSIC in the United States Controlled and Administered by HAPPY ASPEN MUSIC LLC c/o SHAPIRO, BERNSTEIN & CO., INC.

All Rights Reserved Used by Permission

Reprinted by Permission of Hal Leonard LLC

A Fine Romance

from SWING TIME

Words by Dorothy Fields

Music by Jerome Kern

Copyright (c) 1936 UNIVERSAL — POLYGRAM INTERNATIONAL PUBLISHING, DIC. and ALDI MUSIC

Copyright Renewed

Print Rights for ALDI MUSIC in the US. Controlled and Administered by HAPPY ASPEN MUSIC LLC

c/o SHAPIRO, BERNSTEIN & C0, WC.

All Rights Reserved Used by Permission

Reprinted by Permission of Hal Leonard LLC

You Couldn't Be Cuter

from JOY OF LIVING

Lyric by Dorothy Fields

NOTES

Epigraph

1. Adrienne Su, "Address," in Miguel Algarín and Bob Holman, eds., *Aloud: Voices from the Nuyorican Poets Café* (New York: Henry Holt and Company, 1994), 150–1.

Chapter 1

1. This point comes from a recent paper in which three language scholars examined the tweets that Americans produced from October 2013 to November 2014. Because tweets, being geotagged, reveal the locations of their writers, the researchers could track how words traveled, where specific words were popular, and where linguistic innovation was taking place. Jack Grieve, Andrea Nini, and Diansheng Guo, "Analyzing Lexical Emergence in Modern American English Online," *English Language and Linguistics* 21, 1 (2017): 99–127.
2. Another friend likes to say that he got an A.B. from Princeton, a J.D. from Fordham, and an F.U. from New York City.
3. Alan Dershowitz, interview, "If These Knishes Could Talk" (2013). Dershowitz was aware that the response to his "funny" New York accent was also a response to his being Jewish. He added in the interview: "Yale was Yale. It had a motto written in Hebrew, *Urim V'Thummim*, and the joke was, 'If you can read it, you can't go here.'"
4. Richard Ellmann, *Oscar Wilde* (New York: Alfred A. Knopf, 1988), 38.

5. Ann Landers, "Listen to Parents, Says Teen," *Santa Cruz Sentinel* (January 27, 1980), 53. Quoted in Deborah Tannen, "New York Jewish Conversational Style," *International Journal of the Sociology of Language* 30 (1981): 134.

6. Tannen, "New York Jewish Conversational Style," 134.

7. Roosevelt's younger relative Franklin, raised in the same area and in similar circumstances, "would pronounce the words *first* as 'fost,' *thirty* as 'tho'dee' or 'tho'tee,' and *third* as 'tho:d.'" Robert Blumenfeld, *Accents: A Manual for Actors* (New York: Proscenium Publishers, [1998] 2002), 139. See also William Labov, *The Social Stratification of English in New York City* (Washington, DC: Center for Applied Linguistics, [1966] 1982), 345–6.

8. "If These Knishes Could Talk" (2013).

9. Nancy Niedzielski and Dennis Preston, *Folk Linguistics* (Berlin: Mouton de Gruyter, 2000), 63–77. Cited in Michael Newman, *New York City English* (Boston and Berlin: Mouton de Gruyter, 2014), 1–2.

10. The poll surveyed 2,331 adults in the United States. Anonymous, "U.S. Adults Like British Accents, Not NYC," *United Press International* (January 30, 2011).

11. Deborah Tannen, "New York Jewish Conversational Style," 145. As Tannen notes, in 1979, an article in the Associated Press discussed speech clinicians on the West Coast who offered a "cure" for New York speech. Said one clinician, "It's really a drag listening to people from New York talk. It upsets me when I hear a New York accent. . . . We're here to offer a service to newcomers to this area, especially to New Yorkers. . . . When they open their mouths, they alienate everyone. We're here to help them adjust to life in Marin County." Quoted in Ibid., 134.

12. See also Deborah Tannen, "Talking New York: It's Not What You Say, It's the Way You Say It," *New York* (March 30, 1981), 30–3; and Deborah Tannen, *Conversational Style: Analyzing Talk among Friends* (Norwood, NJ: Ablex, 1984). Michael Newman discusses Tannen's work and its legacy in Newman, *New York City English*, 103–6.

13. Tannen, "New York Jewish Conversational Style," 135–7.

14. Ibid., 137. She also discusses this in Deborah Tannen, "Turn-Taking and Intercultural Discourse and Communication," in Christina Bratt Paulston, Scott F. Kiesling, Elizabeth S. Rangel, eds., *The Handbook of Intercultural Discourse and Communication* (Malden, MA: Wiley-Blackwell, 2012): 135–57.

15. Tannen, "Turn-Taking and Intercultural Discourse and Communication," 136–7.

16. Tannen also points out the relative nature of this process. She learned to wait for pauses when talking with a colleague from Michigan: "I learned over time that in conversation with Ron, I had to count to seven after I got the impression that he had nothing to say, in order to give him time to perceive that I was done and he could begin." Yet Ron in turn had the same problem when talking to his spouse, who grew up in Hawaii; she would tell Ron, "You ask me a question, but before I can answer you ask another." And Ron's wife, in turn, had

the same problem while visiting the Arctic Circle; Athabaskans paused for so long that she became the frequent interrupter (in Tannen, "Turn-Taking and Intercultural Discourse and Communication,"136–7).

17. *Latching* is when you begin to speak right away after the last speaker finishes—no overlapping, but also no gap between one speaker and another. Tannen, "Turn-Taking and Intercultural Discourse and Communication," 136–42.

18. Tannen, "New York Jewish Conversational Style," 136–7.

19. Deborah Tannen, "Cultural Patterning in *Language and Woman's Place*," in Robin Lakoff, *Language and Woman's Place: Texts and Commentaries*, ed. Mary Bucholtz (Oxford: Oxford University Press, [1975] 2004), 161.

20. Bill Bryson, *Notes from a Small Island* (New York: Avon Books, [1995] 1997), 216.

21. Tannen, "New York Jewish Conversational Style"; Tannen, "Talking New York."

22. Deborah Schiffrin, "Jewish Argument as Sociability," *Language in Society* 13, 3 (1984): 317–9.

23. Ibid., 318; Tannen, "New York Jewish Conversational Style," 142.

24. Paul Kilpatrick, "Turn and Control in Puerto Rican Spanish Conversation" (Educational Resources Information Center, 1986).

25. Umberto Eco once commented, "Italians interrupt one another . . . Americans speak in turns. . . . It is no accident that the pragmatic theory of 'conversation turns' originated in the United States. Italian researchers who write articles about this matter treat it as an excavation from Mars." Obviously, Eco's characterization of all Americans as alike was premature. Quoted in Gabriela G. Alfaraz, "Conversing Through Overlaps: Information Overlaps and Simultaneous Talk in Cuban Spanish," *Multilingua* 28 (2009): 29. Tannen also notes a 1982 study that observed "two Italian-American children in a suburb of Boston. Their teacher had complained that many students in her class 'interrupted' frequently. The authors, after observing and videotaping the children in their homes and at school, identified differences in turn-taking conventions in these two contexts. In family conversations overlapping speech frequently occurred without anyone reacting as if it were inappropriate. At school, however, when the teacher was enforcing a 'one speaker at a time' rule, she heard children's overlapping speech as 'interrupting' " (in Tannen, "Turn-Taking and Intercultural Discourse and Communication," 147).

26. Alfaraz, "Conversing Through Overlaps," 28–9. See also Anne Berry, "Spanish and American Turn-Taking Styles: A Comparative Study," *Pragmatics and Language Learning* 2 (1994): 180–90.

27. Elizabeth Knutson, "On Being Heard: A Study of Listening Behavior in French Conversation," *The French Review* 82, 6 (May 2009): 1180–93; Molly Wieland, "Turn-Taking as a Source of Misunderstanding in French-American Cross-Cultural Conversation," in Lawrence Bouton and Yamuna Kachru,

eds., *Pragmatics and Language Learning* 2 (Champaign-Urbana: University of Illinois Press, 1991), 101–18.

28. Erving Goffman, in *Forms of Talk* (Philadelphia: University of Pennsylvania Press, 1981), 23. Cited in Gabriela G. Alfaraz, "Conversing Through Overlaps: Information Overlaps and Simultaneous Talk in Cuban Spanish," *Multilingua* 28 (2009), 30.

29. See, for example, Emmanuel A. Schegloff, "Overlapping Talk and the Organization of Turn-Taking for Conversation," *Language in Society* 29 (2000): 1–63; and Alfaraz, "Conversing Through Overlaps."

30. Tannen discusses these features in Tannen, "Talking New York," 30–1.

31. Schiffrin, "Jewish Argument as Sociability," 322.

32. Alfaraz, "Conversing Through Overlaps." For an ethnographic account of this social use of joking, see Samuel C. Heilman, *Synagogue Life: A Study in Symbolic Interaction* (New Brunswick, NJ: Transaction Publishers, [1976] 1998), 198.

33. If a speaker disobeys one of the rules of the Cooperative Principle, he may be trying to convey additional information through this disobedience. For example, if he writes a recommendation letter that merely states that the applicant is punctual, thus disobeying the rule that one's contribution be informative, he is conveying the additional information that the applicant has no relevant merits. Herbert P. Grice, "Logic and Conversation," in Peter Cole and Jerry L. Morgan, eds., *Syntax and Semantics: Speech Acts* (New York: Academic Press, 1975), 45.

34. Alfaraz, "Conversing Through Overlaps," 27.

35. The opening scene in Woody Allen's film *Manhattan* (1979) has a good example of this feature. Allen speaks without emphatic masculine plosives, while some big guys who are unintentionally intimidating him speak with emphatic masculine plosives.

36. Nor were those opponents wrong to guess that Bartholdi was likely to include an anti-slavery message in the statue. Bartholdi's sentiments on slavery, and his respect for African Americans, are well-attested. During an 1871 tour of the States that he took with the aim of gauging American support for the ambitious project, Bartholdi attended a service in an African American church. He wrote to his mother, "It commanded respect, this demonstration by people, slaves only yesterday, who turned their minds to the ideal, who have faith, and who interest themselves so violently in moral questions." Yasmin Sabina Kahn, *Enlightening the World: The Creation of the Statue of Liberty* (Ithaca, NY: Cornell University Press, 2010), 85.

37. Kahn, *Enlightening the World*, 82–111. Incidentally, many older iconographic representations of the figure of Liberty—for example, from the Renaissance—show her with a cat, because cats hate to be contained. In other words, the Statue of Liberty could have had a cat. I estimate that the cat would be about sixteen feet tall, in keeping with the scale of the Liberty figure.

38. See, for example, Noel Ignatiev, *How the Irish Became White* (New York: Routledge, 1995); Jennifer Guglielmo and Salvatore Salerno, eds., *Are Italians White?: How Race Is Made in America* (New York: Routledge, 2003); Eric L. Goldstein, *The Price of Whiteness: Jews, Race, and American Identity* (Princeton, NJ: Princeton University Press, 2006); and Ian Haney Lopez, *White by Law: The Legal Construction of Race* (New York: New York University Press, 2006).

39. See, for example, Nancy Foner, "How Exceptional Is New York? Migration and Multiculturalism in the Empire City," *Ethnic and Racial Studies* 30, 6 (November 2007): 999–1023; Philip Kasinitz, John Mollenkopf, and Mary Waters, "Becoming American/Becoming New Yorkers: Immigrant Incorporation in a Majority Minority City," *The International Migration Review* 36, 4 (2002): 1020; Kevin Keogan, "A Sense of Place: The Politics of Immigration and the Symbolic Construction of Identity in Southern California and the New York Metropolitan Area," *Sociological Forum* 17, 2 (June 2002): 227–8.

40. Tannen, "Ethnicity as Conversational Style," 13.

41. For example, nonrhoticity persists in African American Vernacular English, even as it fades, albeit slowly, in New York City English.

42. This kind of incorrect belief is sometimes known as *folk linguistics.*

43. Kara Becker and Luiza Newlin-Lukowicz, "The Myth of the New York City Borough Accent: Evidence from Perception," *University of Pennsylvania Working Papers in Linguistics* 24, 2 (October 15, 2018): 9.

44. Unsigned, "Tawking the Tawk," *The New Yorker* (November 14, 2005). Cited in Becker and Newlin-Lukowicz, "The Myth of the New York City Borough Accent," 9.

45. Becker and Newlin-Lukowicz, "The Myth of the New York City Borough Accent"; you can take the quiz yourself at www.newyorkcityaccents.com.

46. The researchers defined *native New Yorker* as follows: "For our purposes, being a 'Native New Yorker' means: 1) I was born in New York City or moved to New York City before I was 5 years old, and 2) I have never lived outside of New York City for more than 10 years" (in Becker and Newlin-Lukowicz. "The Myth of the New York City Borough Accent," 11ffn).

47. Becker and Newlin-Lukowicz, "The Myth of the New York City Borough Accent," 14–6. Michael Newman notes some points of difference from the general similarity of speech across the five boroughs—for example, more Standard American English appears in Manhattan and "Brownstone Brooklyn"—in Newman, *New York City English,* 18–20.

48. See also Kara Becker, "The Social Motivations of Reversal: Raised BOUGHT in New York City English," *Language in Society* 43, 3 (2014): 395–420.

49. Unsigned, "Tawking the Tawk"; Sam Roberts, "Unlearning to Tawk Like a New Yorker," *New York Times* (November 19, 2010); Tom Wolfe, *The Bonfire of the Vanities* (New York: Farrar, Straus and Giroux, 1987), 371.

50. Newman, *New York City English*, 45–6; Becker and Newlin-Lukowicz, "The Myth of the New York City Borough Accent," 10–13.

51. William Safire examines the unspoken meanings of *fuhgeddaboutit* in Safire, "Fuhgeddaboutit," *New York Times Magazine* (September 1, 1996). Safire likewise notes the importance of the absent /r/ to the local flavor of the word: "In New York, the r in forget is as lost as that letter in York."

52. Newman, *New York City English*, 78.

53. As the researchers note, some of these pairings are "near-minimal pairs" rather than exact minimal pairs. Becker and Newlin-Lukowicz, "The Myth of the New York City Borough Accent," 12–13.

54. We can also see this ideology at work in a video with more than a million hits on YouTube, "The accents of NYC—a guide and a tour"—which, Kara Becker and Luiza Newlin-Lukowicz note, promotes the myth that New York accents vary by borough. The tour guide in the video claims that speakers from the Bronx, being tough, use tough sounds in their speech—such as strong initial consonants: "First you got the Bronx, you know what I mean, the Bronx is dark, it's in the back of your throat, and you're dropping your final r's, and you have a heavy initial emphasis on your consonants, because the Bronx is a very tough borough, and . . . you punch your initial consonants, you got it? Cause it's tough there." Quoted in Becker and Newlin-Lukowicz, "The Myth of the New York City Borough Accent," 10.

55. Walter Kerr, review of *Fiddler on the Roof, New York Theatre Critics Reviews* 25, 19 (1964): 217; Howard Taubman, "Theater: Mostel as Tevye in 'Fiddler on the Roof,'" *New York Theatre Critics Reviews* 25, 19 (1964): 217–18. Both cited in Henry Bind, *Acting Jewish: Negotiating Ethnicity on the American Stage & Screen* (Ann Arbor: University of Michigan Press, 2005), 67.

56. Bind, *Acting Jewish*, 3.

57. Although they will make exceptions for one another's safety, another example of New York Nice. Recently I was approached on a mostly empty street by a stranger who said, "Hey, be careful. There's a guy over there who looks like he doesn't know where he's at." I looked, and farther down the street was indeed a guy who didn't look like he knew where he was at. I added a curve to my route.

58. Edgar Allan Poe, "The Man of the Crowd," *Burton's Gentleman's Magazine* (December 1840).

59. Nathaniel Hawthorne, "Wakefield" (1835), in *The Portable Hawthorne*, ed. Malcolm Cowley (New York: The Viking Press, [1969] 1983): 151–62.

Chapter 2

1. Thomas Paul Bonfiglio, *Race and the Rise of Standard American* (Berlin and New York: Mouton de Gruyter, 2002), 1–3. See also Newman, *New York City English*, 1–2.

2. When I say "we," I mean people who use a Standard American accent.

3. Bonfiglio, *Race and the Rise of Standard American*, 1. Intrusive /r/ doesn't result from over-correction by speakers worried about their "incorrect" speech, although many people mistakenly think it does. For example, the satirist John Oliver, who is pretty confident about his English accent—as he likes to say, "It has a quiet authority"—uses intrusive /r/ in specific, predictable environments. I am certain that he would pronounce "America Online" as "Americer Online."

4. Bonfiglio, *Race and the Rise of Standard American*, 3.

5. Yakira H. Frank, review of Allan Forbes Hubbell's *The Pronunciation of English in New York City: Consonants and Vowels*, *Language* 28, 2 (April–June 1952): 278–9.

6. S. N. Behrman, "Do or Diaphragm," *The New Yorker* (May 25, 1935): 22–7.

7. John Hurt Fisher, "British and American, Continuity and Divergence," in John Algeo, ed., *The Cambridge History of the English Language*, vol. VI (Cambridge: Cambridge University Press, 2001), 75–9.

8. Some scholars speculate that nonrhoticity spread further in the South than it did in the North because of the "greater prestige of the elite there" (Fisher, "British and American, Continuity and Divergence," 76).

9. Fisher, "British and American, Continuity and Divergence," 75–6. To be sure, not all of the sounds in RP passed into American English (Fisher, "British and American, Continuity and Divergence," 77–8). Nonetheless, much of the sound of cultivated American speech before the 1940s seems to reflect the influence of Received Pronunciation.

10. Fisher, "British and American, Continuity and Divergence," 75–6.

11. Ibid., 75–8.

12. Yakira Hagalili Frank, "The Speech of New York City," dissertation, University of Michigan (1948), 12.

13. It also appears in Henry Roth's novel *Call It Sleep* (1934), about a Jewish boy's experiences on the Lower East Side. "My ticher calls id Xmas, bod de kids call id Chrizmas. Id's a goyish holiday anyways. Wunst I hanged op a stockin' in Brooklyn. Bod mine fodder pud in a eggshells wid terlit paper an' a piece f'om a ol' kendle. So he leffed w'en he seen me. Id ain' no Sendy Klaws, didja know?" Roth perhaps makes the boy's variant rhotic so that it is more "incorrect." Henry Roth, *Call It Sleep: A Novel* (New York: Picador, [1934] 1991), 125.

14. For example, in *Top Hat* (1935), Astaire (who plays an American) says, "I'm sorry, I can't [kɑːnt] do it," with a British vowel, "charming [ˈʧɑːmɪŋ]"; "Well, there you are [ɑː]," with no postvocalic /r/; and "horse [hɔːs]" and "course [kɔːs]." Rogers (who plays an Englishwoman) says "driver [draɪvər], faster [fæstər]," "horse [hɔrs]," "course [kɔrs]," and "can't [kænt]" like an American. However, she uses British pronunciation for "guards [gɑːdz]," "arms [ɑːmz]," and upper-class British pronunciation for "back [bɛk]" and "hat [hɛt]."

15. George Gershwin and Ira Gershwin, "Let's Call the Whole Thing Off," in *Shall We Dance* (1937).

16. See, for example, J. K. Chambers, "'Canadian Dainty': The Rise and Decline of Briticisms in Canada," in Raymond Hickey, ed., *Legacies of Colonial English: Studies in Transported Dialects* (Cambridge: Cambridge University Press, 2004), 224–41.

17. Ibid., 232.

18. For an excellent account of the differences between variants artificially concocted by adults and ones naturally produced by children, see Steven Pinker, *The Language Instinct: How the Mind Creates Language* (New York: Penguin Books, 1994).

19. In 1963, Paul McCartney was leaning so hard on the American /r/ that he sometimes inserted it into words that don't contain it: "I never saw [sɔr] them at all." By 1967, he was proudly Liverpudlian: "Lovely Rita meter [miːtə] maid." Peter Trudgill, "Acts of Conflicting Identity: The Sociolinguistics of British Pop-Song Pronunciation," in Peter Trudgill, *On Dialect: Social and Geographical Perspectives* (New York: New York University Press, 1983), 141–60.

20. As Trudgill notes, British singers who are trying to sound American rely on a handful of pronunciations: the replacement of /t/ with a flap in words like *bottle*, making them sound, to some, like "boddle"; pronouncing the /r/ in words like *girl*, which speakers of nonrhotic English variants normally do not pronounce, with an emphasis that speakers of rhotic English variants do not use; and pronouncing words like *my* and *life* with a monophthong vowel, [a]— a pronunciation familiar in the American South—even though most variants in Britain pronounce those words as diphthongs (Ibid., 141–2).

21. Frank, "The Speech of New York City," 11.

22. Ibid., 25–6.

23. Ibid., 25.

24. Labov, *The Social Stratification of English in New York City*, 345–6.

25. Giles Wilkeson Gray and Claude Merton Wise, *The Bases of Speech* (New York: Harper & Row, [1934] 1959), 314–8.

26. Ibid., 256.

27. Edith Skinner, *The Seven Points for Good Speech in Classic Plays* (Mill Valley, CA: Performance Skills, 1983), 10–26. A Canadian by birth, Skinner attended Columbia University in the 1930s and worked in New York City thereafter.

28. Astaire, in the meanwhile, says *horse* [hɔːs] and *course* [kɔːs].

29. Nancy Elliott, "A Sociolinguistic Study of Rhoticity in American Film Speech from the 1930s to the 1970s," dissertation, Indiana University (2000): 101–2.

30. Gray and Wise, *The Bases of Speech*, 309–14.

31. Arthur Bronstein, "Let's Take Another Look at New York City Speech," *American Speech* 37, 1 (1962): 14–21.

32. Bureau of Speech Improvement, "Suggestions in Speech Improvement for the Use of Classroom Teachers" (Board of Education, The City of New York, 1933 [Reprinted June 1934]), 52–3.

33. Course of the Study and Syllabus in English and Citizenship for Evening Elementary Schools (Board of Education, the City of New York, 1931), 12.

34. Bureau of Speech Improvement, "Suggestions in Speech Improvement for the Use of Classroom Teachers," 54.

35. Many of Franklin Roosevelt's speeches are available as recordings online.

36. Some historians suggest that the nonrhoticity of African American Vernacular English derives from slaves in the Tidewater South imitating the English of whites who were themselves nonrhotic—although AAVE differs from white port-city pronunciation in that speakers drop the /r/ entirely rather than replace it with a schwa (Fisher, "British and American, Continuity and Divergence," 76). If this was the case, influence would soon have gone in both directions. African American speakers in the South likely helped to sustain the nonrhoticity of other Southern variants.

37. Jerome Karabel, *The Chosen: The Hidden History of Admission and Exclusion at Harvard, Yale, and Princeton* (New York: Houghton Mifflin, 2005), 77.

38. Ibid., 86–97.

39. Ibid., 87.

40. Ibid., 77–85.

41. Ibid., 77–84; quotation from *The Passing of the Great Race* is from Ibid., 81.

42. This book argues that "internal Bolshevist disaffection" had already weakened the white race, which was therefore vulnerable to "the rising tide of color" worldwide. Lothrop Stoddard, *The Rising Tide of Color against White World-Supremacy* (New York: Charles Scribner's Sons, 1921), 221. Quoted in Karabel, *The Chosen*, 83–4.

43. Karabel, *The Chosen*, 77–85.

44. The Big Three schools each carried out this program in their own characteristic way. Harvard did it publicly and accidentally set off a national controversy. Yale did it in secret. Princeton did it with collaboration from its students that was slightly frightening in its enthusiasm. When the news emerged that elite schools were imposing a racial quota, the student-run newspaper *The Daily Princetonian* argued in favor of the quota on the grounds that it would ensure that students possessed "such vital factors as character, personality, physical ability, public spirit, and all that goes to make up leadership of the highest type" (Karabel, *The Chosen*, 94–102, 127).

45. Ibid., 99–101.

46. Bonfiglio, *Race and the Rise of Standard American*, 5.

47. In 1939, for example, the employees of CBS included States, Elmer Davis, George Fielding Eliot, Thomas Grandin, H.V. Kaltenborn, Edward R. Murrow, Eric Sevareid, William L. Shirer, and Paul White. "Almost all were young men," as Jeffrey Ian Cole writes. Jeffrey Ian Cole, "Born to the New Art: CBS Correspondents and the Emergence of Broadcast News, 1930–1941," dissertation, University of California, Los Angeles (1985): 146.

48. He continued to serve on the Emergency Committee's board after moving to CBS. See, for example, Laurel Leff, "Rebuffing Refugee Journalists: The Profession's Failure to Help Jews Persecuted by Nazi Germany," *Journalism & Communication Monographs* 17, 3 (2015): 169.

49. Ibid., 87–171.

50. Cole, "Born to the New Art," 171–2.

51. Ibid., 168–72.

52. Ibid., 193.

53. As Cole notes, NBC also reported on the Blitz from London, but nobody remembers NBC's reporting, while everyone remembers Murrow's reporting Cole, "Born to the New Art," 182.

54. Dixon Wecter, "Hearing Is Believing," *The Atlantic Monthly* (August 1945): 59; Cole, "Born to the New Art," 183–5.

55. Ibid., 182, 210–8; Charles Wertenbaker, "The World on His Shoulders," *The New Yorker* (December 26, 1953).

56. Dick Leith, *A Social History of English* (London: Routledge, [1983] 2003), 55.

57. Cole, "Born to the New Art," 230–2.

58. Bonfiglio, *Race and the Rise of Standard American*, 174–5.

59. Cole, "Born to the New Art," 201.

60. These examples are from Frank Colby, "F.D.R. on Radio Has New England Accent," *Daily Boston Globe* (December 29, 1940): 34. Colby reads Roosevelt's nonrhoticity as reflecting "a little of the South (or is it Harvard?)," presumably forgetting that New Yorkers are also nonrhotic.

61. Cole, "Born to the New Art," 204–5.

62. James Bender, *NBC Handbook of Pronunciation* (New York: Thomas Y. Crowell Company, 1943), ix. Quoted in Bonfiglio, *Race and the Rise of Standard American*, 175–6. Soon after publishing this book, Bender resigned from Queens College after having been caught faking academic credentials. See Robert McG. Thomas Jr., "James Bender, 92, Eclectic Educator, Dies," *The New York Times* (November 28, 1997).

63. Bonfiglio, *Race and the Rise of Standard American*, 175–7.

64. Ibid., 184–6.

65. Ibid., 182.

66. Charles Grandgent, "The Dog's Letter," in *Old and New: Sundry Papers* (Cambridge, MA: Harvard University Press, 1920), 56. Quoted in Bonfiglio, *Race and the Rise of Standard American*, 47, 185.

67. Bonfiglio, *Race and the Rise of Standard American*, 187–94; Frederick Jackson Turner, "Social Forces in American History," *American Historical Review* 16, 2 (January 1911): 220–1. Turner's argument connecting the American spirit with the spirit of the frontier—widely known as the Turner Thesis—has its most famous articulation in his 1893 essay, "The Significance of the Frontier in American History."

68. Bonfiglio, *Race and the Rise of Standard American*, 188–209.

69. Ibid., 215–6.
70. Ibid., 216.
71. Allan Forbes Hubbell, *The Pronunciation of English in New York City* (1950), 48; Bonfiglio, *Race and the Rise of Standard American*, 214.
72. The informants were young people entering Queens College from 1947 to 1952. Bronstein, "Let's Take Another Look at New York City Speech," 24–5; Bonfiglio, *Race and the Rise of Standard American*, 214.
73. Ibid., 217.
74. Bonfiglio, *Race and the Rise of Standard American*, 181. On the efforts of elite colleges to recruit more students from the Midwest, see also David Levine, *The American College and the Culture of Aspiration, 1915–1940* (Ithaca, NY: Cornell University Press, 1983), especially 145–50.
75. I'm a big fan of Cap, so this footnote is dedicated to the excellent job Chris Evans has done in representing him on the screen.
76. Bonfiglio, *Race and the Rise of Standard American*, 224. On *Law and Order: Criminal Intent* (2001–11), Detective Robert Goren, who normally spoke Standard American English, would adopt a fake New York accent whenever he wanted a suspect to think he was an asshole.
77. Julia Dobrow and Calvin Gidney, "The Good, the Bad, and the Foreign: The Use of Dialect in Children's Animated Television," *The Annals of the American Academy of Political and Social Science* 557 (May 1998): 105–19.
78. Ibid., 115.
79. Ibid., 116.
80. Leith, *A Social History of English*, 55.
81. Personal communication, Michael Newman (July 17, 2015).
82. Groucho Marx wasn't the only influence from cinema on Bugs Bunny's speech patterns. There's also, for instance, *The Bowery Boys*, a series of popular, low-budget films that ran to 48 installments between 1946 and 1958. These movies, which kept to a steady formula (imagine a more racist *Scooby-Doo*), featured a tough group of young men on the Lower East Side who were forever getting in fights, going after get-rich-quick schemes, and speaking in a New York City variant punctuated with ludicrous solecisms: "Housewives all over da country will put me up on a pedestrian." (Incidentally, *Spook Busters*, one of the earliest Bowery Boys films, had the working title *Ghost Busters*.) This schtick was so popular that other long-running film series used the same premise—notably, *The East Side Kids* (1940–45), which ran for 22 films. In a typical East Side Kids film, *Let's Get Tough!* (1942), the eponymous kids used the Teddy Roosevelt sound, though it was old-fashioned even by then: "They got boined in a very severe fire"; "I'll moider 'im"; "We was just tryin' to be patriotic." In the same film, a policeman uses what was then the contemporary, more modern pronunciation: "se:vice." (Shemp Howard, one of the Three Stooges, cut his teeth as a child actor in another similar series, *The Little Tough Guys*.)

83. John Alberti, *Screen Ages: A Survey of American Cinema* (New York: Routledge, 2015): 130. In *A Wild Hare* (1940), the first Bugs Bunny cartoon, he has the voice of Woody Woodpecker, including the laugh.

84. According to his official biography, Bugs was born on July 27, 1940, under the Brooklyn Dodgers stadium.

85. Kirsten Moana Thompson, "Classical Cel Animation, World War II, and Bambi," in Cynthia Lucia, Roy Grundmann, and Art Simon, eds., *American Film History: Selected Readings, Origins to 1960* (Hoboken, NJ: John Wiley & Sons, 2016), 318.

86. Ibid., 318.

87. Incidentally, I have a vivid childhood memory of my father waking me up in the middle of the night because the radio was playing "Who's on First" and he thought it was an important part of my education. That's what life was like before the internet; you had to take your education piecemeal, adding to it whenever the pieces presented themselves.

88. The illustrator Saul Steinberg, who came to the United States from Eastern Europe, believed that he saw in Mickey Mouse the same inhuman, comical, caricatured features that American culture often gave to African Americans. He believed that "in Walt Disney's head, Mickey Mouse was black . . . half-human, comic, even in the physical way he was represented with big white eyes . . . Comic and moving, but only human in some aspects." Deirdre Bair, *Saul Steinberg: A Biography* (New York: Doubleday, 2012), 88.

89. Rich DesRochers, *The New Humor in the Progressive Era: Americanization and the Vaudeville Comedian* (New York: Palgrave Macmillan, 2014), 2.

90. Alberti, *Screen Ages: A Survey of American Cinema*, 130.

91. Specifically, he imitates Bugs in his suprasegmentals.

92. Darryl Littleton, *Black Comedians on Black Comedy: How African-Americans Taught Us to Laugh* (New York: Applause Theatre and Cinema Books, 2006), 61.

93. Adam Gopnik, "Stand Up Guys," *The New Yorker* (May 12, 2003).

94. At the start of early episodes, the show ran a disclaimer stating, "Warning: The program you are about to see is *All in the Family*. It seeks to throw a humorous spotlight on our frailties, prejudices, and concerns. By making them a source of laughter, we hope to show—in a mature fashion—just how absurd they are." Sean Campbell, *The Sitcoms of Norman Lear* (Jefferson, NC: McFarland, 2007), 10–1.

95. There is no agreed-upon transcription for this sound. Some linguists write it as /eə/.

96. Bill Finger, the Batman writer who named Gotham, has said, "Originally I was going to call Gotham City 'Civic City.' Then I tried 'Capital City,' then 'Coast City.' Then I flipped through the New York City phone book and spotted the name 'Gotham Jewelers' and said, 'That's it,' Gotham City. We didn't call it New York because we wanted anybody in any city to identify with it."

Quoted in Crystal Bell, "Batman's Gotham City Map: What Does the Dark Knight's Home Really Look Like?" *The Huffington Post* (July 17, 2012).

97. Quoted in William Uricchio, "The Batman's Gotham City: Story, Ideology, Performance," in Jörn Ahrens and Arno Meteling, eds., *Comics and the City: Urban Space in Print, Picture, and Sequence* (New York: Continuum, 2010), 121–22.

98. Ibid., 122.

99. Quoted in Ibid., 122.

100. The character's voice actor in the film, Bradley Cooper, chose the New York accent. In the comic books, Rocket Raccoon has a Cockney accent.

101. Brian Jay Jones, *George Lucas: A Life* (New York: Little, Brown, 2016), 208–37.

102. George Lucas, "The Star Wars," dated May 1974.

103. In *Star Wars*, he does not say, "Your kindness is greatly appreciated."

104. "Sɔɪtənli. əm si θri pi oʊ, ˈjumən saɪbɔːg riˈleɪʃənz." The reason I'm using the anachronistic /ɔɪ/ for /r/ is that it feels right for this kind of character.

105. Character summaries for "World of Warcraft: Lord of the Clans," reported in the game blog Warcraftiii.net. Published January 1, 2004. Accessed January 27, 2018: http://archive.is/SK5GQ#selection-1365.0-1365.228.

106. "Goblin," World of Warcraft wiki. Accessed January 27, 2018. http://wow-wiki.wikia.com/wiki/Goblin.

107. To give yet another example of this cultural pressure in action, in *The Maltese Falcon* (1941), Humphrey Bogart, a New York native, refers to the film's MacGuffin as a "black bɝd," using what I have described in these pages as a Woody Allen /r/; nonetheless, some critics, recognizing that he plays a tough guy, have projected onto his speech a more stigmatized usage—"he calls the falcon a 'black boid'"—because that usage is what comes to mind when they imagine a tough New Yorker. James Naremore, "John Huston and *The Maltese Falcon*," in William Luhr, ed., *The Maltese Falcon: John Huston, Director* (New Brunswick, NJ: Rutgers University Press, 1995), 150.

108. Terms *sloppy, careless,* and *very little schooling* are from Labov, *The Social Stratification of English in New York City*, 341–7. In 1996, Dennis Preston conducted a study in which laypersons in South Carolina drew dialect regions onto a map of the United States. They labeled the Midwest with phrases such as "Yak," "No Identity at all," and "doesn't have an accent"; the South with phrases such as "Southern Hospitality," "Courteous and Gentlemanly," "Us—the Good People," "God's People," and "Country As In Music"; and New York and New Jersey with phrases such as "Fast & Rude," "Them—the bad guys," and "Scratch and Claw." I have to believe these maps were drawn with tongue firmly in cheek. Dennis R. Preston, "Where the Worst English Is Spoken," in E. W. Schneider, ed., *Focus on the USA* (Amsterdam, The Netherlands: John Benjamins, 1996), 297–360.

109. He continues, "Psychologists found that the public subconsciously identi-fied the stupid little man with the gun and his counterparts with Hitler, and strongly identified the rabbit—unarmed except for his wits and will to win—with themselves." Quoted in Susan Elizabeth Dalton, "Bugs and Daffy Go to War," *The Velvet Light Trap* 4 (Spring 1972): 44–5.

Chapter 3

1. This epigraph is from Charles Cutler's indispensable book, *O Brave New Words!: Native American Loanwords in Current English* (Norman and London: University of Oklahoma Press, 1994).

2. Nicoline Van der Sijs, *Cookies, Coleslaw, and Stoops: The Influence of Dutch on the North American Languages* (Amsterdam, The Netherlands: Amsterdam University Press, 2009), 26.

3. A compelling account of the circumstances that surrounded Hudson's voyage and Juet's travel writing is Douglas Hunter, *Half Moon: Henry Hudson and the Voyage that Redrew the Map of the New World* (New York: Bloomsbury, 2010).

4. Robert S. Grumet, *Manhattan to Minisink: American Indian Place Names in Greater New York and Vicinity* (Norman: University of Oklahoma Press, 2013), 1–2. See also Eric W. Sanderson, *Mannahatta: A Natural History of New York City* (New York: Abrams, 2009), 102–35.

5. In *synthetic* languages, like English, speakers can add inflections to a morpheme to make an individual word more complex: an English speaker can refer to a *cheese-hat-wearer*, whereas a speaker of French, an *analytic* language, must refer to *un homme qui porte un chapeau de fromage*. All languages from the Americas are polysynthetic.

6. The most famous instance of this kind of myth-making is the claim that the Inuit have a hundred words for snow. One response to this claim is that of course we have more words for things we live with daily, regardless of the language we speak; an English speaker in Alaska can name black ice, blizzards, crud, flurries, freezing fog, hail, powder, sleet, whiteouts, and so forth. But another response is that, because Inuktitut is a polysynthetic language, the Inuit have *infinite* words for snow, for the same boring reason that English speakers can create infinite sentences about snow. In Inuktitut, a word can be a sentence, never spoken before in the history of mankind and never to be spoken again. See, for example, Geoffrey Pollum, "The Great Eskimo Vocabulary Hoax," in *The Great Eskimo Vocabulary Hoax, and Other Irreverent Essays on the Study of Language* (Chicago: University of Chicago Press, 1991), 159–72.

7. Steven H. Jaffe, *New York at War: Four Centuries of Combat, Fear, and Intrigue in Gotham* (New York: Basic Books, 2012), 13. See also, for example, Russell Shorto, *The Island at the Center of the World* (New York: Doubleday, 2005), and Daniel K. Richter, "Brothers, Scoundrels, Metal Makers: Dutch

Constructions of Native American Constructions of the Dutch," *de Halve Maen* 71 (1998), 59–64.

8. Indigenous words and translations are from Grumet, *Manhattan to Minisink*.

9. Anne Raulin, "The Naming of Urban Space: A Study of Manhattan Place Names," dissertation, The New School (1984), 38.

10. Evan T. Pritchard, *Native New Yorkers: The Legacy of the Algonquin People of New York* (San Francisco: Council Oak Books, 2002), 35. See also Grumet, *Manhattan to Minisink*, 77–8.

11. Geoffrey D. Needler, "Three Studies in the Linguistic History of New York City," dissertation, Union Institute and University (1978), 88. See also Raulin, "The Naming of Urban Space," 38; van der Sijs, *Cookies, Coleslaw, and Stoops*, esp. 207; John McNamara, *History in Asphalt: The Origin of Bronx Street and Place Names* (Harrison, NY: Harbor Hill Books, 1978); Henry Moscow, *The Street Book: An Encyclopedia of Manhattan's Street Names and Their Origins* (New York: Fordham University Press, 1978).

12. Needler, "Three Studies in the Linguistic History of New York City," 88.

13. van der Sijs, *Cookies, Coleslaw, and Stoops*, 202–10. *Rhode Island*, originally *Roodt Eylandt*, likely has a similar origin for its name. Ibid., 51.

14. Ibid., 207.

15. Washington Irving, *Knickerbocker's History of New York*, vol. 1 (London: Cassell & Company, [1809] 1891), 83–4.

16. Thomas Campanella, *Brooklyn: The Once and Future City* (Princeton, NJ: Princeton University Press, 2019), 197.

17. Raulin, "Naming New York," 153.

18. Needler, "Three Studies in the Linguistic History of New York City," 31, 41.

19. Raulin, "The Naming of Urban Space," 71–5.

20. The island was renamed Liberty Island in 1956 in honor of its famous resident.

21. Riker's Island also contains a nursery, which produces trees for New York City's green spaces. McNamara, *History in Asphalt*, 194–5.

22. The families were Dutch, English, French, German, and Belgian, although the street names were sometimes later anglicized. Raulin, "The Naming of Urban Space," 68–81; Grumet, *Manhattan to Minisink*, 58–9.

23. New Netherland, the name for the larger governing area, became the Province of New York.

24. Raulin explains how street names were Anglicized: for Dutch names, the particle "van" was removed, as in the case of Cortlandt, or was run into the word, as in the case of Vandam. For French names, the particle "de" got the same treatment. And most names had alterations of sound and spelling, as in the case of William from its Dutch equivalent (Raulin, "The Naming of Urban Space," 125).

25. Needler, "Three Studies in the Linguistic History of New York City," 40–2.

26. Ibid., 40. See also Carl Horton Pierce, William Pennington Toler, and Harmon De Pau Nutting, *New Harlem Past and Present* (New York: New Harlem Publishing Company, 1903), 145–6.

27. Raulin, "The Naming of Urban Space," 136–45; Fierstein, *Naming New York,* 25, 61.

28. Ibid., 38–9. The name Staten Island became official in 1975.

29. Ibid., 152–79. The mansion named Chelsea was passed down to Clement Clarke Moore, who wrote the 1823 poem "A Visit from St. Nicholas" while living there.

30. Bruce Clark, *Native Liberty, Crown Sovereignty: The Existing Aboriginal Right of Self-Government in Canada* (Montreal: McGill-Queen's University Press, 1990), 99.

31. On the appropriation of native land as one of the rationales for the American Revolution, see, for example, Thomas P. Abernethy, *Western Lands and the American Revolution* (New York: Russell and Russell, [1937] 1959); Daniel M. Friedenberg, *Life, Liberty, and the Pursuit of Land* (Buffalo, NY: Prometheus Books, 1992); and Woody Holton, *Forced Founders: Indians, Debtors, Slaves, and the Making of the American Revolution in Virginia* (Chapel Hill: University of North Carolina Press, 1999). I am grateful to Jon W. Parmenter of Cornell University for directing me to this literature.

32. See, for example, Ruma Chopra, *Unnatural Rebellion: Loyalists in New York City during the Revolution* (Charlottesville: University of Virginia Press, 2011); and Judith Van Buskirk, *Generous Enemies: Patriots and Loyalists in Revolutionary New York* (Philadelphia: University of Pennsylvania Press, 2002).

33. Maya Jasanoff, *Liberty's Exiles: American Loyalists in the Revolutionary World* (New York: Vintage Books, 2011), 5–6, 91–4.

34. New York City remained the federal capital until 1790, when the capital moved farther south.

35. Raulin, "The Naming of Urban Space," 54, 113; Leonard Benardo and Jennifer Weiss, *Brooklyn by Name: How the Neighborhoods, Streets, Parks, Bridges, and More Got Their Names* (New York: New York University Press, 2006), 2; Fierstein, *Naming New York.*

36. Raulin, "The Naming of Urban Space," 147–9. See also Fierstein, *Naming New York.*

37. Raulin, "The Naming of Urban Space," 41–6.

38. T. J. C. Brasser, "The Coastal Algonkians," in Eleanor Leacock and Nancy Lurie, eds., *North American Indians in Historical Perspective* (New York: Random House, 1971), 83. Washington Irving, "To the Editor of *The Knickerbocker,*" in *The Works of Washington Irving,* vol. 4 (New York: Peter Fenelon Collier, 1897), 437–40. Raulin discusses both authors in "The Naming of Urban Space," 45–51.

39. Quoted in Phyllis Lee Levin, *Abigail Adams: A Biography* (New York: St. Martin's Press, [1987] 2001), 91.

40. George Washington, letter to New York City mayor James Duane (April 10, 1785).

41. Gerard Koeppel, *City on a Grid: How New York Became New York* (New York: Perseus Books, 2015), 11–6.

42. Ibid., 18–28.

43. Ibid., 20–34. In one proposal for New York City's street system, New York would have been a grid—a necessary rationalization of the land, since the land was being sold in lots—but many streets would have taken acute rather than right angles, and would have curved around natural hills (Koeppel, *City on a Grid*, 119–20). See also Gerard Koeppel, "How New York City Could Have Looked Like Paris," *The New York Post* (November 8, 2015).

44. Koeppel, *City on a Grid*, 119–20. See also Robert T. Augustyn and Paul E. Cohen, *Manhattan in Maps, 1587–2014* (Mineola, NY: Dover Publications, 2014) 86–8.

45. Andrea Renner, "Opening First Avenue," in Hillary Ballon, ed., *The Greatest Grid: The Master Plan of Manhattan, 1811–2011* (New York: Museum of the City of New York/Columbia University Press, 2012), 74–5; Reuben Rose-Redwood, "How Manhattan's Topography Changed and Stayed the Same," in *The Greatest Grid*, 80; Carolyn Yerkes, "Rocks on 81st Street," in *The Greatest Grid*, 83.

46. Sibyl Moholy-Nagy, *Matrix of Man: An Illustrated History of Urban Environment* (New York: Frederick A. Praeger, 1968), 227. Quoted in Raulin, "The Naming of Urban Space," 161.

47. Raulin, "The Naming of Urban Space," 136–41; Fierstein, *Naming New York*, 35, 66.

48. Work on Central Park began in 1856. Writes one historian, "if this move had been delayed for as little as ten years, there probably would have been no park at all; the land would have become too precious." Stephen Birmingham, *"Our Crowd": The Great Jewish Families of New York* (New York: Macmillan, [1967] 2015), 84. On the building of Central Park, see, for example, Roy Rosenzweig and Elizabeth Blackmar, *The Park and the People: A History of Central Park* (Ithaca, NY: Cornell University Press, 1992), and Morrison H. Heckscher, *Creating Central Park* (New Haven, CT: Yale University Press, 2008).

49. Sanderson, *Mannahatta*, 82.

50. Raulin, "The Naming of Urban Space," 177–9.

51. *30 Rock*, "The Tuxedo Begins" (February 16, 2012).

52. To extend an old saw: in England, you have to hear a man speak to know whether you despise him; in America, you have to see him; in New York, you have to know his nearest cross-street.

53. On the relationship between the grid system and Manhattan's rapacious real-estate market, see Max Page, *The Creative Destruction of Manhattan, 1900–1940* (Chicago: University of Chicago Press, 1999).

54. Jeff Nunokawa, writing in London, is, as usual, apt: "The first thing you notice here is the real estate. Not just what's for sale and for how much, but what could be and for how much. One of the things that charter'd means is zoned for commercial purposes, and one of the things that Blake is saying is that everything is nowadays. (The word used to have a little more nobility: it was supposed to be some kind of royal contract.) By calling both the streets and the river that runs through it charter'd, Blake is basically saying that all maps are basically real estate apps.: nothing's charted, not even a river as old as the hills, older even than the ancient Romans who first charted it, that's not also charter'd—going back to the ancient Romans who first charter'd it as a means of expanding their tax base. You wander the streets around here and you think the same thing you think wandering around any capital type city—*wow! this must cost a fortune!*" Jeff Nunokawa, Facebook (August 20, 2017), "4850. Introduction to London Real Estate."

55. Kate Simon, *Fifth Avenue: A Very Social History* (New York: Harcourt Brace Jovanovich, 1978), 22.

56. Ibid., 88–95.

57. James Trager, *Park Avenue: Street of Dreams* (New York: Atheneum, 1990), 2.

58. In the 1840's, the city lowered the tracks into a cut in the road to prevent further accidents from trains hitting people and animals. "The Fourth Avenue Boys, a gang of thugs, lived in holes dug into the sides of the cut." Trager, *Park Avenue* 2–29.

59. Ibid., 29; Raulin, "The Naming of Urban Space," 142–3.

60. Raulin, "The Naming of Urban Space," 142–3.

61. Kurt Schlichting, *Grand Central Terminal: Railroads, Engineering, and Architecture in New York City* (Baltimore, MD: Johns Hopkins University Press, 2001), 50–60.

62. As suggested, for instance, in the 1927 *New York Times* article quoted in Peter Bearman, *Doormen* (Chicago: University of Chicago Press, 2005), 1ff.

63. Renner, "Shacks on Fifth Avenue," in *The Greatest Grid*, 98.

64. Ibid.

65. See, for example, Tyler Anbinder, *Five Points: The 19th-Century New York City Neighborhood That Invented Tap Dance, Stole Elections, and Became the World's Most Notorious Slum* (New York: The Free Press, 2001).

66. Timothy J. Gilfoyle, *City of Eros: New York City, Prostitution, and the Commercialization of Sex, 1790–1920* (New York: W. W. Norton, 1992), 50–3.

67. "Even allowing for the exaggerated claims of the guidebook, most of the dwellings in Corlears Hook were devoted to the sale of sex" (Gilfoyle, *City of Eros*, 52).

68. Quoted in Irving Lewis Allen, *The City in Slang: New York Life and Popular Speech* (Oxford: Oxford University Press, 1993), 185.

69. Gilfoyle, *City of Eros*, 49–50.

70. David L. Gold, "Towards a Dossier of the Still Unclear Immediate Etymon(s?) of American English Slang *Hooker* 'Whore' (With Remarks on the Origin of

American English Barnegat, Dixie, Fly ~Vlei ~Vley ~Vlaie ~Vly, Gramercy Park, Hell Gate, Jazz, Sloughter, and Spuyten Duyvil)," in David L. Gold, *Studies in Etymology and Etiology*, ed. Félix Rodríguez González and Antonio Lillo Buadez (San Vicente, Spain: Publicaciones de la Universidad de Alciante, 2009), 110.

71. Charles Dickens, *American Notes for General Circulation*, 2nd ed., vol. 1 (London: Chapman and Hall, 1842), 212. Quoted in (Anbinder, *Five Points*, 32–3).

72. Anbinder, *Five Points*, 32–4.

73. Ibid., 176–89.

74. Quoted in the Oxford English Dictionary.

75. Joseph J. Varga, *Hell's Kitchen and the Battle for Urban Space: Class Struggle and Progressive Reform in New York City, 1894–1914* (New York: Monthly Review Press, 2013), 18–21; Fierstein, *Naming New York*, 123–4.

76. The *New York Herald* began using the term *Tenderloin* in reference to a police precinct in 1880: "What is the matter in the Twenty-ninth precinct, 'the tenderloin steak of the city?' Portions of it average more dangerous characters than an equal amount of space in Sing Sing prison, but they have done so for a long time without causing as much nuisance and bold crime as at present." "The Twenty-Ninth Precinct," *The New York Herald* (September 4, 1880).

77. Marcy S. Sacks, *Before Harlem: The Black Experience in New York City before World War I* (Philadelphia: University of Pennsylvania Press, 1996), 95–6.

78. Rose-Redwood, "How Manhattan's Topography Changed and Stayed the Same," in *The Greatest Grid*, 80.

79. Anbinder, *Five Points*, 46.

80. Rose-Redwood, "Numbering and Naming Manhattan's Streets," in *The Greatest Grid*, 95.

81. Anonymous, "Counterpoint: Broadway," in *The Greatest Grid*, 155.

82. Ibid.

83. Anonymous, "Counterpoint: Broadway," in *The Greatest Grid*, 155; Michael Miscione, "Promenading and Biking on the Boulevard," in *The Greatest Grid*, 159.

84. The city initially planned to call Union Square *Union Place*. Fierstein, *Naming New York*, 98–106.

85. See, for example, Lynne B. Sagalyn, *Times Square Roulette: Rethinking the City Icon* (Cambridge, MA: MIT Press, 2001).

86. Lynne B. Sagalyn, *Times Square Roulette: Rethinking the City Icon* (Cambridge, MA: MIT Press, 2001), 37–8.

87. Maurer, *Argot of the Racetrack*, 3.

88. John McNamara, *History in Asphalt: The Origin of Bronx Street and Place Names* (The Bronx, NY: The Bronx County Historical Society [1978] 2010), 116. Jerome also helped to establish the American Jockey Club itself.

89. Quoted in Barry Popik, "First 'Big Apple' Explanation: February 18, 1924," The Big Apple website (July 11, 2004). Gerald Cohen identifies the first published usage of the term *Big Apple*, applied to New York City, in a 1921 column about horseracing in the New York *Morning Telegraph*: "J. P. Smith, with Tippity Witchet and others of the L. T. Bauer string, is scheduled to start for 'the big apple' to-morrow after a most prosperous Spring campaign at Bowie and Havre de Grace." John J. Fitz Gerald, New York *Morning Telegraph* (May 3, 1921); cited in Gerald Leonard Cohen, *Origin of New York City's Nickname "The Big Apple"* (New York: Peter Lang, 1991), 16–7.

90. The original line is, "What news on the Rialto?" William Shakespeare, *The Merchant of Venice*, Act 3, Scene 1, line 1.

91. Sagalyn, *Times Square Roulette*, 37–8.

92. When, in 1928, the Times Tower inaugurated a new form of news delivery, the *electric zipper*—"a five-foot-high, 360-foot long ribbon of 14,800 electric-light bulbs that wrapped around the base of the building and spelled out the news in traveling headlines"—the effect was to affirm the identity of the square as a place of light (Sagalyn, *Times Square Roulette*, 33–40).

93. Tim Edensor, "Lights, City, Action . . .," in John Hannigan and Greg Richards. eds., *The SAGE Handbook of New Urban Studies* (London: SAGE Publications, 2017), 219.

94. Sagalyn, *Times Square Roulette*, 39–40.

95. "In the four-year period between 1856 and 1860, one-half of all the immigrants arriving to the United States remained in New York City" (in Frank, "The Speech of New York City," 11–8). See also Bonfiglio, *Race and the Rise of Standard American*, 51.

96. Paul Moses, *An Unlikely Union: The Love-Hate Story of New York's Irish and Italians* (New York: New York University Press, 2015), 89–94.

97. See McNamara, *History in Asphalt*.

98. In 2011, the demographic scholar Andrew Beveridge embarked on a "New Littles" project, which used population data to identify emerging ethnic enclaves in New York City—including Little Thailand, Little Greece, Little Bangladesh, Little Peru, and Little British West Indies. The project's website is https://project.wnyc.org/census-maps/littles/littles.html.

99. Fierstein, *Naming New York*, 56–7.

100. Bernardo and Weiss, *Brooklyn by Name*, 3.

101. In 1945, as a celebration of the United States's friendship with Latin American nations, the city changed Sixth Avenue to *Avenue of the Americas*.

102. Place names and histories are from Fierstein, *Naming New York*.

103. William Wallace Tooker, *The Indian Place-Names on Long Island and Islands Adjacent, with Their Probable Significations*, ed. Alexander F. Chamberlain (New York: G. P. Putnam's Sons, 1911), xiii.

104. See, for example, Wilbur Zelinsky, *Nation into State: The Shifting Symbolic Foundations of American Nationalism* (Chapel Hill: University of North Carolina Press, 1988).

105. See, for example, Mary Waters and Philip Kasinitz, "Immigrants in New York City: Reaping the Benefits of Continuous Immigration," *Daedalus* 142, 3 (2013): 92–106; Philip Kasinitz, John Mollenkopf, and Mary Waters, "Becoming American/Becoming New Yorkers: Immigrant Incorporation in a Majority Minority City," *The International Migration Review* 36, 4 (2002): 1020–36; Foner, "How Exceptional Is New York?," 999–1023; and Keogan, "A Sense of Place," 223–53.

106. David Dinkins, *A Mayor's Life: Governing New York's Gorgeous Mosaic* (New York: PublicAffairs, 2013), 162.

107. Saul Steinberg, "View of the World from 9th Avenue" (1976).

108. Kasinitz et al., "Becoming American/Becoming New Yorkers," 1022–34.

Chapter 4

1. Edith Wharton, *A Backward Glance* (New York: D. Appleton–Century Company, 1934), 55.

2. Charles G. Shaw, "Out-of-Towner," *The New Yorker* (November 6, 1926): 23.

3. Allen, *The City in Slang*, 200.

4. Gunther Barth, *City People: The Rise of Modern City Culture in the Nineteenth Century* (Oxford: Oxford University Press, 1982), 66–7.

5. David Maurer comments that the professional language of criminals "appears to be pretty well standardized from coast to coast and from the Gulf well into Canada." David W. Maurer, *Language of the Underworld* (Lexington: The University Press of Kentucky, 1981), 39. The words in **bold lettering** in this chapter are those I have found first attested in New York City, either in or out of the Oxford English Dictionary.

6. Michael Adams, *Slang: The People's Poetry* (Oxford, UK: Oxford University Press, 2009), 8–9; 49. The word *cant*, which has been used to denote thieves' language since the Renaissance, originated as a word for *song*.

7. Adams quotes the complaint of Amy March in the novel *Little Women*: "Jo does use such slang words." The implication is that boys can use slang, but not young ladies. Quoted in Adams, *Slang*, 78.

8. Jonathan Lighter, "Slang," in John Algeo, ed., *Cambridge History of the English Language*, volume 6: North America (2001), 220. Quoted in Adams, *Slang*, 48–9.

9. Consider, for example, the term *poppycock*, which derives from a Dutch word meaning *shit* (specifically, *soft shit*). If the First Lady of the United States were to say "poppycock," nobody would care; the word has become respectable. But in 2004, when Teresa Heinz Kerry, the wife of a presidential candidate, used the word "scumbag" in a television interview, the media rioted; evidently, the word still carried too much residue of its origins as a slang word for *condom*. See, for example, Judith Thurman, "The Candidate's Wife," *The New Yorker* (September 27, 2004).

10. This term may have originated in carnival lingo mimicking banjo music; as David Maurer discusses, traveling carnivals had a substantial grift culture. Maurer, *Language of the Underworld*. See also David W. Maurer, *Whiz Mob: A Correlation of the Technical Argot of Pickpockets with Their Behavior Pattern* (New Haven, CT: College & University Press, 1964).

11. I draw extensively on Maurer, *Whiz Mob*, and Maurer, *Language of the Underworld*, for examples of slang in this chapter. For the definition of "shoo-in," see David Maurer, *Argot of the Racetrack* (Tuscaloosa, Alabama: American Dialect Society, 1951), 58.

12. Dick Leith, *A Social History of English* (New York: Routledge, 1983), 83.

13. Slang terms for money in 19th- and early 20th-century America include, and were far from limited to, *ace, balsam, blunt, brads, brass, bumblebee, can, case, case-note, century, chicken feed, chink, chinkers, chips, clover, c-note, coachwheel, dace, darby, deuce, dews, dibs, dots, double saw, double sawbuck, dragons, duce, fat, fin, finniff, g-note, gelter, goldfinch, greed, hard cole, honey, iron men, iron money, jack, kale, lush green, moolah, monkey, muck, Ned, negotiable grass, new light, ochre, plate, poney, posh, push-note, quetor, quids, q.v., rag, ready, red, rhino, ridge, sawbuck, scratch, screaves, screen, sicer, skinny, slat, smackers, smelts, soap, soft, Spanish, sprat, stuff, sucrose, sugar, ten yards, threswins, tizzy, thrums, spondulicks, wad, wind, x-ray, XX,* and *yard.*

14. Lawrence Friedman, "Crimes of Mobility," *Stanford Law Review* 43 (1991): 638. Friedman quotes Anthony Trollope's comment that Americans were not "fixed in their employment. . . . If a young Benedict cannot get along as a lawyer at Salem, perhaps he may thrive as a shoemaker at Thermopylae. Jefferson B. Johnson fails in the lumber line at Eleutheria, but hearing of an opening for a Baptist preacher at Big Mud Creek moves himself off with his wife and three children at a week's notice" (quoted in Friedman, "Crimes of Mobility," 639–40ff). Incidentally, this comment ridicules American conventions of naming people and places, which seemed to some commentators to be pretty highfalutin' for the frontier.

15. Phineas Taylor Barnum, *The Life of P. T. Barnum: Written by Himself* (London: Sampson Low, Son, & Co., 1855), 28–36, 143.

16. "A Swindler," *New York Journal and Patriotic Register*, New York, New York (February 22, 1800), 3. A money order could be cashed at any store, whereas a check had to be cashed at a bank.

17. "The Swindler Detected," *The True American*, Trenton, New Jersey (August 27, 1810), 2.

18. "Patterson Falls," *New York Journal*, New York, New York (September 1, 1810), 2.

19. "A Swindler," *Albany Gazette*, Albany, New York (July 25, 1820), 2.

20. Lawrence Friedman, *Guarding Life's Dark Secrets: Legal and Social Controls over Reputation, Propriety, and Privacy* (Stanford, CA: Stanford University Press, 2007), 30; Friedman, "Crimes of Mobility," 650–3.

21. "Arrest of the Confidence Man," *New-York Herald* (July 8, 1849).

22. Friedman comments that this number is "surely the tip of the iceberg," given that many crimes went uncaught. Friedman, "Crimes of Mobility," 651–53.

23. These descriptions are from George W. Matsell, *Vocabulum; or, the Rogue's Lexicon* (New York: George W. Matsell & Co., 1859).

24. Poe, in "Diddling Considered as One of the Exact Sciences," first published under the title "Raising the Wind; or, Diddling Considered as One of the Exact Sciences" in the Philadelphia *Saturday Courier* of October 14, 1843, and reprinted in *The Broadway Journal* of September 13, 1845.

25. See, for example, *The New York Times*, "Confidence Man Jailed; McCloundy, Who Once Sold the Brooklyn Bridge, Faces Life Term" (July 8, 1928), 21.

26. Edward Berenson, *The Trial of Madame Caillaux* (Berkeley: University of California Press, [1992] 1993), 211.

27. Michel Foucault, *Discipline and Punish: The Birth of the Prison*, trans. Alan Sheridan (New York: Vintage Books, 1975), 69.

28. Crime stories were of course not new in themselves; see, for example, John Brewer, *A Sentimental Murder: Love and Madness in the Eighteenth Century* (New York: Farrar, Straus and Giroux, 2004).

29. She inspired Edgar Allan Poe's pioneering detective story, "The Mystery of Marie Rogêt." While *romans-feuilletons* eventually went out of style, this style of crime reporting never quite did; we can see it, for example, in coverage of the 1989 case of the Central Park Jogger. A classic essay on the news coverage of the jogger case is Joan Didion, "New York: Sentimental Journeys," *The New York Review of Books* (January 17, 1991).

30. Benedict Anderson, *Imagined Communities: Reflections on the Origin and Spread of Nationalism* (London: Verso, [1983] 2006), 35.

31. "The Arrest of the Confidence Man."

32. Matsell, *Vocabulum*, 6.

33. Ned Buntline, *The Mysteries and Miseries of New York: A Story of Real Life* (New York: W. W. Burgess, 1849), 5.

34. The terms given as examples in this paragraph are just a few of many.

35. "Caveat Emptor," *The New Yorker* (December 28, 1929): 13. To this reader, *The New Yorker* in its early years resembled the early *Gawker*, at least in its dim view of human nature and its interest in bad behavior.

36. See, for example, Glenn Shirley, *Hello, Sucker!: The Story of Texas Guinan* (New York: Eakin Press, 1989).

37. I like a quip published in the *National Police Gazette* in 1882: "We're not going to deny the devil nor go back on him in any way. He's got too big a pull in New York and in the world generally."

38. Simon, *Fifth Avenue*, 134–6; Stephen Leacock, "A Hero in Homespun: or, the Life Struggle of Hezekiah Hayloft," in *Nonsense Novels* (New York: John Lane Company, 1920), 94.

39. See, for example, Katharine Fullerton Gerould, "The Nature of Hokum," *Harper's Magazine* (August 1927), 285–90.

40. H.L. Mencken, *The American Language* (New York: Alfred A. Knopf, [1919] 2006), 200.

41. A *ringer*, incidentally, meant a good horse that races under a false identity, allowing a big payout for a win.

42. George Randolph Chester, *Get-Rich-Quick Wallingford: A Cheerful Account of the Rise and Fall of an American Business Buccaneer.*

43. Ned Buntline describes "gnof" as slang for *pickpocket*, which must be a case of his mishearing the same word. Matsell is prone to the same parochialisms; he defines "gonnoff" as "a thief that has attained the higher walks of his profession" and "romoney" as "a gipsy."

44. *Faker*, for street peddler, adapts the Arabic *fakir*, but this certainly came directly from thieves' cant in England rather than from New Yorkers who spoke Arabic.

45. Kevin Kenny, "Labor and Labor Organizations," in Marion Casey and J. J. Lee, eds., *Making the Irish American: History and Heritage of the Irish in the United States* (New York: New York University Press, 2006), 356–7.

46. Allen, *The City in Slang*, 46.

47. My thanks to Barry McCrea for this observation.

48. Ibid., 213–4.

49. *Bull* derives from the Spanish Romani *bul* (Allen, *The City in Slang*, 213).

50. *Copper* is a borrowing from underworld slang in London. Allen, *The City in Slang*, 214.

51. Robert Darnton, *The Great Cat Massacre and Other Episodes in French Cultural History* (New York: Basic Books, 1984), 53–61.

52. "Fraud," *New-York Spectator*, New York, New York (September 29, 1829), 1.

53. "Personal Intelligence," *New York Herald*, New York, New York (November 6, 1875), 6.

54. "New Dorp Club Grounds," *New York Herald*, New York, New York (November 15, 1874); "Cocking on Long Island a Rattling Series of Battles on Newtown Creek," *New York Herald*, New York, New York (January 31, 1877); "Bond Negotiators Arrested," *The New York Herald*, New York, New York (July 26, 1877).

55. See, for example, Jackson Lears, *Fables of Abundance: A Cultural History of Advertising in America* (New York: Basic Books, 1994).

56. See, for example, Karen Halttunen, *Confidence Men and the Painted Women: A Study of Middle-Class Culture in America, 1830–1870* (New Haven, CT: Yale University Press, 1982). See also William Leach, *Land of Desire: Merchants, Power, and the Rise of a New American Culture* (New York: Vintage, 1993), and Jackson Lears, *Something for Nothing: Luck in America* (New York: Viking, 2003).

57. See, for example, James W. Cook, *The Arts of Deception: Playing with Fraud in the Age of Barnum* (Cambridge, MA: Harvard University Press, 2001).

58. P. T. Barnum, *The Life of P. T. Barnum: Written by Himself* (London: Sampson Low, Son, & Co., 1855), 22.

59. Andree Brooks, "Debunking the Myth of P. T. Barnum," *The New York Times* (October 3, 1982). Retrieved April 27, 2016.

60. P. T. Barnum, *The Humbugs of the World: An Account of Humbugs, Delusions, Impositions, Quackeries, Deceits, and Deceivers Generally, in All Ages* (New York: Carleton, 1866), 12–3.

61. For example, during the exhibition of Joice Heth—a slave, purported to be 161 years old, whom Barnum purchased and took on tour under the claim that she had been George Washington's nurse—Barnum had a letter published, under an anonymous signature, that declared the famous woman to be no woman at all, but a "curiously constructed automaton." Writes Harris, "The crowds who had seen the slave once immediately returned to check out their possible deception." Neil Harris, *Humbug: The Art of P. T. Barnum* (Chicago: The University of Chicago Press, 1973), 23.

62. Quoted in Ibid., 54–5.

63. Ibid., 61.

64. P. T. Barnum, *The Life of P. T. Barnum: Written by Himself* (London: Sampson Low, Son, & Co., 1855).

65. Kenneth Burke, "Literature as Equipment for Living," in David H. Richter, ed., *The Critical Tradition: Classic Texts and Contemporary Trends*, 2nd. ed. (Boston: Bedford Books, 1998), 596.

66. Richards, "The Yankee Schoolboy," *The Magnet* 150, 5 (December 24, 1910), cover.

67. Richards, "The Yankee Schoolboy," 8. A great deal of comedy in the story comes from the English boys' inability to understand, and Fish's unwillingness to depart from, the language that he calls "Plain United States."

68. "hustle, v.". OED Online. September 2019. Oxford University Press. https://www-oed-com.proxy.library.stonybrook.edu/view/Entry/89734?rskey=aiWjhw&result=2&isAdvanced=false (accessed November 28, 2019).

69. P. T. Barnum, *The Art of Money-Getting: Or, Golden Rules for Making Money* (Bedford, MA: Applewood Books, [1880] 1999), 42. Stories of good hustles became celebrated throughout American culture. As another example, when Jenny Lind, a famous singer known as "The Swedish Nightingale," came to America on tour, the hatter John Genin, whose establishment stood near Barnum's on Broadway, sent her a riding hat as a gift. When she accepted it, he advertised hats of the same make at his store as "Jenny Lind Riding Hats." No swindle here; just a good, sharp hustle. Barbara Penner, "'Colleges for the Teaching of Extravagance': New York Palace Hotels," *Winterthur Portfolio* 44, 2–3 (Summer/Autumn 2010): 174.

70. Brittany Lewis, "The Secrets behind Young Jeezy's Hustle & Ambition," *Global Grind* (December 18, 2011).

71. I sometimes hear the kids in my neighborhood shouting, "John Cena! John Cena!" as they play.

72. Allen, *The City in Slang*, 15.
73. Many slang words came from the profession of sailing, for New York was a seafaring town, and shipbuilding and sailing were big industries. For example, *reef*, a sailing term for the action of drawing, as in drawing up a rope, was a verb referring to lifting a purse to steal.

Chapter 5

1. "Although plugging could take place anywhere, pluggers' most important and regular locales were music and department stores, nickelodeons and later movie houses, and restaurants, cafes, and dance halls." David Suisman, *Selling Sounds: The Commercial Revolution in American Music* (Cambridge, MA: Harvard University Press, 2009), 64, 77–8. If you hate Muzak in department stores now, imagine the late 19th century, when kids would sing by the makeup counter.
2. Quoted in Ben Yagoda, *The B Side: The Death of Tin Pan Alley and the Rebirth of the Great American Song* (New York: Penguin, 2015), 33.
3. Suisman, *Selling Sounds*, 58.
4. Isaac Goldberg, *Tin Pan Alley: A Chronicle of American Popular Music* ([New York: John Day, 1930], New York: Frederick Ungar, 1961), 211. Quoted in (Suisman, *Selling Sounds*, 11).
5. Gradually, the actual location of Tin Pan Alley moved north up Broadway (Suisman, *Selling Sounds*, 17–22).
6. Charles Hamm, quoted in Philip Furia, *The Poets of Tin Pan Alley: A History of America's Great Lyricists* (Oxford, UK: Oxford University Press, [1990] 1922), 22.
7. Suisman, *Selling Sounds*; Ben Yagoda, *The B Side: The Death of Tin Pan Alley and the Rebirth of the Great American Song* (New York: Penguin, 2015).
8. William Zinsser, *Easy to Remember: The Great American Songwriters and their Songs* (Boston: David R. Godine, 2001), 72–104.
9. Suisman, *Selling Sounds*, 34. See also Berndt Ostendorf, " 'The Diluted Second Generation': German-Americans in Music, 1870–1920," in Hartmut Keil, ed., *German Workers' Culture in the United States, 1850 to 1920* (Washington, DC: Smithsonian, 1988), 261–87.
10. Suisman, *Selling Sounds*, 34–5.
11. See, for example, Suisman, *Selling Sounds*, 34–5 and Neal Gabler, *An Empire of Their Own: How the Jews Invented Hollywood* (New York: Crown Publishers, 1988).
12. See, for example, Roberta Pearson and William Uricchio, "How Many Times Shall Caesar Bleed in Sport: Shakespeare and the Cultural Debate about Moving Pictures," in Lee Grieveson and Peter Kramer, eds., *The Silent Cinema Reader* (New York: Routledge, 2004), 155–68.

13. See, for example, *Course of Study in Literature for Elementary Schools Grades 1A–8B, As Adopted by the Board of Education July 13, 1927, with a Syllabus as Adopted by the Board of Superintendents June 30, 1927* (Board of Education, The City of New York, 1927).

14. Meredith Martin's *The Rise and Fall of Meter: Poetry and English National Culture, 1860–1930* (Princeton, NJ: Princeton University Press, 2012) and Catherine Robson's *Heart Beats: Everyday Life and the Memorized Poem* (Princeton, NJ: Princeton University Press, 2012) examine schoolroom memorization in a mostly British context. The practice persisted in North America for decades after it declined in Britain.

15. Harriet Hyman Alonso, *Yip Harburg: Legendary Lyricist and Human Rights Activist* (Middletown, CT: Wesleyan University Press, 2012), 9.

16. Ibid., 14; Philip Furia, *Ira Gershwin: The Art of the Lyricist* (Oxford: Oxford University Press, [1996] 1997), 9–10.

17. Furia, *Ira Gershwin*, 7. Harburg's parents were immigrants from Russia. His father read him Shalom Aleichem and took him to the Yiddish theater on the weekends, telling Harburg's mother that they were going to synagogue. Harburg later told an interviewer, "My parents were Orthodox Jews, though not as strict as the Hasidim. To some extent they were tongue-in-cheek Orthodox" (Alonso, *Yip Harburg*, 5–6).

18. Ibid., 21–3; Zinsser, *Easy to Remember*, 145–6.

19. Alonso, *Yip Harburg*, 24–5.

20. As with today's book publishing business, Tin Pan Alley publishers relied on occasional hits to survive. "For every ten songs a Tin Pan Alley firm issued, nine might recoup only half the publisher's expenditures—which consisted principally of the purchase of the song or payment of an advance on royalties; printing; lithography expenses for the sheet music cover; and—by far the biggest expense—advertising and promotion. This revenue, however, might be enough to cover the firm's fixed costs (rent, wages, and so on), that is, to keep the publisher in business. Then, if one of the ten songs was even a modest success (yielding, say, fifty thousand copies sold), it would cover the cost of publishing all ten tunes and return a small profit"(Suisman, *Selling Sounds*, 42–4).

21. Alonso, *Yip Harburg*, 102.

22. Sondheim went so far as to say that the clues in a good crossword "have many characteristics of a literary manner: cleverness, humor, even a pseudo-aphoristic grace." He compared the authors of crosswords to Oscar Wilde and Somerset Maugham, legendary playwrights of wit and elegance. Stephen Sondheim, "How to Do a Real Crossword Puzzle," *New York* (April 8, 1968); Samuel G. Freedman, "The Words and Music of Stephen Sondheim," *The New York Times* (April 1, 1984).

23. His schooling included a "rigorous training in classical poetic forms." " 'We were well-versed,' a classmate recalled, 'in the ballad, the triolet, the rondo, the villanelle, the sonnet. We were highly disciplined. We were never permitted

to use an oracular rhyme or a tonal rhyme like *home* and *tone*'" (Furia, *Ira Gershwin*, 8–10).

24. Alonso, *Yip Harburg*, x.
25. Suisman, *Selling Sounds*, 49.
26. Ibid., 50.
27. Less often, the sequence may be A-B-A-B or A-B-A-C, where C is basically A with jazz hands.
28. Furia, *Ira Gershwin*, 9.
29. Zinsser, *Easy to Remember*, 40–7.
30. Stephen Sondheim, "Theater Lyrics," in *Playwrights, Lyricists, Composers on Theater*, ed. Otis L. Guernsey, Jr. (New York: Dodd, Mead and Co., 1974), 64.
31. Charlotte Greenspan, *Pick Yourself Up: Dorothy Fields and the American Musical* (Oxford: Oxford University Press, 2008), 28–9.
32. Furia, *Ira Gershwin*, 9.
33. Zinsser, *Easy to Remember*, 26.
34. Both groups would come to have the same nickname for the period of increased migration to the city: "The Great Migration."
35. Deborah Grace Winer, *On the Sunny Side of the Street: The Life and Lyrics of Dorothy Fields* (New York: Schirmer, 1997), 36.
36. A generation earlier, the enormous success of Irving Berlin's "Alexander's Ragtime Band" (1911), which some historians have used as a signpost marking the end of the dominance of the waltz meter in popular songs and the start of the dominance of syncopated rhythm, earned Berlin the nickname "The Ragtime King." Suisman, *Selling Sounds*, 53–5.
37. "New" refers not to the date of coinage, but to the spiking popularity of these terms in the early 20th century. Zinsser, *Easy to Remember*, 27–8.
38. Quoted in Zinsser, *Easy to Remember*, 88.
39. Furia, *The Poets of Tin Pan Alley*, 12–13, 145–9; Winer, *On the Sunny Side of the Street*, 70.
40. Zinsser, *Easy to Remember*, 47.
41. See, for example, John Seabrook, *The Song Machine: Inside the Hit Factory* (New York: Norton, 2015).
42. Her account of her first songwriting contract, with Mills Music, offers a useful glimpse into the factory side of Tin Pan Alley. "Mills Music," she said, "was the kind of firm that when Valentino died, the next day they had a song out, 'There's a New Star in Heaven since Valentino passed Away.' When Caruso died, the next day there was 'A Songbird in Heaven Named Caruso.' Now, at this time a lady named Ruth Elder was going to fly the Atlantic. So Mills says, 'She's going to fly today and we have to have a song. I'll help you out. I'll give you fifty dollars to do this if you can do it by tomorrow. I'll even give you a title—'Our American Girl.'" After that, Fields started writing for Mills full-time: "I became their fifty dollars a night girl. For fifty dollars they got a hundred words" (Greenspan, *Pick Yourself Up*, 27).

43. Greenspan, *Pick Yourself Up*, xv.

44. Winer, *On the Sunny Side of the Street*, 48.

45. He was not going to a ballgame at the time; when he wrote the lyrics, he had never *been* to a ballgame.

46. Alonso, *Yip Harburg*, 28.

47. Ibid., 88.

48. Ibid., 86.

49. Edwin Milton Royle, "The Vaudeville Theatre," *Scribner's Magazine* 26 (October 1899): 495.

50. Harold Arlen recalled this commuting culture as a small, clubby world: "It was a great period! Maybe it was the accident of all of us working there because of the Depression. Practically every talent you can name. So many. Jerry Kern, Harry Warren, the Gershwins, Dorothy Fields and Jimmy McHugh. Oscar Hammerstein—even Berlin, although he didn't stick around. All of us, writing pictures so well. We were all on the weekly radio Hit Parade" (Alonso, *Yip Harburg*, 104).

51. Freedman, "The Words and Music of Stephen Sondheim." See also Mark Eden Horowitz, *Sondheim on Music: Minor Details and Major Decisions* (Lanham, MD, and Oxford: The Scarecrow Press, 2003).

52. At Williams College, he apprenticed under the composer Milton Babbitt, who made him take a metaphorical ruler and graph paper to the music of Mozart and Jerome Kern, and Robert Barrow, a music professor who showed him the power of Apollonian form and control. "Barrow made me realize that all my Romantic views of art were nonsense," Sondheim later said. "I had always thought an angel came and sat down on your shoulder and whispered in your ear, 'Dah-dah-dah-*dum*.' It never occurred to me that art was something worked out. And suddenly it was skies opening up. As soon as you find out what a leading tone is, you think, oh my God. What a diatonic scale is—oh, my God! The logic of it. And, of course, what that meant to me was: well, I can do that. Because you just don't know. You think it's a talent, you think you're born with this thing. What I've found out and what I believed is that everyone is talented. It's just that some people get it developed and some don't." Quoted in Stephen Schiff, "Deconstructing Sondheim," in *The Sondheim Review* 17, 2 (2010): 16.

53. Stephen Sondheim, *Finishing the Hat: Collected Lyrics (1954–1981) with Attendant Comments, Principles, Heresies, Grudges, Whines, and Anecdotes* (New York: Alfred A. Knopf, 2010), xviii, footnote.

54. Sondheim, *Finishing the Hat*, 30.

55. See, for example, Ada Calhoun, "Where Musical-Makers Audition Their Ideas," *The New York Times* (November 28, 2004). I am not referring here to *developmental workshops*, in which creators already in the process of getting a play produced hire actors and start to develop the play on a bare-bones basis.

56. Interview with Greg Pliska, New York City (May 4, 2016).

57. See, for example, Dick Hebdige, *Cut 'n' Mix: Culture, Identity, and Caribbean Music* (London: Methuen, 1987); Tricia Rose, *Black Noise: Rap Music and Black Culture in Contemporary America* (Middletown, CT: Wesleyan University Press, 1994); Cheryl Keyes, *Rap Music and Street Consciousness* (Urbana: University of Illinois Press, 2002); Jeff Chang, *Can't Stop Won't Stop: A History of the Hip-Hop Generation* (New York: St. Martin's Press, 2005).

58. Joseph C. Ewoodzie, Jr., *Break Beats in the Bronx: Rediscovering Hip-Hop's Early Years* (Chapel Hill: University of North Carolina Press, 2017), 17, 64–5. DJs often looped these passages in records to extend breaks further. Adam Bradley, *Book of Rhymes: The Poetics of Hip-Hop* (New York: Perseus Books, 2009), 13.

59. Mark Katz, *Groove Music: The Art and Culture of the Hip-Hop DJ* (Oxford, UK: Oxford University Press, 2012), 4. One early hip-hop dancing group, the Harlem Pop Lockers, began dancing in the streets in 1972, according to András Tokaji. One tradition holds that, in dance competitions held at St. Martin Church in the Bronx, "it was the priests who served as referees." András Tokaji, "The Meeting of Sacred and Profane in New York's Music: Robert Moses, Lincoln Center, and Hip-Hop," *Journal of American Studies* 29, 1 (April 1995): 103.

60. David Sköld and Alf Rehn, "Makin' It, By Keeping It Real: Street Talk, Rap Music, and the Forgotten Entrepreneurship from 'The 'Hood,'" *Group & Organization Management* 32, 1 (February 2007): 50–78.

61. See, for example, Dan Charnas, *The Big Payback: The History of the Business of Hip-Hop* (New York: New American Library, 2010).

62. Numbers are from the blog of a former market researcher for Seagram's: Arthur Shapiro, "Seagram's Gin," Booze Business website (January 14, 2012).

63. In the musical *Hamilton* (2015), Hercules Mulligan rhymes *daughters, horses, intercourse, four sets,* and *corsets,* a string of rhymes that works better with a New York City accent.

64. My thanks to Mark Aronoff for bringing this feature to my attention.

65. Grandmaster Flash and the Furious Five, "The Message" (1982).

66. Tokaji, "The Meeting of Sacred and Profane in New York's Music: Robert Moses, Lincoln Center, and Hip-Hop," 99.

67. Joanna Teresa Demers, "Sampling as Lineage in Hip-Hop," dissertation, Princeton University (2002). The term *funk,* as a name or descriptive term for a certain kind of jazz, is first recorded in New York City. The Oxford English Dictionary offers as the first recorded use of the musical term *funk* Horace Silver's 1954 recording "Opus de Funk," which was created in New York City. Presumably, the word was already in common use. For more on funk, see Ricky Vincent, *Funk: The Music, the People, and the Rhythm of the One* (New York: St. Martin's Press, 1996).

68. Adam Bradley, *Book of Rhymes: The Poetics of Hip-Hop* (New York: Perseus Books, 2009), xviii–xix.

69. Ibid., xviii. However, a growing number of writers report using the Notes app on their phones for this purpose.

70. Mickey Hess, "Book of Rhymes," in Mickey Hess, ed., *Icons of Hip-Hop*, Vol. 2 (Westport, CT: Greenwood Press, 2007), 359–60.

71. Bradley, *Book of Rhymes*, xviii–xx.

72. William Jelani Cobb, *To the Break of Dawn: A Freestyle on the Hip Hop Aesthetic* (New York: New York University Press, 2007), 87; Bradley, *Book of Rhymes*, xix–33. Sondheim discusses the challenges of patterning vowel and consonant sounds in patter songs in Sondheim, *Finishing the Hat*, 184.

73. The Notorious B.I.G., "I Love the Dough" (1997).

74. Juelz Santana, "I Am Crack" (2005). Quoted in Bradley, *Book of Rhymes*, 98.

75. Salt-N-Pepa, "Shoop" (1993). These lyrics sample—play with the exact words of—Cole Porter's "You Do Something to Me" (1929).

76. Bradley, *Book of Rhymes*, 91.

77. Quoted in Dick Hebdige, *Subculture: The Meaning of Style* (New York: Routledge, [1979] 2013), 105.

78. Bradley, *Book of Rhymes*, 111.

79. For more on ciphers, see, for example, Michael Newman, "Rap as Literacy: A Genre Analysis of Hip-Hop Ciphers," *Text* 25, 3 (2005): 399–436; Marcyliena Morgan, *The Real Hiphop: Battling for Knowledge, Power, and Respect in the LA Underground* (Durham, NC: Duke University Press, 2009); and James Peterson, *The Hip-Hop Underground and African American Culture: Beneath the Surface* (New York: Palgrave Macmillan, 2014).

80. Jooyoung Lee, *Blowin' Up: Rap Dreams in South Central* (Chicago: University of Chicago Press, 2016), esp. 82–107.

81. Bradley, *Book of Rhymes*, 87–8.

82. Quoted in Christopher Weimer, "One-Handed Catch," *The Sondheim Review* 15, 4 (Summer 2009): 18.

83. Colleen L. Rua, "Coming Home: US-Latinos on the Broadway Stage," dissertation, Tufts University (2014): 99–101.

84. Billy Strayhorn wrote "Take the 'A' Train" and Duke Ellington performed it.

85. Miranda later performed the same move by calling Alexander Hamilton "my man Hamilton." Lin-Manuel Miranda, performance at White House, 2009.

86. KRS-One, "South Bronx" (1986).

87. Grandmaster Flash and the Furious Five, "The Message" (1982).

88. See, for example, Cornel West, "On Afro-American Music: From Bebop to Rap," *The Cornel West Reader* (New York: Basic Civitas, 1999), 474–84; Rose, *Black Noise*; Bakari Kitwana, *Hip-Hop Activism in the Obama Era* (Chicago: Third World Press, 2018); Chang, *Can't Stop Won't Stop*.

89. Shaheem Reid, "MTV News Exclusive: Nas Previews *Hip-Hop Is Dead*," *MTV. com* (October 9, 2006).

90. See, for example, Lin-Manuel Miranda and Jeremy McCarter, *Hamilton: The Revolution* (New York: Grand Central Publishing, 2016), 94–5, 172–5. The

play's acknowledgment of predecessors in both hip-hop and Broadway tradition is especially apparent in the character descriptions that Miranda included in a casting call in 2015. They describe Alexander Hamilton as "Eminem meets Sweeney Todd"; Eliza Hamilton as "Alicia Keys meets Elphaba"; Angelica Schuyler as "Nicki Minaj meets Desiree Armfeldt"; Aaron Burr as "Javert meets Mos Def"; George Washington as "John Legend meets Mufasa"; Marquis de Lafayette as "Lancelot meets Ludacris"; Thomas Jefferson as "Harold Hill meets Drake"; Hercules Mulligan as "Busta Rhymes meets Donald O'Connor"; James Madison as "RZA meets Zach from Chorus Line"; John Laurens as "Nas meets Elder Price"; Philip Hamilton as "Tupac meets J. Pierrepont Finch"; Peggy Schuyler as "The Michelle Williams of Destiny's Child"; Maria Reynolds as "Jasmine Sullivan meets Carla from Nine"; and King George as "Rufus Wainwright meets King Herod in JCS." "*Hamilton* to hold Broadway Auditions this Month; Read Lin-Manuel Miranda's Character Descriptions!" BBW News Desk, *Broadway World* (March 12, 2015).

91. Referring to Sondheim as a god is a minor tradition in musical theater. Recently, a playwright of my acquaintance wrote on Facebook that he had spotted Sondheim in the audience at a theater: "Well, intermission of 'Into the Woods' opening and we're seated two rows behind God and His Grandson. Needless to say, I've been watching Him and not the show. I can report that He laughs at His own jokes" Drew Fornarola, Facebook (January 22, 2015).

92. For Sondheim on perfect rhymes, see, for example, Sondheim, *Finishing the Hat*, xxv–xxvi.

93. Edward Delman, "How Lin-Manuel Miranda Shapes History," *The Atlantic* (September 29, 2015).

94. Lin-Manuel Miranda, performance at White House, 2009.

Chapter 6

1. Ana Celia Zentella, *Growing Up Bilingual: Puerto Rican Children in New York* (Malden, MA: Blackwell, 1997), 1.

2. Ingrid Gould Ellen, Katherine O'Regan, Amy Ellen Schwartz, and Leanna Stiefel, "Immigrant Children and New York City Schools: Segregation and Its Consequences," in William G. Gale and Janet Rothenberg Pack, *Brookings-Wharton Papers on Urban Affairs* (2002): 184.

3. Emerson Palmer, *The New York Public School: Being a History of Free Education in the City of New York* (New York: The Macmillan Company, 1905), 11–4.

4. The city first opened evening schools in 1833 but decided to save money by not paying the teachers. The schools closed within a few years, to reopen later under a better administration (Palmer, *The New York Public School*, 14, 88–9).

5. Melissa F. Weiner, *Power, Protest, and the Public Schools: Jewish and African American Struggles in New York City* (New Brunswick, NJ: Rutgers University

Press, 2010), 27. At the time, many Americans did not consider Jewish people to be white. See, for example, Eric Goldstein, *The Price of Whiteness: Jews, Race, and American Identity* (Princeton, NJ: Princeton University Press, 2006); and Newman, *New York City English*, 2, 36–8.

6. See, for example, Weiner, *Power, Protest, and the Public Schools*.

7. Weiner, *Power, Protest, and the Public Schools*, 26–9. See also Diane Ravitch, *The Great School Wars: A History of the Public Schools as Battlefield of Social Change* (New York: Basic Books, 1974); and Stephan Brumberg, *Going to America, Going to School: The Jewish Immigrant Public School Encounters in Turn-of-the-Century New York City* (New York: Praeger, 1986).

8. See, for example, a 1927 booklet issued to the teachers of elementary schools: *Course of Study in Literature for Elementary Schools, Grades 1A–8B* (Board of Education, the City of New York, 1927). The supplementary readings included many books on immigration. Among them: Hasanovitz; *Out of the Shadow*—Cohen; *The Promised Land*—Antin; *My Mother and I*—Stern; *Americanization of Edward Bok; From the Bottom Up*—Irvine; *Story of My Boyhood and Youth*—Muir; *An American in the Making*—Ravage; *A Far Journey*—Rihbany; *Making of an American*—Riis; *From Alien to Citizen*—Steiner; *Life Stories of Undistinguished Americans*—Holt; *Americans by Adoption*—Husband; *Pilgrims of To-day*—Wade. (Board of Education 1927, 52).

9. *Course of the Study and Syllabus in English and Citizenship for Evening Elementary Schools* (Board of Education, the City of New York, 1931). Board of Education, *Course of Study in Literature for Elementary Schools* (1927), 24–5.

10. In sixth grade, they started being reassessed on "The American's Creed": "I therefore believe it is my duty to my country to love it; to support its Constitution; to obey its laws; to respect its flag; and to defend it against all enemies.—William Tyler Page."

11. Board of Education, *Course of the Study and Syllabus in English*, 9–12.

12. On the fluency of children speaking their native languages, see, for example, Pinker, *The Language Instinct*. On the disconnect between human genetic variation and the racial categories belonging to the United States in the past or present, see, for example, Evelynn Hammonds, "Straw Men and Their Followers: The Return of Biological Race," Social Science Research Council website (June 7, 2006).

13. Those challenges meant, for example, that officials consistently moved funds away from black schools, and that schools with large black student populations stressed vocational over scholarly education (Weiner, *Power, Protest, and the Public Schools*, 29–30).

14. Language Policy Task Force, "Language Policy and the Puerto Rican Community," *Bilingual Review / La Revista Bilingüe* 5, 1/2 (January–August 1978): 13.

15. See Deborah Dash Moore, Jeffrey S. Gurock, Annie Polland, Howard B. Rock, and Daniel Soyer, *Jewish New York: The Remarkable Story of a City and a People* (New York: New York University Press, 2017), 256.

16. Ravitch, *The Great School Wars*, 253.

17. John Kucsera with Gary Orfied, "New York State's Extreme School Segregation," report for the Civil Rights Project at the University of California, Los Angeles (March 2014), 57. According to data from the 2010 census, one segment of the New York metropolitan region is, in terms of housing, "the third most segregated such region in the US after portions of Detroit and Milwaukee" (Newman 2014, 41).

18. Eliza Shapiro, "Segregation Has Been the Story of New York City's Schools for 50 Years," *The New York Times* (March 26, 2019).

19. Over the past few decades, contact between these groups has only grown; in Spanish Harlem, neighborhoods that had only Puerto Rican residents now house many African Americans as well. Cara Shousterman, "Speaking English in Spanish Harlem: Language Change in Puerto Rican English," dissertation in linguistics, New York University (2015): 13–4.

20. Ibid., 8–9.

21. Ibid., 55; John Lipski, *A History of Afro-Hispanic Language: Five Centuries, Five Continents* (Cambridge, UK: Cambridge University Press, 2005), 260–3.

22. Shousterman, "Speaking English in Spanish Harlem: Language Change in Puerto Rican English," 63; Newman, *New York City English*, 87.

23. The linguist Michael Newman examines this relationship in much of his work, including Newman, " 'I Represent Me': Identity Construction in a Teenage Rap Crew" (Austin: Proceedings from the Ninth Annual Symposium about Language and Society, 2001); Newman, "Rap as Literacy," 399–436; and Newman, *New York City English*.

24. Walt Wolfram, *Sociolinguistic Aspects of Assimilation: Puerto Rican English in New York City* (Arlington, VA: Center for Applied Linguistics, 1974), 199–200; Pinker, *The Language Instinct*, 30; Shousterman, "Speaking English in Spanish Harlem: Language Change in Puerto Rican English," 10–1. See also Peter Slomanson and Michael Newman, "Peer Group Identification and Variation in New York Latino English Laterals," *English Worldwide* 25 (2004): 199–216.

25. Zentella had trouble establishing rapport at first because speakers assumed that, as a teacher, she must be concerned with proper speech. While she was still introducing herself around the neighborhood, one child told an elder who asked why she had a tape recorder that she was studying children "*a ver si hablan bien el inglés o el español*, you know, *ella es como una maestra*": "to see if they speak English or Spanish well, you know, she is like a teacher." Even after she became a trusted acquaintance, when she knocked at the doors of local families, "Children greeted me in English because they knew that I was a teacher, but they ran to call an adult in Spanish" (Zentella, *Growing Up Bilingual*, 8–9, 56).

26. Zentella, *Growing Up Bilingual*, 46–55, 114.

27. Wolfram, *Sociolinguistic Aspects of Assimilation*, 2.

28. Tonya Wolford and Keelan Evanini, "Features of AAVE as Features of PRE: A Study of Adolescents in Philadelphia," *University of Pennsylvania Working Papers in Linguistics* 12, 2 (2006). See also Wolfram, *Sociolinguistic Aspects of Assimilation*; Stuart Silverman, "The Learning of Black English by Puerto Ricans in New York City," in J. L. Dillard, ed., *Perspectives on Black English* (The Hague: Mouton, 1975), 331–57; and Slomanson and Newman, "Peer Group Identification and Variation in New York Latino English Laterals," 205.

29. See, for example, D'Vera Cohn, "Census History: Counting Hispanics," Pew Research Center website (March 3, 2010). https://www.pewsocialtrends.org/2010/03/03/census-history-counting-hispanics-2/.

30. Raquel Z. Rivera, *New York Ricans from the Hip Hop Zone* (New York: Palgrave Macmillan, 2003), 29. Rivera is discussing Douglas Massey and Nancy Denton, "Trends in the Residential Segregation of Blacks, Hispanics and Asians 1970–1980," in *Majority and Minority: The Dynamics of Race and Ethnicity in American Life*, ed. Norman Yetman (Boston: Allyn and Bacon, 1991), 352–78.

31. John Edwards, *Language Diversity in the Classroom* (Bristol, UK, Buffalo, New York, and Toronto, Canada: Multilingual Matters, 2010), 170. In fact— as linguists have known for more than half a century—AAVE is a full language with systematic rules. See, for example, J. R. Rickford and R. J. Rickford, *Spoken Soul* (New York: John Wiley, 2000).

32. William Labov, *Language in the Inner City: Studies in the Black English Vernacular* (Philadelphia: University of Pennsylvania Press, 1972), 4. See also William Labov, "Can Reading Failure Be Reversed? A Linguistic Approach to the Question," in Vivian Gadsen and Daniel Wagner, eds., *Literacy among African American Youth* (Creskill, NJ: Hampton Press, 1995), 39–68.

33. Quoted in Rickford and Rickford, *Spoken Soul*, 4–5.

34. These examples and glosses are quoted directly from (Rickford and Rickford, *Spoken Soul*, 119).

35. See, for example, J. Cramer and J. Hallett, "From Chi-Town to the Dirty-Dirty: Regional Identity Markers in U.S. Hip Hop," in M. Terkourafi, ed., *The Languages of Global Hip Hop* (New York: Continuum, 2010), 256–76.

36. The reason the final "g" of *getting* is absent in this example is that speakers of AAVE may simplify consonant clusters: *past* becomes *pass, willing* becomes *willin'*. This is also a phonological feature of Japanese.

37. Michael Newman, "Focusing, Implicational Scaling, and the Variant Status of New York Latino English," *Journal of Sociolinguistics* 14, 2 (2010): 208.

38. Newman, *New York City English*, 82–3; Slomanson and Newman, "Peer Group Identification and Variation in New York Latino English Laterals," 199–216; and Newman, "Focusing, Implicational Scaling, and the Dialect Status of New York Latino English," 207–39.

39. Slomanson and Newman, "Peer Group Identification and Variation in New York Latino English Laterals," 199–216.

40. Labov, *Language in the Inner City*, 255–86.

41. Labov, "Can Reading Failure Be Reversed?," 42.

42. Labov, *Language in the Inner City*, 255–86; Jeff Siegel, *Second Dialect Acquisition* (Cambridge: Cambridge University Press, 2010), 171.

43. Language Policy Task Force, "Language Policy and the Puerto Rican Community," 14-5.

44. Judith Harris, *The Nurture Assumption: Why Children Turn Out the Way They Do* (New York: Free Press, [1998] 2009), 151–3, 185, 204–5.

45. Zentella, *Growing Up Bilingual*, 39–41.

46. Ana Celia Zentella, "Individual Differences in Growing Up Bilingual," in *Cross-Cultural Literacy: Ethnographies of Communication in Multiethnic Classrooms*, ed. Marietta Saravia-Shore and Steven F. Arvizu (New York: Garland, 1992), 221.

47. Paul H. Anisman, "Some Aspects of Code Switching in New York Puerto Rican English," *Bilingual Review* 2, 1 & 2 (1975): 56–85.

48. Shana Poplack, "Sometimes I'll Start a Sentence in Spanish *y Termino en Español*: Toward a Typology of Code-Switching," *Linguistics* 18, 7–8 (1980): 581–618. Some examples are taken from this article. Shousterman discusses Anisman and Poplack in Shousterman, "Speaking English in Spanish Harlem," 36-8.

49. Lakoff, *Language and Woman's Place*, 41–7.

50. A useful term for this concept is *intersectionality*, which Kimberly Crenshaw first used in 1989 to describe the intersection of identities—and discrimination—based on sexual, racial, and gender terms. Kimberly Crenshaw, "Demarginalizing the Intersection of Race and Sex: A Black Feminist Critique of Antidiscrimination Doctrine, Feminist Theory, and Antiracist Politics," *University of Chicago Legal Forum* (1989): 139–67. See also Kimberly Crenshaw, "Mapping the Margins: Intersectionality, Identity Politics, and Violence against Women of Color," *Stanford Law Review* 43, 6 (1991): 1241–99.

51. Evan Bartlett Page and Jimmie Manning, quoted in Erik Piepenburg, "So What's Wrong with a Little Lisp?" *Out* (February 2006): 36–9.

52. Willi Ninja, quoted in Jennie Livingston, *Paris Is Burning*, film, 1990; Burbank, CA: Miramax Films, 2005.

53. On ballroom culture, see also Marlon Bailey, *Butch Queens Up in Pumps: Gender, Performance, and Ballroom Culture in Detroit* (Ann Arbor: University of Michigan Press, 2013); Eric Garber, "A Spectacle in Color: The Lesbian and Gay Subculture of Jazz Age Harlem," in *Hidden from History: Reclaiming the Gay and Lesbian Past* (New York: Penguin Books, [1989] 1990), 318–31; Gerard Gaskin, *Legendary: Inside the House Ballroom Scene* (Durham, NC: Duke University Press, 2013); Jonathan David Jackson, "The Social World of Voguing," *Journal for the Anthropological Study of Human Movement*

12, 2 (2002): 26–42; and Lucas Hilderbrand, *Paris Is Burning: A Queer Film Classic* (Vancouver, BC: Arsenal Pulp Press, 2013).

54. In 2015, a computational dialectologist listed *unbothered* among ten "emerging words" that seemed newly coined, having just become fashionable on Twitter that year. In *Paris Is Burning*, ball children use the similar term *not bothered*, which also appears in Jennie Livingston's remarks for an early media kit for the documentary: "I had my own prejudices about what oppression does to people, but my cultural assumptions were overturned when I realized that these men and women had adopted attitudes based on the certainty that they—in the expression of the ball world—were *not bothered*." Quoted in Hilderbrand, *Paris Is Burning*, 26. Jack Greive, Diansheng Guo, and Alice Kasakoff, "Mapping Lexical Spread in American English," paper presented at American Dialect Society Annual Meeting, Portland, Oregon (January 8, 2015). See also Nikhil Sonnad, "How Brand-New Words Are Spreading across America," *Quartz* (July 29, 2015); Jack Grieve, Andrea Nini, and Diansheng Guo, "Mapping Lexical Innovation on American Social Media," *Journal of English Linguistics* 46, 4 (2018): 293–319; and Nikhil Sonnad, "America Can Thank Black Twitter for All Those New Words," *Quartz* (September 20, 2018).

55. On the spread of slang from drag culture to mainstream youth culture, see, for example, Lexi Pandell, "How RuPaul's Drag Race Fueled Pop Culture's Dominant Slang Engine," *Wired* (March 22, 2018).

56. Rusty Barrett, *From Drag Queens to Leathermen: Language, Gender, and Gay Male Subcultures* (Oxford: Oxford University Press, 2017), 40–8; Rusty Barrett, "Indexing Polyphonous Identity in the Speech of African-American Drag Queens," in Mary Bucholtz, Anita Liang, and Laurel Sutton, eds., *Reinventing Identities: The Gendered Self in Discourse* (New York: Oxford University Press, 1999), 313–31; and Rusty Barrett, " 'She Is *Not* White Woman': Appropriation of White Women's Language by African American Drag Queens," in Mary Bucholtz, Anita C. Liang, Laurel A. Sutton, and Caitlin Hines, eds., *Cultural Performances: Proceedings of the Third Berkeley Women and Language Conference* (Berkeley, CA: Berkeley Women and Language Group, 1994), 1–14.

57. Polyphony is not restricted to this group, of course. Zentella similarly argues that New York Puerto Ricans, as part of their everyday expression, may draw upon repertoires from both outside groups and overlapping aspects of their own identities: "It is precisely the ability to co-author and co-interpret conversations against a multicultural and multidialectical backdrop that enables NYPRs [New York Puerto Ricans] to identify each other. Like basketball players who know where to hit the backboard in order to score a point, or *salsa* dancers who can follow a new partner's every turn, their interactions rely on shared linguistic and cultural knowledge of standard and non-standard Puerto Rican Spanish, Puerto Rican English, African American Vernacular English,

Hispanized English, and standard NYC English, among other dialects" (Zentella, *Growing Up Bilingual*, 3).

58. Madonna, "Vogue," video; directed by David Fincher; 1991; copyright WMA, 2006.

59. Livingston, *Paris Is Burning*.

60. See, for example, Robert Evans and Harry Collins, in "Interactional Expertise and the Imitation Game," in Michael E. Gorman, ed., *Trading Zones and Interactional Expertise: Creating New Kinds of Collaboration* (Cambridge, MA: MIT Press, 2010), 53–70.

61. Stephen Colbert was once named an "honorary woman" by *Maxim* magazine. Look at videos of the event; look at how genuinely happy he is. I live for that.

62. This was the argument of Pierre Bourdieu in his famous book *Distinction: A Social Critique of the Judgement of Taste*, trans. Richard Nice (London: Routledge, 1984). Originally published in French in 1979.

63. Harris, *The Nurture Assumption*, 226. See also Malcolm Gladwell, "Do Parents Matter?", *The New Yorker* (August 17, 1998).

64. Quoted in Harris, *The Nurture Assumption*, 62.

65. Zentella, *Growing Up Bilingual*, 2.

66. Kenneth Barrios, "New York, Puerto Rico, and English Proper: A Regimen for Success," November 30, 2016. I am grateful to Kenneth Barrios for his permission to quote this passage.

Chapter 7

1. The term *department store* was widespread by the 1890s, with *department* referencing the novel practice of having specialty stores within a store.

2. Mona Domosh, *Invented Cities: The Creation of Landscape in Nineteenth-Century New York* (New Haven, CT: Yale University Press, 1996), 36; Amy Merrick, "The End of Saks as We Knew It," *The New Yorker* (July 30, 2013).

3. Jan Whitaker, *Service and Style: How the American Department Store Fashioned the Middle Class* (New York: St. Martin's Press, 2006), 109–29.

4. Labov, *The Social Stratification of English in New York City*, 45.

5. Newman discusses Labov's department store study and its successors in Newman, *New York City English*, 45–51.

6. For a thoroughly charming memoir from a personal shopper at Bergdorf Goodman, see Betty Halbreich, *I'll Drink to That: A Life in Style, with a Twist* (New York: Penguin Books, 2014).

7. This actually happened—see Noam Scheiber, "Freaks and Geeks," *The New Republic* (April 2, 2007).

8. Labov estimated that Saks employees made less money than Macy's employees, but reckoned that, in the eyes of the employees, the "greater prestige" of

Saks made up for the difference. Labov, *The Social Stratification of English in New York City*, 45.

9. Ibid., 45.
10. Ibid., 43–6.
11. Ibid., 46–8.
12. Research with human subjects now requires informed consent.
13. Labov, *The Social Stratification of English in New York City*, 48–50.
14. Even so, S. Klein employees showed the lowest voicing of /r/ among the three stores for both casual and careful speech. Ibid., 48–50.
15. Ibid., 341–4.
16. Kara Becker, "/r/ and the Construction of Place Identity on New York City's Lower East Side," *Journal of Sociolinguistics* 13, 5 (2009): 644–5. Definition of "New Yorkah" on the crowd-sourced website Urban Dictionary. Published May 23, 2005. Accessed December 10, 2019. urbandictionary.com/define. php?term=New%20Yorkah.
17. Crawford Feagin, "The Dynamics of a Sound Change in Southern States English: From R-less to R-ful in Three Generations," in J. A. Edmondson, Crawford Feagin, and P. Muhlhausler, eds., *Development and Diversity: Language Variation across Time and Space* (Arlington: The Summer Institute of Linguistics and The University of Texas at Arlington, 1990), 130–8. Quoted, as a point of comparison with the rate of change that Labov's Department Store Study and its successors chart, in Kara Becker, "(r) we there yet? The Change to Rhoticity in New York City English," *Language Variation and Change* 26, 2 (July 2014): 145.
18. In Labov, *The Social Stratification of English in New York City*, 55–6.
19. Ibid., 53.
20. Patrick-André Mather, "The Social Stratification of /r/ in New York City: Labov's Department Store Study Revisited," *Journal of English Linguistics* 40 (2012): 340–3.
21. Ibid., 352–3.
22. Ibid., 348.
23. Ibid., 342–53.
24. Ibid., 338–51.
25. Maeve Eberhardt and Corrine Downs, "A Department Store Study for the 21st Century: /r/ Vocalization on TLC's Say Yes to the Dress," *University of Pennsylvania Working Papers in Linguistics* 41 19, 2 (2013): 51–60.
26. Ibid., 50–2.
27. They coded each token as rhotic or nonrhotic. They also recorded such variables as whether the /r/ phoneme began with an unstressed vowel (as in *square*); whether the /r/ phoneme began with a stressed vowel (as in *fur*); whether the /r/ phoneme ended with a consonant, a vowel, or a pause; "whether the word was lexical or functional, and whether the syllable in which /r/ occurred was stressed or unstressed" (Eberhardt and Downs, "A Department Store Study for

the 21st Century," 51–3). Here, I am discussing only the findings that connect directly to Labov's original study.

28. Eberhardt and Downs, "A Department Store Study for the 21st Century," 54–5.

29. See, for example, Mather, "The Social Stratification of /r/ in New York City: Labov's Department Store Study Revisited," 347–8.

30. Eberhardt and Downs, "A Department Store Study for the 21st Century," 57.

31. Ibid., 58–9.

32. Newman briefly discusses the phenomenon of "covert prestige"—the idea that a speaker who uses a speech form like New York City English can seem "cooler, more down-to-earth, more one of us, and/or tougher than one who does not." Newman, *New York City English*, 9–10.

33. Becker, "/r/ and the Construction of Place Identity on New York City's Lower East Side," 643–4.

34. He added, "The small rate of increase of 1.5 percent a year reported above is largely due to the behavior of the younger upper middle class speakers. For others, r-constriction shows an increase only in careful styles, and this tendency is greatest in middle-aged rather than younger speakers." William Labov, Sharon Ash, and Charles Boberg, *The Atlas of North American English: Phonetics, Phonology, and Sound Change*, vol. 1 (Berlin, Germany: Walter de Gruyter, 2006), 48. Cited in Becker, "/r/ and the Construction of Place Identity on New York City's Lower East Side," 644.

35. Kara Becker, "(r) we there yet?," 141–68.

36. Fifteen participants identified their ethnicity as Jewish and therefore (she notes) did not identify exactly as white. The participants she classified as African American all had ancestral ties to the American South. She used the term *Puerto Rican* to refer to heritage, not necessarily to people directly from Puerto Rico (in Becker, "(r) we there yet?," 151).

37. Becker, "(r) we there yet?," 147.

38. Ibid., 148–64.

39. Becker, "/r/ and the Construction of Place Identity on New York City's Lower East Side," 634–58.

40. Ibid., 646–50.

41. William Labov, "The Social History of a Sound Change on the Island of Martha's Vineyard, Massachusetts," master's essay, Columbia University (1962). See also William Labov, "The Social Motivation of a Sound Change," in Labov, *Sociolinguistic Patterns*, 1–42; and William Labov, "The Social Setting of Linguistic Change," in Labov, *Sociolinguistic Patterns*, 260–325.

42. Becker, "/r/ and the Construction of Place Identity on New York City's Lower East Side," 638.

43. Barbara Johnstone, Neeta Bhasin, and Denise Wittkofski, "'Dahntahn' Pittsburgh: Monophthongal /aw/ and Representations of Localness in Southwestern Pennsylvania," *American Speech* 77, 2 (2002): 160. Quoted in

Becker, "/r/ and the Construction of Place Identity on New York City's Lower East Side," 653.

44. Johnstone, Bhasin, and Wittkofski, " 'Dahntahn' Pittsburgh," 148, 159. Cited in Becker, "/r/ and the Construction of Place Identity on New York City's Lower East Side," 654.

45. Becker, "(r) we there yet?," 146.

46. On perpetuating stereotypes, see, for example, Christopher Mele, *Selling the Lower East Side: Culture, Real Estate, and Resistance in New York City* (Minneapolis: University of Minnesota Press, 2000), 27.

Epilogue

1. Kolker notes that the New York of *The Hours, Mean Streets, Raging Bull*, and *Taxi Driver*, "a place of tough people, crowded streets, fights, and whores," is "much different from the New York created by Woody Allen, whose streets and apartments are comfortable habitations for walking and conversation." Robert Phillip Kolker, *A Cinema of Loneliness: Penn, Kubrick, Scorsese, Spielberg, Altman* (New York and Oxford: Oxford University Press, 1988), 164.

2. Martin Scorsese, *Taxi Driver* (Columbia Pictures, 1976).

3. Paul Schrader, quoted in Richard Thompson, "Screen Writer: *Taxi Driver*'s Paul Schrader," *Film Comment* (March–April 1976): 11.

4. Kolker, *A Cinema of Loneliness*, 194.

5. Paul Schrader, "Taxi Driver," screenplay (April 29, 1975). Harry Ransom Center, University of Texas at Austin.

6. Steve Wilson, "You Talkin' to Me?," blog post, *Ransom Center Magazine*, University of Texas at Austin (October 13, 2016).

7. "New York Citizens Direct Traffic after Power Cut Hits Manhattan—Video," *The Guardian* website (July 14, 2019); Coralie Carlson and Jonathan Dienst, "Power Restored after Blackout Hits 73K Manhattan Customers: Con Ed," NBC New York website (July 14, 2019).

8. Sophie Vershbow, @svershbow, Twitter (July 13, 2019).

REFERENCES

30 Rock, "The Tuxedo Begins," Broadway Video, Little Stranger, NBC Studios, Universal Television (February 16, 2012).

Abernethy, Thomas P., *Western Lands and the American Revolution* (New York: Russell and Russell, [1937] 1959).

Adams, Michael, *Slang: The People's Poetry* (Oxford, UK: Oxford University Press, 2009).

Alberti, John, *Screen Ages: A Survey of American Cinema* (London: Routledge, 2015).

Alfaraz, Gabriela G., "Conversing Through Overlaps: Information Overlaps and Simultaneous Talk in Cuban Spanish," *Multilingua* 28 (2009): 25–43.

Alim, H. Samy, *Rock the Mic Right: The Language of Hip Hop Culture* (London: Routledge, 2006).

Allen, Irving Lewis, *The City in Slang: New York Life and Popular Speech* (Oxford, UK: Oxford University Press, 1993).

Allen, Woody, *Manhattan*, United Artists (1979).

Alonso, Harriet Hyman, *Yip Harburg: Legendary Lyricist and Human Rights Activist* (Middletown, CT: Wesleyan University Press, 2012).

Anbinder, Tyler, *Five Points: The 19th-Century New York City Neighborhood That Invented Tap Dance, Stole Elections, and Became the World's Most Notorious Slum* (New York: The Free Press, 2001).

Anderson, Benedict, *Imagined Communities: Reflections on the Origin and Spread of Nationalism* (London: Verso, [1983] 2006).

Anisman, Paul H. "Some Aspects of Code Switching in New York Puerto Rican English," *Bilingual Review* 2, 1 & 2 (1975): 56–85.

Anonymous, "Arrest of the Confidence Man," *New-York Herald* (July 8, 1849).

Anonymous, "Bond Negotiators Arrested," *The New York Herald*, New York, New York (July 26, 1877).

Anonymous, "Caveat Emptor," *The New Yorker* (December 28, 1929): 13.

Anonymous, "Cocking on Long Island a Rattling Series of Battles on Newtown Creek," *New York Herald*, New York, New York (January 31, 1877).

Anonymous, "Confidence Man Jailed; McCloundy, Who Once Sold the Brooklyn Bridge, Faces Life Term," *The New York Times* (July 8, 1928): 21.

Anonymous, "Fraud," *New-York Spectator*, New York, New York (September 29, 1829): 1.

Anonymous, "*Hamilton* to hold Broadway Auditions this Month; Read Lin-Manuel Miranda's Character Descriptions!" BBW News Desk, *Broadway World* (March 12, 2015).

Anonymous, "New Dorp Club Grounds," *New York Herald*, New York, New York (November 15, 1874).

Anonymous, "New York Citizens Direct Traffic After Power Cut Hits Manhattan—Video," *The Guardian* website (July 14, 2019).

Anonymous, "Patterson Falls," *New York Journal*, New York, New York (September 1, 1810): 2.

Anonymous, "Personal Intelligence," *New York Herald*, New York, New York (November 6, 1875): 6.

Anonymous, "A Swindler," *Albany Gazette*, Albany, New York (July 25, 1820): 2.

Anonymous, "A Swindler," *New York Journal and Patriotic Register*, New York, New York (February 22, 1800): 3.

Anonymous, "The Swindler Detected," *The True American*, Trenton, New Jersey (August 27, 1810): 2.

Anonymous, "Tawking the Tawk," *The New Yorker* (November 14, 2005).

Anonymous, "The Twenty-Ninth Precinct," *The New York Herald* (September 4, 1880).

Anonymous, "U.S. Adults Like British Accents, Not NYC," *United Press International* (January 30, 2011).

Augustyn, Robert T., and Paul E. Cohen, *Manhattan in Maps, 1587–2014* (Mineola, NY: Dover Publications, 2014).

Bailey, Marlon, *Butch Queens Up in Pumps: Gender, Performance, and Ballroom Culture in Detroit* (Ann Arbor: University of Michigan Press, 2013).

Bair, Deirdre, *Saul Steinberg: A Biography* (New York: Doubleday, 2012).

Ballon, Hillary, editor, *The Greatest Grid: The Master Plan of Manhattan, 1811–2011* (New York: Museum of the City of New York/Columbia University Press, 2012).

Bakari Kitwana, *Hip-Hop Activism in the Obama Era* (Chicago: Third World Press, 2018).

Barnum, P. T., *The Art of Money-Getting: Or, Golden Rules for Making Money* (Bedford, MA: Applewood Books, [1880] 1999).

Barnum, P. T., *The Humbugs of the World: An Account of Humbugs, Delusions, Impositions, Quackeries, Deceits, and Deceivers Generally, in All Ages* (New York: Carleton, 1866).

Barnum, P. T., *The Life of P. T. Barnum: Written by Himself* (London: Sampson Low, Son, & Co., 1855).

Barnum, P. T., *Struggles and Triumphs: Or, Sixty Years' Recollections of P. T. Barnum* (London: Sampson Low, Son, & Co., 1855).

Barrett, Rusty, *From Drag Queens to Leathermen: Language, Gender, and Gay Male Subcultures* (Oxford, UK: Oxford University Press, 2017).

Barrett, Rusty, "Indexing Polyphonous Identity in the Speech of African-American Drag Queens," in Mary Bucholtz, Anita Liang, and Laurel Sutton, eds., *Reinventing Identities: The Gendered Self in Discourse* (New York: Oxford University Press, 1999): 313–31.

Barrett, Rusty, "'She Is *Not* White Woman': Appropriation of White Women's Language by African American Drag Queens," in Mary Bucholtz, Anita C. Liang, Laurel A. Sutton, and Caitlin Hines, eds., *Cultural Performances: Proceedings of the Third Berkeley Women and Language Conference* (Berkeley, CA: Berkeley Women and Language Group, 1994): 1–14.

Barth, Gunther, *City People: The Rise of Modern City Culture in the Nineteenth Century* (Oxford, UK: Oxford University Press, 1982).

Bearman, Peter, *Doormen* (Chicago: University of Chicago Press, 2005).

Becker, Kara, "/r/ and the Construction of Place Identity on New York City's Lower East Side," *Journal of Sociolinguistics* 13, 5 (2009): 634–58.

Becker, Kara, "(r) we there yet? The Change to Rhoticity in New York City English," *Language Variation and Change* 26, 2 (July 2014): 141–68.

Becker, Kara, "The Social Motivations of Reversal: Raised BOUGHT in New York City English," *Language in Society* 43, 3 (2014): 395–420.

Becker Kara, and Elizabeth L. Coggshall, "The Sociolinguistics of Ethnicity in New York City," *Language and Linguistics Compass* 3, 3 (2009): 751–66.

Becker, Kara, and Luiza Newlin-Lukowicz, "The Myth of the New York City Borough Accent: Evidence from Perception," *University of Pennsylvania Working Papers in Linguistics* 24, 2 (October 15, 2018): 8–17.

Behrman, S. N., "Do or Diaphragm," *The New Yorker* (May 25, 1935): 22–7.

Bell, Crystal, "Batman's Gotham City Map: What Does the Dark Knight's Home Really Look Like?" *The Huffington Post* (July 17, 2012).

Benardo, Leonard, and Jennifer Weiss, *Brooklyn by Name: How the Neighborhoods, Streets, Parks, Bridges, and More Got Their Names* (New York: New York University Press, 2006).

Bender, James, *NBC Handbook of Pronunciation* (New York: Thomas Y. Crowell Company, 1943).

Berenson, Edward, *The Trial of Madame Caillaux* (Berkeley: University of California Press, [1992] 1993).

Berry, Anne, "Spanish and American Turn-Taking Styles: A Comparative Study," *Pragmatics and Language Learning* 5 (1994): 180–90.

Bind, Henry, *Acting Jewish: Negotiating Ethnicity on the American Stage & Screen* (Ann Arbor: University of Michigan Press, 2005).

Birmingham, Stephen, *"Our Crowd": The Great Jewish Families of New York* (New York: Macmillan, [1967] 2015).

Blumenfeld, Robert, *Accents: A Manual for Actors* (New York: Proscenium Publishers, [1998] 2002).

Bonfiglio, Thomas Paul, *Race and the Rise of Standard American* (Berlin and New York: Mouton de Gruyter, 2002).

Bourdieu, Pierre, *Distinction: A Social Critique of the Judgement of Taste*, trans. Richard Nice (London: Routledge, 1984).

Bradley, Adam, *Book of Rhymes: The Poetics of Hip-Hop* (New York: Perseus Books, 2009).

Brasser, T.J.C., "The Coastal Algonkians," in Eleanor Leacock and Nancy Lurie, eds., *North American Indians in Historical Perspective* (New York: Random House, 1971), 64–91.

Brewer, John, *A Sentimental Murder: Love and Madness in the Eighteenth Century* (New York: Farrar, Straus and Giroux, 2004).

Bronstein, Arthur J., "Let's Take Another Look at New York City Speech," *American Speech* 37, 1 (February 1962): 13–26.

Brooks, Andree, "Debunking the Myth of P. T. Barnum," *The New York Times* (October 3, 1982).

Bryson, Bill, *Notes from a Small Island* (New York: Avon Books, [1995] 1997).

Brumberg, Stephan, *Going to America, Going to School: The Jewish Immigrant Public School Encounters in Turn-of-the-Century New York City* (New York: Praeger, 1986).

Buntline, Ned, *The Mysteries and Miseries of New York: A Story of Real Life* (New York: W. W. Burgess, 1849).

Bureau of Speech Improvement, "Suggestions in Speech Improvement for the Use of Classroom Teachers" (Board of Education, The City of New York, 1933 [reprinted June 1934]).

Burke, Kenneth, "Literature as Equipment for Living," in David H. Richter, ed., *The Critical Tradition: Classic Texts and Contemporary Trends*, 2nd ed. (Boston: Bedford Books, 1998), 593–8.

Calhoun, Ada, "Where Musical-Makers Audition Their Ideas," *The New York Times* (November 28, 2004).

Campanella, Thomas, *Brooklyn: The Once and Future City* (Princeton, NJ: Princeton University Press, 2019).

Campbell, Sean, *The Sitcoms of Norman Lear* (Jefferson, NC: McFarland, 2007).

Carlson, Coralie, and Jonathan Dienst, "Power Restored after Blackout Hits 73K Manhattan Customers: Con Ed," NBC New York website (July 14, 2019).

Chambers, J. K., " 'Canadian Dainty': The Rise and Decline of Briticisms in Canada," in Raymond Hickey, ed., *Legacies of Colonial English: A Study in Transported Dialects* (Cambridge, UK: Cambridge University Press, 2004), 224–41.

Chang, Jeff, *Can't Stop Won't Stop: A History of the Hip-Hop Generation* (New York: St. Martin's Press, 2005).

Charnas, Dan, *The Big Payback: The History of the Business of Hip-Hop* (New York: New American Library, 2010).

Chester, George Randolph, *Get-Rich-Quick Wallingford: A Cheerful Account of the Rise and Fall of an American Business Buccaneer* (Indianapolis: The Bobbs-Merrill Company, [1907] 1908).

Chopra, Ruma, *Unnatural Rebellion: Loyalists in New York City during the Revolution* (Charlottesville: University of Virginia Press, 2011).

Clark, Bruce, *Native Liberty, Crown Sovereignty: The Existing Aboriginal Right of Self-Government in Canada* (Montreal: McGill-Queen's University Press, 1990).

Cobb, William Jelani, *To the Break of Dawn: A Freestyle on the Hip Hop Aesthetic* (New York: New York University Press, 2007).

Cohen, Gerald Leonard, *Origin of New York City's Nickname "The Big Apple"* (New York: Peter Lang, 1991).

Cohn, D'Vera, "Census History: Counting Hispanics," Pew Research Center website (March 3, 2010). https://www.pewsocialtrends.org/2010/03/03/census-history-counting-hispanics-2/.

Colby, Frank, "F.D.R. on Radio Has New England Accent," *Daily Boston Globe* (December 29, 1940): 34.

Cole, Jeffrey Ian, "Born to the New Art: CBS Correspondents and the Emergence of Broadcast News, 19301941," dissertation, University of California, Los Angeles (1985).

Cook, James W., *The Arts of Deception: Playing with Fraud in the Age of Barnum* (Cambridge, MA: Harvard University Press, 2001).

Course of Study in Literature for Elementary Schools, Grades 1A–8B (Board of Education, the City of New York, 1927).

Course of the Study and Syllabus in English and Citizenship for Evening Elementary Schools (Board of Education, the City of New York, 1931).

Cowley, Malcolm, ed., *The Portable Hawthorne* (New York: The Viking Press, [1969] 1983).

Cramer, J., and J. Hallett, "From Chi-Town to the Dirty-Dirty: Regional Identity Markers in U.S. Hip Hop," in M. Terkourafi, ed., *The Languages of Global Hip Hop* (New York: Continuum, 2010): 256–76.

Crenshaw, Kimberly, "Demarginalizing the Intersection of Race and Sex: A Black Feminist Critique of Antidiscrimination Doctrine, Feminist Theory, and Antiracist Politics," *University of Chicago Legal Forum* (1989): 139–67.

Crenshaw, Kimberly, "Mapping the Margins: Intersectionality, Identity Politics, and Violence against Women of Color," *Stanford Law Review* 43, 6 (1991): 1241–99.

Cutler, Charles, *O Brave New Words!: Native American Loanwords in Current English* (Norman and London: University of Oklahoma Press, 1994).

Dalton, Susan Elizabeth, "Bugs and Daffy Go to War," *The Velvet Light Trap* 4 (Spring 1972).

Darnton, Robert, *The Great Cat Massacre and Other Episodes in French Cultural History* (New York: Basic Books, 1984).

Delman, Edward, "How Lin-Manuel Miranda Shapes History," *The Atlantic* (September 29, 2015).

Demers, Joanna Teresa, "Sampling as Lineage in Hip-Hop," dissertation, Princeton University, Princeton, New Jersey (2002).

DesRochers, Rich, *The New Humor in the Progressive Era: Americanization and the Vaudeville Comedian* (New York: Palgrave Macmillan, 2014).

Dickens, Charles, *American Notes for General Circulation*, 2nd ed., vol. 1 (London: Chapman and Hall, 1842).

Didion, Joan, "New York: Sentimental Journeys," *The New York Review of Books* (January 17, 1991).

Dillard, Joey Lee, ed., *Perspectives on American English* (The Hague, Netherlands: Mouton Publishers, 1980).

Dinkins, David, *A Mayor's Life: Governing New York's Gorgeous Mosaic* (New York: PublicAffairs, 2013).

Dobrow, Julia, and Calvin Gidney, "The Good, the Bad, and the Foreign: The Use of Dialect in Children's Animated Television," *The Annals of the American Academy of Political and Social Science* 557 (May 1998): 105–19.

Domosh, Mona, *Invented Cities: The Creation of Landscape in Nineteenth-Century New York* (New Haven, CT: Yale University Press, 1996).

Eberhardt, Maeve, and Corrine Downs, "A Department Store Study for the 21st Century: /r/ Vocalization on TLC's Say Yes to the Dress," *University of Pennsylvania Working Papers in Linguistics* 41 19, 2 (2013): 51–60.

Edensor, Tim, "Lights, City, Action . . .," in John Hannigan and Greg Richards, eds., *The SAGE Handbook of New Urban Studies* (London: SAGE Publications, 2017): 217–31.

Edwards, John, *Language Diversity in the Classroom* (Bristol, UK, Buffalo, New York, and Toronto, Canada: Multilingual Matters, 2010).

Ewoodzie, Jr., Joseph C., *Break Beats in the Bronx: Rediscovering Hip-Hop's Early Years* (Chapel Hill: The University of North Carolina Press, 2017).

Ellen, Ingrid Gould, Katherine O'Regan, Amy Ellen Schwartz, and Leanna Stiefel, "Immigrant Children and New York City Schools: Segregation and Its Consequences," in William G. Gale and Janet Rothenberg Pack, *Brookings-Wharton Papers on Urban Affairs* (2002): 183–214.

Elliott, Nancy, "A Sociolinguistic Study of Rhoticity in American Film Speech from the 1930s to the 1970s," dissertation, Indiana University, Bloomington (2000).

Ellmann, Richard, *Oscar Wilde* (New York: Alfred A. Knopf, 1988).

Evans, Robert, and Harry Collins, "Interactional Expertise and the Imitation Game," in Michael E. Gorman, ed., *Trading Zones and Interactional Expertise: Creating New Kinds of Collaboration* (Cambridge, MA: MIT Press, 2010): 53–70.

Feagin, Crawford, "The Dynamics of a Sound Change in Southern States English: From R-less to R-ful in Three Generations," in J. A. Edmondson, Crawford Feagin, and P. Muhlhausler, eds., *Development and Diversity: Language Variation across Time and Space* (Arlington: The Summer Institute of Linguistics and The University of Texas at Arlington, 1990): 130–8.

Fierstein, Sanna, *Naming New York: Manhattan Places and How They Got Their Names* (New York: New York University Press, 2001).

Fisher, John Hurt, "British and American, Continuity and Divergence," in John Algeo, ed., *The Cambridge History of the English Language*, vol. VI (Cambridge, UK: Cambridge University Press, 2001): 59–85.

Foner, Nancy, "How Exceptional Is New York? Migration and Multiculturalism in the Empire City," *Ethnic and Racial Studies* 30, 6 (November 2007): 999–1023.

Foucault, Michel, *Discipline and Punish: The Birth of the Prison*, trans. Alan Sheridan (New York: Vintage Books, 1975).

Frank, Yakira Hagalili, review of Allan Forbes Hubbell's *The Pronunciation of English in New York City: Consonants and Vowels, Language* 28, 2 (April–June 1952): 278–83.

Frank, Yakira Hagalili, "The Speech of New York City," dissertation, University of Michigan, Ann Arbor (1948).

Freedman, Samuel, "The Words and Music of Stephen Sondheim," *The New York Times* (April 1, 1984).

Friedenberg, Daniel M., *Life, Liberty, and the Pursuit of Land* (Buffalo, NY: Prometheus Books, 1992).

Friedman, Lawrence, "Crimes of Mobility," *Stanford Law Review* 43 (1991): 637–58.

Friedman, Lawrence, *Guarding Life's Dark Secrets: Legal and Social Controls over Reputation, Propriety, and Privacy* (Stanford, CA: Stanford University Press, 2007).

Furia, Philip, *Ira Gershwin: The Art of the Lyricist* (Oxford, UK: Oxford University Press, [1996] 1997).

Furia, Philip, *The Poets of Tin Pan Alley: A History of America's Great Lyricists* (Oxford, UK: Oxford University Press, [1990] 1922).

Gabler, Neal, *An Empire of Their Own: How the Jews Invented Hollywood* (New York: Crown Publishers, 1988).

Garber, Eric, "A Spectacle in Color: The Lesbian and Gay Subculture of Jazz Age Harlem," in *Hidden from History: Reclaiming the Gay and Lesbian Past* (New York: Penguin Books, [1989] 1990): 318–31.

Gaskin, Gerard, *Legendary: Inside the House Ballroom Scene* (Durham, NC: Duke University Press, 2013).

Gerould, Katharine Fullerton, "The Nature of Hokum," *Harper's Magazine* (August 1927), 285–90.

Gilfoyle, Timothy J. *City of Eros: New York City, Prostitution, and the Commercialization of Sex, 1790–1920* (New York: W. W. Norton, 1992).

Gladwell, Malcolm, "Do Parents Matter?," *The New Yorker* (August 17, 1998).

Gray, Giles Wilkeson, and Claude Merton Wise, *The Bases of Speech* (New York: Harper & Row, [1934] 1959).

Goffman, Erving, *Forms of Talk* (Philadelphia: University of Pennsylvania Press, 1981).

Gold, David L., "Towards a Dossier of the Still Unclear Immediate Etymon(s?) of American English Slang *Hooker* 'Whore' (With Remarks on the Origin of American English Barnegat, Dixie, Fly ~Vlei ~Vley ~Vlaie ~Vly, Gramercy Park, Hell Gate, Jazz, Sloughter, and Spuyten Duyvil)," in Félix Rodríguez González and Antonio Lillo Buadez, eds., *Studies in Etymology and Etiology* (San Vicente, Spain: Publicaciones de la Universidad de Alciante, 2009): 105–62.

Goldstein, Eric L., *The Price of Whiteness: Jews, Race, and American Identity* (Princeton, NJ: Princeton University Press, 2006).

Grandgent, Charles, "The Dog's Letter," in *Old and New: Sundry Papers* (Cambridge, MA: Harvard University Press, 1920).

Grant, Madison, *The Passing of the Great Race: Or, the Racial Basis of European History* (New York: Charles Scribner's Sons, [1916] 1922).

Grice, Herbert P., "Logic and Conversation," in Peter Cole and Jerry L. Morgan, eds., *Syntax and Semantics: Speech Acts* (New York: Academic Press, 1975): 41–58.

Grieve, Jack, Andrea Nini, and Diansheng Guo, "Analyzing Lexical Emergence in Modern American English Online," *English Language and Linguistics* 21, 1 (2017): 99–127.

Goldstein, Eric, *The Price of Whiteness: Jews, Race, and American Identity* (Princeton, NJ: Princeton University Press, 2006).

Gopnik, Adam, "Stand Up Guys," *The New Yorker* (May 12, 2003).

Goldberg, Isaac, *Tin Pan Alley: A Chronicle of American Popular Music* ([New York: John Day, 1930], New York: Frederick Ungar, 1961).

Grandmaster Flash and the Furious Five, "The Message," Sugar Hill Records (1982).

Greenspan, Charlotte, *Pick Yourself Up: Dorothy Fields and the American Musical* (Oxford, UK: Oxford University Press, 2010).

Grieve, Jack, Diansheng Guo, and Alice Kasakoff, "Mapping Lexical Spread in American English," paper presented at American Dialect Society Annual Meeting, Portland, Oregon (January 8, 2015).

Grieve, Jack, Andrea Nini, and Diansheng Guo, "Mapping Lexical Innovation on American Social Media," *Journal of English Linguistics* 46, 4 (2018): 293–319.

Grumet, Robert S., *Manhattan to Minisink: American Indian Place Names in Greater New York and Vicinity* (Norman: University of Oklahoma Press, 2013).

Guglielmo, Jennifer, and Salvatore Salerno, eds., *Are Italians White?: How Race Is Made in America* (New York: Routledge, 2003).

Halbreich, Betty, *I'll Drink to That: A Life in Style, with a Twist* (New York: Penguin Books, 2014).

Halttunen, Karen, *Confidence Men and the Painted Women: A Study of Middle-Class Culture in America, 1830–1870* (New Haven, CT: Yale University Press, 1982).

Hammonds, Evelynn, "Straw Men and Their Followers: The Return of Biological Race," Social Science Research Council website (June 7, 2006).

Harris, Judith, *The Nurture Assumption: Why Children Turn Out the Way They Do* (New York: Free Press, [1998] 2009).

Harris, Neil, *Humbug: The Art of P.T. Barnum* (Chicago: The University of Chicago Press, 1973).

Hawthorne, Nathaniel, "Wakefield" (1835), in Malcolm Cowley ed., *The Portable Hawthorne*, (New York: The Viking Press, [1969] 1983): 151–62.

Hebdige, Dick, *Cut 'n' Mix: Culture, Identity, and Caribbean Music* (London: Methuen, 1987).

Hebdige, Dick, *Subculture: The Meaning of Style* (New York: Routledge, [1979] 2013).

Heckscher, Morrison H., *Creating Central Park* (New Haven, CT: Yale University Press, 2008).

Heilman, Samuel C., *Synagogue Life: A Study in Symbolic Interaction* (New Brunswick, NJ: Transaction Publishers, [1976] 1998).

Hess, Mickey, "Book of Rhymes," in Mickey Hess, ed., *Icons of Hip-Hop*, vol. 2 (Westport, CT: Greenwood Press, 2007): 359–60.

Hilderbrand, Lucas, *Paris Is Burning: A Queer Film Classic* (Vancouver, BC: Arsenal Pulp Press, 2013).

Holton, Woody, *Forced Founders: Indians, Debtors, Slaves, and the Making of the American Revolution in Virginia* (Chapel Hill: University of North Carolina Press, 1999).

Horowitz, Mark Eden, *Sondheim on Music: Minor Details and Major Decisions* (Lanham, MD, and Oxford, UK: The Scarecrow Press, Inc., 2003).

Hubbell, Allan Forbes, *The Pronunciation of English in New York City* (New York: King's Crown Press, 1950).

Hunter, Douglas, *Half Moon: Henry Hudson and the Voyage that Redrew the Map of the World* (New York: Bloomsbury, 2010).

Ignatiev, Noel, *How the Irish Became White* (New York: Routledge, 1995).

Irving, Washington, *Knickerbocker's History of New York*, vol. 1 (London: Cassell & Company, [1809] 1891).

Irving, Washington, "To the Editor of *The Knickerbocker*," in *The Works of Washington Irving*, vol. 4 (New York: Peter Fenelon Collier, 1897), 436–42.

Jackson, Jonathan David, "The Social World of Voguing," *Journal for the Anthropological Study of Human Movement* 12, 2 (2002): 26–42.

Jaffe, Steven H., *New York at War: Four Centuries of Combat, Fear, and Intrigue in Gotham* (New York: Basic Books, 2012).

Jasanoff, Maya, *Liberty's Exiles: American Loyalists in the Revolutionary World* (New York: Vintage Books, 2011).

Johnstone, Barbara, Neeta Bhasin, and Denise Wittkofski, "'Dahntahn' Pittsburgh: Monophthongal /aw/ and Representations of Localness in Southwestern Pennsylvania," *American Speech* 77, 2 (2002): 148–66.

Jones, Brian Jay, *George Lucas: A Life* (New York: Little, Brown, 2016).

Kahn, Yasmin Sabina, *Enlightening the World: The Creation of the Statue of Liberty* (Ithaca, NY: Cornell University Press, 2010).

Karabel, Jerome, *The Chosen: The Hidden History of Admission and Exclusion at Harvard, Yale, and Princeton* (New York: Houghton Mifflin, 2005).

Kasinitz, Philip, John Mollenkopf, and Mary Waters, "Becoming American/ Becoming New Yorkers: Immigrant Incorporation in a Majority Minority City," *The International Migration Review* 36, 4 (2002): 1020–36.

Katz, Mark, *Groove Music: The Art and Culture of the Hip-Hop DJ* (Oxford, UK: Oxford University Press, 2012).

Kenny, Kevin, "Labor and Labor Organizations," in Marion Casey and J. J. Lee, eds., *Making the Irish American: History and Heritage of the Irish in the United States* (New York: New York University Press, 2006) 354–63.

Keogan, Kevin, "A Sense of Place: The Politics of Immigration and the Symbolic Construction of Identity in Southern California and the New York Metropolitan Area," *Sociological Forum* 17, 2 (2002): 223–53.

Kerr, Walter, review of *Fiddler on the Roof*, *New York Theatre Critics Reviews* 25, 19 (1964): 217.

Keyes, Cheryl, *Rap Music and Street Consciousness* (Urbana: University of Illinois Press, 2002).

Kilpatrick, Paul, "Turn and Control in Puerto Rican Spanish Conversation" (Educational Resources Information Center, 1986).

Knutson, Elizabeth, "On Being Heard: A Study of Listening Behavior in French Conversation," *The French Review* 82, 6 (May 2009): 1180–93.

KRS-One, "South Bronx," B-Boy (1986).

Koeppel, Gerard, *City on a Grid: How New York Became New York* (New York: Perseus Books, 2015).

Koeppel, Gerard, "How New York City Could Have Looked Like Paris," *The New York Post* (November 8, 2015).

Kolker, Robert Phillip, *A Cinema of Loneliness: Penn, Kubrick, Scorsese, Spielberg, Altman* (New York and Oxford, UK: Oxford University Press, 1988).

Kucsera, John, and Gary Orfied, "New York State's Extreme School Segregation," report for the Civil Rights Project at the University of California, Los Angeles (March 2014).

Labov, William, "Can Reading Failure Be Reversed? A Linguistic Approach to the Question," in Vivian Gadsen and Daniel Wagner, eds., *Literacy Among African American Youth* (Creskill, NJ: Hampton Press, 1995): 39–68.

Labov, William, *Language in the Inner City: Studies in the Black English Vernacular* (Philadelphia: University of Pennsylvania Press, 1972).

Labov, William, "The Social History of a Sound Change on the Island of Martha's Vineyard, Massachusetts," master's essay, Columbia University, New York (1962).

Labov, William, *The Social Stratification of English in New York City* (Washington, DC: Center for Applied Linguistics, [1966] 1982).

Labov, William, *Sociolinguistic Patterns* (Philadelphia: University of Pennsylvania Press, 1972).

Labov, William, Sharon Ash, and Charles Boberg, *The Atlas of North American English: Phonetics, Phonology, and Sound Change*, vol. 1 (Berlin, Germany: Walter de Gruyter, 2006).

Lakoff, Robin, *Language and Woman's Place: Texts and Commentaries*, ed. Mary Bucholtz (Oxford, UK: Oxford University Press, [1975] 2004).

Language Policy Task Force, "Language Policy and the Puerto Rican Community," *Bilingual Review / La Revista Bilingüe* 5, 1/2 (January–August 1978): 1–39.

Leach, William, *Land of Desire: Merchants, Power, and the Rise of a New American Culture* (New York: Vintage, 1993).

Leacock, Stephen, *Nonsense Novels* (New York: John Lane Company, 1920).

Lears, Jackson, *Fables of Abundance: A Cultural History of Advertising in America* (New York: Basic Books, 1994).

Lears, Jackson, *Something for Nothing: Luck in America* (New York: Viking, 2003).

Lee, Jooyoung, *Blowin' Up: Rap Dreams in South Central* (Chicago: University of Chicago Press, 2016).

Leff, Laurel, "Rebuffing Refugee Journalists: The Profession's Failure to Help Jews Persecuted by Nazi Germany," *Journalism & Communication Monographs* 17, 3 (2015): 149–218.

Leith, Dick, *A Social History of English* (New York: Routledge, [1983] 2003).

Let's Get Tough!, film Monogram Pictures Corporation (1942).

Levin, Phyllis Lee, *Abigail Adams: A Biography* (New York: St. Martin's Press, [1987] 2001).

Levine, David, *The American College and the Culture of Aspiration, 1915–1940* (Ithaca, NY: Cornell University Press, 1983).

Lewis, Brittany, "The Secrets behind Young Jeezy's Hustle & Ambition," *Global Grind* (December 18, 2011).

Lipski, John, *A History of Afro-Hispanic Language: Five Centuries, Five Continents* (Cambridge, UK: Cambridge University Press, 2005).

Littleton, Darryl, *Black Comedians on Black Comedy: How African-Americans Taught Us to Laugh* (New York: Applause Theatre and Cinema Books, 2006).

Livingston, Jennie, *Paris Is Burning*, film (1990). Burbank, CA: Miramax Films, 2005.

Lopez, Ian Haney, *White by Law: The Legal Construction of Race* (New York: New York University Press, 2006).

Lucas, George, "The Star Wars," screenplay dated May 1974.

McNamara, John, *History in Asphalt: The Origin of Bronx Street and Place Names* (The Bronx, NY: The Bronx County Historical Society, [1978] 2010).

Madonna, "Vogue," video; directed by David Fincher (1991); copyright WMA, 2006.

Martin, Meredith, *The Rise and Fall of Meter: Poetry and English National Culture, 1860–1930* (Princeton, NJ: Princeton University Press, 2012).

Massey, Douglas, and Nancy Denton, "Trends in the Residential Segregation of Blacks, Hispanics and Asians 1970–1980," in Norman Yetman ed., *Majority and Minority: The Dynamics of Race and Ethnicity in American Life* (Boston: Allyn and Bacon, 1991): 352–78.

Mather, Patrick-André, "The Social Stratification of /r/ in New York City: Labov's Department Store Study Revisited," *Journal of English Linguistics* 40 (2012): 338–56.

Matsell, George W., *Vocabulum; or, the Rogue's Lexicon* (New York: George W. Matsell & Co., 1859).

Maurer, David W., *Argot of the Racetrack* (Tuscaloosa, Alabama: American Dialect Society, 1951).

Maurer, David W., *Language of the Underworld* (Lexington: The University Press of Kentucky, 1981).

Maurer, David W., *Whiz Mob: A Correlation of the Technical Argot of Pickpockets with Their Behavior Pattern* (New Haven, CT: College & University Press, 1964).

Mele, Christopher, *Selling the Lower East Side: Culture, Real Estate, and Resistance in New York City* (Minneapolis: University of Minnesota Press, 2000).

Mencken, H.L., *The American Language* (New York: Alfred A. Knopf, [1919] 2006).

Merrick, Amy, "The End of Saks as We Knew It," *The New Yorker* (July 30, 2013).

Miranda, Lin-Manuel, and Jeremy McCarter, *Hamilton: The Revolution* (New York: Grand Central Publishing, 2016).

Moholy-Nagy, Sibyl, *Matrix of Man: An Illustrated History of Urban Environment* (New York: Frederick A. Praeger, 1968).

Moore, Deborah Dash, Jeffrey S. Gurock, Annie Polland, Howard B. Rock, and Daniel Soyer, *Jewish New York: The Remarkable Story of a City and a People* (New York: New York University Press, 2017).

Morgan, Marcyliena, *The Real Hiphop: Battling for Knowledge, Power, and Respect in the LA Underground* (Durham, NC: Duke University Press, 2009).

Moscow, Henry, *The Street Book: An Encyclopedia of Manhattan's Street Names and Their Origins* (New York: Fordham University Press, 1978).

Moses, Paul, *An Unlikely Union: The Love-Hate Story of New York's Irish and Italians* (New York: New York University Press, 2015).

Naremore, James, "John Huston and *The Maltese Falcon*," in William Luhr, ed., *The Maltese Falcon: John Huston, Director* (New Brunswick, NJ: Rutgers University Press, 1995): 149–60.

Needler, Geoffrey D., "Three Studies in the Linguistic History of New York City," dissertation, Union Institute and University, Cincinnati, Ohio (1978): 88.

Newman, Michael, "Focusing, Implicational Scaling, and the Dialect Status of New York Latino English," *Journal of Sociolinguistics* 14, 2 (2010): 207–39.

Newman, Michael, "'I Represent Me': Identity Construction in a Teenage Rap Crew" (Austin, TX: Proceedings from the Ninth Annual Symposium about Language and Society, 2001).

Newman, Michael, *New York City English* (Boston and Berlin, Germany: Mouton de Gruyter, 2014).

Newman, Michael, "Rap as Literacy: A Genre Analysis of Hip-Hop Ciphers," *Text* 25, 3 (2005): 399–436.

Niedzielski, Nancy, and Dennis Preston, *Folk Linguistics* (Berlin, Germany: Mouton de Gruyter, 2000).

The Notorious B.I.G., "I Love the Dough," Bad Boy Entertainment and Arista Records (1997).

Nunokawa, Jeff, "4850. Introduction to London Real Estate," Facebook (August 20, 2017).

Oliver, John, "New York's Port Authority," *Last Week Tonight* (August 3, 2014).

Ostendorf, Berndt, "'The Diluted Second Generation': German-Americans in Music, 1870–1920," in Hartmut Keil, ed., *German Workers' Culture in the United States, 1850 to 1920* (Washington, DC: Smithsonian, 1988): 261–87.

Page, Evan Bartlett, and Jimmie Manning, quoted in Erik Piepenburg, "So What's Wrong with a Little Lisp?" *Out* (February 2006): 36–9.

Page, Max, *The Creative Destruction of Manhattan, 1900–1940* (Chicago: University of Chicago Press, 1999).

Palmer, Emerson, *The New York Public School: Being a History of Free Education in the City of New York* (New York: The Macmillan Company, 1905).

Pandell, Lexi, "How RuPaul's Drag Race Fueled Pop Culture's Dominant Slang Engine," *Wired* (March 22, 2018).

Patterson, Jerry, *Fifth Avenue: The Best Address* (New York: Rizzoli, 1998).

Pearson, Roberta, and William Uricchio, "How Many Times Shall Caesar Bleed in Sport: Shakespeare and the Cultural Debate About Moving Pictures," in Lee Grieveson and Peter Kramer, eds., *The Silent Cinema Reader* (New York: Routledge, 2004): 155–68.

Penner, Barbara, "'Colleges for the Teaching of Extravagance': New York Palace Hotels," *Winterthur Portfolio* 44, 2–3 (Summer/Autumn 2010): 159–92.

Peterson, James, *The Hip-Hop Underground and African American Culture: Beneath the Surface* (New York: Palgrave Macmillan, 2014).

Pierce, Carl Horton, William Pennington Toler, and Harmon De Pau Nutting, *New Harlem Past and Present* (New York: New Harlem Publishing Company, 1903).

Pinker, Steven, *The Language Instinct: How the Mind Creates Language* (New York: Penguin Books, 1994).

Poe, Edgar Allan, "Diddling Considered as One of the Exact Sciences." Short story first published under the title "Raising the Wind; or, Diddling Considered as

One of the Exact Sciences," in the *Philadelphia Saturday Courier* of October 14, 1843 and reprinted in *The Broadway Journal* of September 13, 1845.

Poe, Edgar Allan, "The Man of the Crowd," *Burton's Gentleman's Magazine* (December 1840).

Pollum, Geoffrey, *The Great Eskimo Vocabulary Hoax, and Other Irreverent Essays on the Study of Language* (Chicago: University of Chicago Press, 1991).

Popik, Barry, "First 'Big Apple' Explanation: February 18, 1924," The Big Apple website (July 11, 2004).

Poplack, Shana, "Sometimes I'll Start a Sentence in Spanish *y Termino en Español*: Toward a Typology of Code-Switching," *Linguistics* 18, 7-8 (1980): 581–618.

Preston, Dennis R., "Where the Worst English Is Spoken," in E. W. Schneider, ed., *Focus on the USA* (Amsterdam, The Netherlands: John Benjamins, 1996): 297–360.

Pritchard, Evan T., *Native New Yorkers: The Legacy of the Algonquin People of New York* (San Francisco: Council Oak Books, 2002).

Quinlan, Heather, "If These Knishes Could Talk," FilmRise documentary film (2013).

Raulin, Anne, "The Naming of Urban Space: A Study of Manhattan Place Names," dissertation, The New School for Social Research, New York (1984).

Ravitch, Diane, *The Great School Wars: A History of the New York Public Schools* (New York: Basic Books, 1974).

Reid, Shaheem, "MTV News Exclusive: Nas Previews *Hip-Hop Is Dead*," *MTV.com* (October 9, 2006).

Renner, Andrea, in Hillary Ballon, ed., *The Greatest Grid: The Master Plan of Manhattan, 1811–2011* (New York: Museum of the City of New York/ Columbia University Press, 2012).

Richards, Frank, "The Yankee Schoolboy," *The Magnet* 150, 5 (December 24, 1910).

Richter, Daniel K., "Brothers, Scoundrels, Metal Makers: Dutch Constructions of Native American Constructions of the Dutch," *de Halve Maen* 71 (1998), 59–64.

Rickford, J. R., and R. J. Rickford, *Spoken Soul* (New York: John Wiley, 2000).

Rivera, Raquel Z., *New York Ricans from the Hip Hop Zone* (New York: Palgrave Macmillan, 2003).

Roberts, Sam, "Unlearning to Tawk like a New Yorker," *The New York Times* (November 19, 2010).

Robson, Catherine, *Heart Beats: Everyday Life and the Memorized Poem* (Princeton, NJ: Princeton University Press, 2012).

Rogin, Michael, *Blackface, White Noise: How Jewish Performers Used Blackface Minstrelsy to Negotiate Their Own Relationship with Whiteness* (Berkeley: University of California Press, 1996).

Roosevelt, Theodore, *The Winning of the West: In the Current of the Revolution* (New York: G. P. Putnam's Sons, [1889] 1900).

Rose, Tricia, *Black Noise: Rap Music and Black Culture in Contemporary America* (Middletown, CT: Wesleyan University Press, 1994).

Rosenzweig, Roy, and Elizabeth Blackmar, *The Park and the People: A History of Central Park* (Ithaca, NY: Cornell University Press, 1992).

Roth, Henry, *Call It Sleep: A Novel* (New York: Picador [1934] 1991).

Royle, Edwin Milton, "The Vaudeville Theatre," *Scribner's Magazine* 26 (October 1899): 485–95.

Rua, Colleen L., "Coming Home: US-Latinos on the Broadway Stage," dissertation, Tufts University, Medford, Massachusetts (2014).

Sacks, Harvey, Emanuel A. Schegloff, and Gail Jefferson, "A Simplest Systematics for the Organization of Turn-Taking for Conversation," *Language* 50 (1974): 696–735.

Sacks, Marcy S., *Before Harlem: The Black Experience in New York City before World War I* (Philadelphia: University of Pennsylvania Press, 1996).

Safire, William, "Fuhgeddaboutit," *The New York Times Magazine* (September 1, 1996).

Sagalyn, Lynne B., *Times Square Roulette: Rethinking the City Icon* (Cambridge, MA: MIT Press, 2001).

Sanderson, Eric W., *Mannahatta: A Natural History of New York City* (New York: Abrams, 2009).

Saville-Troike, Muriel, *The Ethnography of Communication: An Introduction* (Oxford, UK: Basil Blackwell, 1982).

Schegloff, Emmanuel A., "Overlapping Talk and the Organization of Turn-Taking for Conversation," *Language in Society* 29 (2000): 1–63.

Scheiber, Noam, "Freaks and Geeks," *The New Republic* (April 2, 2007).

Schiffrin, Deborah, "Jewish Argument as Sociability," in *Language in Society* 13, 3 (1984): 311–35.

Salt-N-Pepa, "Shoop," Next Plateau (1993).

Santana, Juelz, "I Am Crack," Diplomat Records and Def Jam Recordings (2005).

Schiff, Stephen, "Deconstructing Sondheim," in *The Sondheim Review* 17, 2 (2010): 16.

Schiffrin, Deborah, "Jewish Argument as Sociability," *Language in Society* 13, 3 (1984): 311–35.

Schlichting, Kurt, *Grand Central Terminal: Railroads, Engineering, and Architecture in New York City* (Baltimore, MD: Johns Hopkins University Press, 2001).

Schrader, Paul, "Taxi Driver," screenplay (April 29, 1975), Harry Ransom Center, University of Texas at Austin.

Scorsese, Martin, *Taxi Driver*, film (Columbia Pictures, 1976).

Seabrook, John, *The Song Machine: Inside the Hit Factory* (New York: Norton, 2015).

Shall We Dance, film. RKO Radio Pictures (1937).

Shakespeare, William, *The Merchant of Venice*. Act 3, Scene 1, line 1.

Shapiro, Arthur, "Seagram's Gin," Booze Business website (January 14, 2012).

Eliza Shapiro, "Segregation Has Been the Story of New York City's Schools for 50 Years," *The New York Times* (March 26, 2019).

Shaw, Charles G., "Out-of-Towner," *The New Yorker* (November 6, 1926): 23.

Shirley, Glenn, *Hello, Sucker!: The Story of Texas Guinan* (New York: Eakin Press, 1989).

Shorto, Russell, *The Island at the Center of the World* (New York: Doubleday, 2005).

Shousterman, Cara, "Speaking English in Spanish Harlem: Language Change in Puerto Rican English," dissertation in linguistics, New York University, New York (2015).

Siegel, Jeff, *Second Dialect Acquisition* (Cambridge, UK: Cambridge University Press, 2010).

Silverman, Stuart, "The Learning of Black English by Puerto Ricans in New York City," in J. L. Dillard, ed., *Perspectives on Black English* (The Hague, The Netherlands: Mouton, 1975).

Simon, Kate, *Fifth Avenue: A Very Social History* (New York: Harcourt Brace Jovanovich, 1978).

Skinner, Edith, *The Seven Points for Good Speech in Classic Plays* (Mill Valley, CA: Performance Skills, 1983).

Sköld, David, and Alf Rehn, "Makin' It, by Keeping It Real: Street Talk, Rap Music, and the Forgotten Entrepreneurship from 'The 'Hood,' " *Group & Organization Management* 32, 1 (February 2007): 50–78.

Slomanson, Peter, and Michael Newman, "Peer Group Identification and Variation in New York Latino English Laterals," *English Worldwide* 25 (2004): 199–216.

Sondheim, Stephen, *Finishing the Hat: Collected Lyrics (1954–1981) with Attendant Comments, Principles, Heresies, Grudges, Whines, and Anecdotes* (New York: Alfred A. Knopf, 2010).

Sondheim, Stephen, "How to Do a Real Crossword Puzzle," *New York* (April 8, 1968).

Sondheim, Stephen, "Theater Lyrics," in Otis L. Guernsey, Jr., ed., *Playwrights, Lyricists, Composers on Theater* (New York: Dodd, Mead and Co., 1974), 61–97.

Sonnad, Nikhil, "America Can Thank Black Twitter for All Those New Words," *Quartz* (September 20, 2018).

Sonnad, Nikhil, "How Brand-New Words Are Spreading across America," *Quartz* (July 29, 2015).

Steinberg, Saul, "View of the World from 9th Avenue" (1976).

Stoddard, Lothrop, *The Rising Tide of Color Against White World-Supremacy* (New York: Charles Scribner's Sons, 1921).

Suisman, David, *Selling Sounds: The Commercial Revolution in American Music* (Cambridge, MA: Harvard University Press, 2009).

Tannen, Deborah, *Conversational Style: Analyzing Talk among Friends* (Norwood, NJ: Ablex, 1984).

Tannen, Deborah "Ethnicity as Conversational Style," *Working Papers in Sociolinguistics* 55 (Austin, Texas: Southwest Educational Development Laboratory, January 1979).

Tannen, Deborah, "New York Jewish Conversational Style," *International Journal of the Sociology of Language* 30 (1981): 133–49.

Tannen, Deborah, "Talking New York: It's Not What You Say, It's the Way You Say It," *New York* (March 30, 1981): 30–3.

Tannen, Deborah, "Turn-Taking and Intercultural Discourse and Communication," in Christina Bratt Paulston, Scott F. Kiesling, Elizabeth S. Rangel, eds., *The Handbook of Intercultural Discourse and Communication* (Malden, MA: Wiley-Blackwell, 2012): 135–57.

Taubman, Howard, "Theater: Mostel as Tevye in 'Fiddler on the Roof,'" *New York Theatre Critics Reviews* 25, 19 (1964): 217–18.

Thomas, Robert McG., Jr., "James Bender, 92, Eclectic Educator, Dies," *The New York Times* (November 28, 1997).

Thompson, Kirsten Moana, "Classical Cel Animation, World War II, and Bambi," in Cynthia Lucia, Roy Grundmann, and Art Simon, eds., *American Film History: Selected Readings, Origins to 1960* (New York: John Wiley & Sons, 2016): 311–25.

Thompson, Richard, "Screen Writer: *Taxi Driver*'s Paul Schrader," *Film Comment* (March–April 1976): 6–19.

Thurman, Judith, "The Candidate's Wife," *The New Yorker* (September 27, 2004).

Tokaji, András, "The Meeting of Sacred and Profane in New York's Music: Robert Moses, Lincoln Center, and Hip-Hop," *Journal of American Studies* 29, 1 (April 1995): 97–103.

Tooker, William Wallace, *The Indian Place-Names on Long Island and Islands Adjacent, with Their Probable Significations*, ed. Alexander F. Chamberlain (New York: G. P. Putnam's Sons, 1911).

Top Hat, film. RKO Radio Pictures (1935).

Trager, James, *Park Avenue: Street of Dreams* (New York: Atheneum, 1990).

Trudgill, Peter, "Acts of Conflicting Identity: The Sociolinguistics of British Pop-Song Pronunciation," in Peter Trudgill, *On Dialect: Social and Geographical Perspectives* (New York: New York University Press, 1983): 141–60.

Turner, Frederick Jackson, "Social Forces in American History," *American Historical Review* 16, 2 (January 1911): 217–33.

Uricchio, William, "The Batman's Gotham City: Story, Ideology, Performance," in Jörn Ahrens and Arno Meteling, eds., *Comics and the City: Urban Space in Print, Picture, and Sequence* (New York: Continuum, 2010): 119–32.

Van Buskirk, Judith, *Generous Enemies: Patriots and Loyalists in Revolutionary New York* (Philadelphia: University of Pennsylvania Press, 2002).

Van der Sijs, Nicoline, *Cookies, Coleslaw, and Stoops: The Influence of Dutch on the North American Languages* (Amsterdam, The Netherlands: Amsterdam University Press, 2009).

Varga, Joseph J., *Hell's Kitchen and the Battle for Urban Space: Class Struggle and Progressive Reform in New York City, 1894–1914* (New York: Monthly Review Press, 2013).

Vincent, Ricky, *Funk: The Music, the People, and the Rhythm of the One* (New York: St. Martin's Press, 1996).

Washington, George, letter to New York City mayor James Duane (April 10, 1785).

Waters, Mary, and Philip Kasinitz, "Immigrants in New York City: Reaping the Benefits of Continuous Immigration," *Daedalus* 142, 3 (2013): 92–106.

Wecter, Dixon, "Hearing Is Believing," *The Atlantic Monthly* (August 1945): 54–61.

Weimer, Christopher, "One-Handed Catch," *The Sondheim Review* 15, 4 (Summer 2009): 18–19.

Weiner, Melissa F., *Power, Protest and the Public Schools: Jewish and African American Struggles in New York City* (New Brunswick, NJ: Rutgers University Press, 2010).

Wertenbaker, Charles, "The World on His Shoulders," *The New Yorker* (December 26, 1953).

West, Cornel, "On Afro-American Music: From Bebop to Rap," *The Cornel West Reader* (New York: Basic Civitas, 1999): 474–84.

Wharton, Edith, *A Backward Glance* (New York: D. Appleton–Century Company, 1934).

Whitaker, Jan, *Service and Style: How the American Department Store Fashioned the Middle Class* (New York: St. Martin's Press, 2006).

Wieland, Molly, "Turn-Taking as a Source of Misunderstanding in French-American Cross-Cultural Conversation," in Lawrence Bouton and Yamuna Kachru, eds., *Pragmatics and Language Learning* 2 (Champaign-Urbana: University of Illinois Press, 1991): 101–18.

A Wild Hare (Bugs Bunny cartoon, Warner Bros. Pictures and The Vitaphone Corporation, 1940).

Winer, Deborah Grace, *On the Sunny Side of the Street: The Life and Lyrics of Dorothy Fields* (New York: Schirmer, 1997).

Wilson, Steve, "You Talkin' to Me?," blog post, *Ransom Center Magazine*, University of Texas at Austin (October 13, 2016).

Wolfe, Tom, *The Bonfire of the Vanities* (New York: Farrar, Straus and Giroux, 1987).

Wolford, Tonya, and Keelan Evanini, "Features of AAVE as Features of PRE: A Study of Adolescents in Philadelphia," *University of Pennsylvania Working Papers in Linguistics* 12, 2 (2006).

Wolfram, Walt, *Sociolinguistic Aspects of Assimilation: Puerto Rican English in New York City* (Arlington, VA: Center for Applied Linguistics, 1974).

Wolfram, Walt, "Sociolinguistic Folklore in the Study of African American English," *Language and Linguistic Compass* 1, 4 (2007): 292–313.

Yagoda, Ben, *The B Side: The Death of Tin Pan Alley and the Rebirth of the Great American Song* (New York: Penguin, 2015).

Zelinsky, Wilbur, *Nation into State: The Shifting Symbolic Foundations of American Nationalism* (Chapel Hill: University of North Carolina Press, 1988).

Zentella, Ana Celia, *Growing Up Bilingual: Puerto Rican Children in New York* (Malden, MA: Blackwell, 1997).

Zentella, Ana Celia, "Individual Differences in Growing Up Bilingual," in Marietta Saravia-Shore and Steven F. Arvizu ed., *Cross-Cultural Literacy: Ethnographies of Communication in Multiethnic Classrooms*, (New York: Garland, 1992), 211–26.

Zinsser, William, *Easy to Remember: The Great American Songwriters and their Songs* (Boston: David R. Godine, 2001).

IMAGE CREDITS

Chapter 1 opener:
Artem Avetisyan/Shutterstock.

Chapter 2 opener:
The Miriam and Ira D. Wallach Division of Art, Prints and Photographs: Photography Collection, The New York Public Library. "Assemblage of the Statue of Liberty in Paris, showing the bottom half of the statue erect under scaffolding, the head and torch at its feet." New York Public Library Digital Collections.

Chapter 3 opener:
Goran Bogicevic/Shutterstock.

Chapter 4 opener:
Art and Picture Collection, The New York Public Library. "Confidence man : I seen him first, Joe; His pal : let's toss for him." New York Public Library Digital Collections.

Chapter 5 opener:
Photo by Laura Levine/Corbis via Getty Images.

Chapter 6 opener:
PYMCA/Universal Images Group via Getty Images.

Chapter 7 opener:
Collins, Marjory, photographer. *New York, New York. Corset display at R. H. Macy and department store during the week before Christmas.* New York, New York State. United States, 1942. Dec. Photograph. https://www.loc.gov/item/2017841516/.

Epilogue:
Henry W. and Albert A. Berg Collection of English and American Literature, The New York Public Library. "Fuck You." New York Public Library Digital Collections. Accessed August 1, 2019. http://digitalcollections.nypl.org/items/aa2c5690-6b46-0135-047e-53ac359131b2.

INDEX

For the benefit of digital users, indexed terms that span two pages (e.g., 52–53) may, on occasion, appear on only one of those pages.

White, Paul, 227n47
Wilde, Oscar, 4–5, 165, 245n22
Williams College, 247n52
William Street, 79, 83–84
Wilson, Rex, 34–35
Winchell, Walter, 119, 238n89
window shopping, use of term, 191
Winston Churchill Square, 96–97
within-turn pauses, 8
Wolfe, Tom, 21
Wolfram, Walt, 173
Woollcott, Alexander, 137–38
Working Girl (film), 4–5, 63
World of Warcraft, 67–69

Wu-Tang Clan (hip-hop artists),
    158–59

Yagoda, Ben, 135
Yale Law School, 4
Yale University, 42–43, 227n44
Yonkers, 79
York County, 80–82
Young Jeezy (hip-hop artist), 129–30

Zentella, Ana Celia, 165, 172–73, 177,
    252n25, 255–56n57
Zexu, Lin, 101
Zinsser, William, 140–43